Brimming Bowls

{ a gluten-free treasury }

Charlene Kennell

foreword by Wm. D. Spontak M.A., D.C.

Quote on page 2 reprinted from *Kitchen Essays* by Agnes Jekyll, copyright The Estate of Lady Jekyll, published by Persephone Books Ltd, London.

Quote on page 40, author unknown, reprinted from *More With Less Cookbook* by Doris Janzen Longacre. Copyright 1976, 2000, 2011 by Herald Press, Harrisonburg, VA.

Quote page 114, by Christopher Kimball, reprinted from *Cook's Illustrated Magazine*, Issue 38,   copyright 1999 Boston Common Press Limited Partnership, Brookline, MA.

Quote page 236, by Celia Barbour, reprinted from *Martha Stewart Living*, copyright Martha Stewart Living Omnimedia LLC, New York, NY.

Quote page 270, author unknown, reprinted from *Martha Stewart Comfort Foods*, copyright 1999 Martha Stewart Living Omnimedia LLC, New York, NY.

After due diligence, we have been unable to contact several copyright owners, and have set aside the standard license/usage fee should they come forward with claim to its rights.

ISBN: 978-0-692-01862-0

Copyright 2012 by Charlene Kennell
Illustrations and text by Charlene Kennell
Design by Colleen Miller and Abigail Troyer
Printed by InnerWorkings, Grand Rapids, MI
1220827

Contact Sparrowsong Press 2153 County Rd D, South Wayne, WI 53587

Thanks to...

...Dad (farmer, supporter) for giving advise, driving me to InnerWorkings, and eating up the scraps.

...Mom (champion gardener, home-featherer) for growing good food, and washing all those dishes.

...My circle of sisters, all fabulous five: Denise (capable editor, word-brain) for all that concise, sensitive editing (and Jeremy, for liking coffee, too).

...Loretta (creative designer, fellow GF cook) for anchoring me through the tough decisions (and Larry, for sharing my "perfect recipe" syndrome).

...Jeanette (dedicated home-keeper) for being interested and supportive (and Abel, for driving me to the publishers).

...Rosanna (teacher, poetry reader), for being a sounding board, and for knowing when I needed a touch of her incomparable sense of humor.

...Hannah (little model housekeeper), for keeping my papers and pens together, and shining up the kitchen after I'd been through it.

...And brother Paul (machinist, finance-brain), for being an appreciative eater, and helping me muddle though the arithmetic of publishing.

...My sweet little nieces (Susannah and Emily) for being themselves.

...All my nephews (Jonathan, Josiah, David, Caleb, Japheth, Matthias, Benjamin, Nathanael, and Jesse), for always being happy eaters.

....Grandma Hobbs (great Southern cook), for all her cooking advise.

...Grandpa and Grandma Kennell (encouragers), for being with me at the beginning...

...Cousin Dawn (Kitchen Queen), for the foodie conversations and the Hearty Peasant Soup.

...Cousin Sarah (singer, teacher, friend), for encouraging and for tossing aside a crowded schedule to help me pull together last details.

continued

Thanks to...

...The whole circle of aunts, uncles, and cousins for support and the no-research-needed, Thanksgiving-at-our-house story.

...Lyle and Ethel Hostetler, (writers, publishers, friends), for capably coaching me in the details.

...Rinck Heule of InnerWorkings for pulling me through boggling decisions, and making my book really happen.

...Colleen Miller (designing genius) for converting my nebulous dreams to happy reality.

...Dr. Hostetler, for starting me on the gluten-free road, and Dr. Anderson, for guiding me through the rough spots.

...The Yoders in West Virginia, for bailing me out of swampy WP moments.

... "Sister" Adina and her sweet mom Mimi, for adopting us, and sharing a new food culture.

... Dr. Spontak (fellow foodie, family friend), for supporting, researching, and writing the foreword for this book.

...The wide network of celiac friends, known and unknown, linked by letters, calls, prayers, recipes.

...Jesus Christ (Savior, Rock, Provider). "For He satisfieth the longing soul, and filleth the hungry soul with goodness." Psalm 107: 9

Table of Contents

Introduction

I once thought life was a series of empty bowls. Especially at pizza suppers or s'more roasts. Or birthday parties, when everyone else got a big slice of the cake. I'd forget my trusty motto "Way-Down-in-Africa-Babies-are-Really-Starving". I'd forget I'd gained 12 pounds and wasn't a skeleton anymore. I'd forget I could, at the very least, snitch a cherry off the top of the cake. I'd think, "I'm the hungriest person in the world right now! If I could just have one big fat slice of chocolate cake!"

Maybe you've been there, too. Maybe you are holding a dessert dish, or a soup bowl, or a pasta plate with nary a crumb in it. And maybe it all began like this...

"You're gluten-intolerant. Absolutely don't eat wheat, rye, oats or barley for the rest of your life. Try it for three months, and you'll be yourself again," your doctor says.

You drag home from his office, thanking God that after ten years, fifteen doctors and fifty tests, the answer is this simple. Maybe now you'll get some energy, get rid of the nagging pain, and put on some weight so your family will stop saying that you look like a starving refugee. But it's been a long day. You stumble into the house and search for comfort food – something to satisfy the deep, nauseous hunger that never seems to go away. Bread and butter? Zucchini cake? Saltines and cheese? No, no, no. Panic closes in. Wait – you think of your home-canned vegetable soup. It would be filling, soothing. You heat it and lift a steaming spoonful to your mouth. You hand freezes midair. Didn't you – yes, you thickened the soup with flour. Suddenly you feel surrounded. Gluten is everywhere. You feel like an alien in a gluten-saturated world.

Take heart – others have been there! Five of my family members and I have been, plus countless friends. Some doctors think that one in every 133 Americans are gluten-intolerant. No, you're definitely not alone!

I was the first of my family to be diagnosed. I was a teenager, and didn't even know what the word "gluten" meant. I felt like a creature from another tribe. My favorite breakfast of three slices of toast, supper of pizza, and dessert of chocolate cake were suddenly taboo. What in the world could I eat? What couldn't I eat? How did I make things I could eat?

That was 13 years ago, and the Lord has led me through some twisting paths. But the victories! The other day I held a piece of warm chocolate cake in my hand – moist, sweet, topped with gooey frosting. I ate that piece of cake, plus (shhh!) two more.

Learning to live without gluten was a challenge – no, much more than a challenge. It was a mental shift. How could wheat make anyone sick – those red-brown kernels of wheat that Dad grew on the sun-tossed prairie, and Mom made into hearty bread – twice a week, five loaves at a time? For this farmer's daughter, it nullified all the eating values I'd ever learned.

What was I supposed to eat now? I wasn't sure. For a while I scraped by without desserts, without bread – and within weeks I was feeling better. In a few months I had more energy, my weight leveled to normal, but best of all, I gradually left behind the burning abdominal pain that shadowed my days.

But I was so hungry for the gluten-filled, satisfying breads, cakes, and cookies I'd grown up on. Could I possibly be cured someday? After several rather lean years, I decided to find out. I snitched here, sampled there, and then those chocolate chip cookies and slices of wheaty bread were so good I threw caution to the wind. My family warned me, but I was drunk with new liberty. "I'm doing okay on this," I'd retort – "don't worry! I think I'm cured!" Several weeks later, I collapsed under a wave of stomach pain and terrible, aching weakness. I spent part of the summer on the couch, existing on tiny bites of cooked carrots and applesauce, regretting that splurge with the deepest shades of regret. No more had the tummy ache abated, when a strange joint stiffness set in, debilitating me in weeks to a pain-racked, rheumatic Grandma. Unable to ease shoes on my swollen feet, I made a pair of soft moccasins that I wore wherever I could hobble. The doctor tested for rheumatoid arthritis, I tried to prepare myself for a life in a wheel chair, my nephews found me an evergreen branch shaped like a cane, and I shuffled around, a twenty-three-year-old going on 100.

"Your test is negative," the doctor said, "the high level of inflammation in your intestinal tract entered the bloodstream and traveled to your joints." "Enteropathic arthritis", a chiropractor later called it. My doctor prescribed a blend of herbs for inflammation, and soon the joint pain and swelling were almost gone. Suddenly young again, I ran everywhere, skated whole evenings, hiked miles with friends. My health, like a shining, bow-wrapped present, had been handed back to me. I dove headlong into life, thanking the Lord with every breath. And my diet? I resisted gluten in any and every form. This girl was a little wiser, I think.

Obviously, my gluten-free diet was going to be long-term. I had to live with it – and make it livable, somehow. About this time my sister was diagnosed with food allergies, and later, my two nephews. I wasn't an alien anymore. I was part of a club, a pizza-and-chocolate-chip-cookie-and-bread-hungry club, and what we needed most were recipes.

Recipes! Recipes! It's the plea of all newly-diagnosed celiacs. We're hungry, maybe still malnourished and sick, and we'd empty our purses in exchange for a few bites of real comfort food. I now have celiac friends everywhere, and as they are diagnosed, we console each other recipes. But back then I was alone in my quest. To complicate things further, my sister, nephews and myself all had multiple allergies as well. Gluten-intolerance, especially if undiagnosed too long, often pairs with other allergies. "Allergies to wheat, egg and dairy are common," my doctor told me. "You're not alone in this. These three allergies are making people sick across the nation." What a few eggs wouldn't do for a flat gluten-free loaf of bread! Or sour cream for a crumbly gluten-free cake! I scoured libraries, finding mostly institutional-style books, with a lot of text and few recipes – recipes like potato "droppies" and broiled fish topped with crisp rice. Obviously other cooks hadn't found the answer to real gluten-free, allergy free comfort food either.

I tested and tested in a wearying process, with three failures for every dubious success. I tried quinoa, millet, potato, sorghum, soy and bean flours, and tapioca, corn, arrowroot and potato starch. Each has benefits, and still I use them occasionally. But I kept zeroing in on white rice flour – its was relatively cheap, mild and easy to digest. But it was bland and gritty. Biscuits wouldn't rise, and cakes crumbled into powder. I knew there had to be a better way. I finally met another celiac, and quizzed her about her flours. I searched everywhere a cook could search, and clutched every new recipe like a long-awaited friend. Still I looked for the keys to good gluten-free baking.

Suddenly, like another shining gift, we had it: xanthan gum and brown rice flour. Brown rice flour is finer, lighter, and tastier than its counterpart, and xanthan gum is a vegetable gum that mimics gluten. Over and over this combination was a winner. It made tall biscuits, spongy cakes, cookies with crunch and chew. One more step, and we discovered a combination of flours that made beautiful bread...yes, bread. A new world swung wide its doors. Now Sis and her family sit down to a supper of onion-cheese biscuits with salad, while I, at home, serve up pizza – and eat it, too.

Our bowls are full now. New recipes fill notebooks, drawers, clipboards, and now, finally, are contained between the covers of one book. I feel so blessed as I hold this 10-year work in my hands. Riffling through it, and seeing these recipes in print, I know the famine is past.

May God grant contentment in your heart and brimming bowls in your hands.

Charlene Kennell

Foreword

Never before in human history has the need for this compilation of information and recipes for a gluten-free diet been so essential. There has been an unprecedented rise in the number of people diagnosed with gluten intolerance in the past 60 years.

A study using frozen blood samples taken from Air Force recruits 60 years ago found that intolerance to wheat gluten is four times more common today than it was in the 1950s. According to statistics from the University of Chicago Celiac Disease Center, an average of 1 out of every 133 otherwise healthy people in the United States suffers from the digestive disease known as celiac disease. One study suggests that just a decade ago, gluten intolerance incidence was found to be 1 in 2,500 worldwide. Previous studies have found that this number may be as high as 1 in 33. Some researchers have suggested that up to 10-15% of persons may have some form of gluten intolerance, but most of them either have no digestive-tract symptoms at all or they are so minor that the symptoms remain unnoticed. The rising prevalence of celiac disease is an indicator that our bodies are not designed to eat large amounts of starch and sugar-rich foods.

Unfortunately, despite its increasing prevalence, diagnosis of gluten intolerance takes an average of four years. This delay in an accurate diagnosis increases the risk of developing other disorders such as autoimmune disorders, neurological problems, osteoporosis and even cancer. In addition, it was found that undiagnosed gluten intolerance was associated with a nearly fourfold increased risk of premature death.

Gluten intolerance or celiac disease occurs when your body cannot digest gluten, a protein most commonly found in wheat, rye and barley. Other grains such as oats and spelt also contain gluten. Gluten can also be found in countless processed foods without being labeled as such. These proteins damage the small finger-like projections called villi that line the small intestine and play a major role in digestion. When damaged and inflamed, the villi are not able to absorb vitamins, water and other nutrients. This causes the celiac to be susceptible to a variety of other conditions related to malabsorption, including lactose intolerance.

Gluten sensitivity can develop at any point in life and symptomatic disease may appear years after the disease develops. This undigested gluten then triggers your immune system to attack the lining of your small intestine which may result in symptoms such as abdominal pain, diarrhea or constipation. Over time, the small intestine is damaged and no longer able to absorb important nutrients.

There are several general theories proposed for the upsurge in the incidence of celiac disease:

· Genetic susceptibility to the illness

· Stress, an environmental agent, or pregnancy can be possible triggers

· Possible exposure to gluten as a young baby before the gut barrier has fully developed.

Most of the attention in research and studies appear to be focused on environmental factors. It is speculated that the damage to gut flora is on the rise in our society because of sugar, alcohol, antibiotics, environmental toxins and other allergens (such as the introduction of GMOs to our food over the last 15 years). According to research posted at the Weston A Price Foundation's website, modern wheat varieties are very different than more traditional varieties. Simply put, modern wheat is not the same plant that it used to be.

Celiac disease has many varied symptoms, with the symptoms of an adult differing from those of children. Diarrhea is one of the more common symptoms associated with the disease. Adults may lose weight and children may not gain weight or grow properly. This malabsorption may cause anemia, leaving people tired and weak. Some may not experience many bowel problems but have other symptoms such as depression, bone pain/fractures, ulcers in the mouth or blistering, itchy skin and rashes. Some women may have difficulty getting pregnant with recurring miscarriages. Additional symptoms that can complicate the diagnostic process include abdominal pain, bloating, gas, or indigestion, constipation, lactose intolerance, nausea and vomiting, floating stools, bruising easily, hair loss, muscle cramps, nosebleeds, seizures, peripheral neuropathies and fatigue.

As part of the diagnosis process, your physician should review your lab results for albumin, alkaline phosphatase, clotting factor, cholesterol, complete blood count, liver enzymes, and prothrombin time, to suggest a few. Blood serum antibody tests (endomysial, reticulin (IgA) and gliadin are used to measure the gluten antibody levels. Blood tests can also detect several special antibodies as tTGA and EMA. If these tests are positive, they may do an endoscopy with a tissue biopsy from the upper small intestine. Genetic testing of the blood is also available to aid in the determination of those that may be at risk.

Celiac disease cannot be cured. The symptoms will go away and the villi in the lining of the intestines will heal if you follow a lifelong gluten-free diet. Do not eat foods, beverages, and medications that contain wheat, barley, rye and possibly oats. Gluten may be hidden in some processed foods like ready-made soups, luncheon meats, candies, soy sauce and various low- and no-fat products labeled as natural flavoring, Texturized vegetable protein (TVP), Hydrolyzed vegetable protein (HVP), starches and malts. More information about hidden gluten can be found at www.celiac.com.

This book should be of interest to everyone and not just those who seek a gluten-free diet. The evidence is clear that we consume too much gluten in our current diets and are keeping ourselves in an "inflamed" state by our high consumption of omega-6 fatty acids from the refined wheat, grains and legumes. Limiting our intake, even if we are symptom free, must become a priority before we would develop problems.

Knowing firsthand the personal struggles, frustrations and confusion that Ms. Kennell endured over the years as she sought to define, diagnose, and treat her various symptoms adds to the personal significance and importance which motivated the construction of this wonderful book.

This book is an inspired work that was motivated by personal sacrifice and spiritual purpose in order to provide direction, help and relief to those who are looking for answers. Through years of tireless exploration of new recipes, Ms. Kennell is offering this convenient reference in the hope that her experiences will help lessen the burden on others as they struggle for answers and look for a solution to alternative food ideas. It is my opinion that this book is extremely timely. I feel that we should all begin to introduce gluten-free foods to our diets. There has been no other time in history where this issue has been such a vital concern. I am excited for this book and grateful for all of her hard work.

William D. Spontak, M.A., D.C.
Nutritional Counselor

Packable, Snackable Treats

{Nibbles, Dips, Crackers, Candies,
and Beverages, Hot and Cold}

Old Fashion Lemonade, Gardener's Hats, Fudgy Fridgies, Maple-Butter Popcorn, Garlic Foccacia

The true spiritual home of the teapot *is surely in a softly lighted room between a deep armchair and a sofa, two cups only, awaiting their* fragrant infusion, *whilst the clock points nearer to six than five, and a woodfire* flickers sympathetically *on the hearth.*

–Agnes Jekyll

chapter one

Packable, Snackable Treats
{Nibbles, Dips, Crackers, Candies and Beverages, Hot and Cold}

A snack, translated, means an interval of eatable pleasure in a long day. It means icy lemonade on a porch swing, hot cider by a campfire, truffles by candlelight, or a plate of nibbles after a Sunday evening hymn sing.

A snack isn't breakfast, lunch or supper; it's something in between. It's not strictly salty or sweet or puckery or spicy, and sometimes (like a garlicky sweet pickle) it's all four at once. A snack can whet the appetite or satisfy it; warm us up or cool us down. And just one chocolate can cure many things— among them a midnight snack attack called "I-need-a-little-something-sweet-to-go-with-this-enthralling-book".

Eating together is synonymous with fellowship. There's no better way to connect with your neighbor than to sit down with warm mugs of tea or bowls of crispy popcorn. Try it—they'll begin on the tea, and before they leave, you'll likely have shared in their latest joy, sorrow, fear or aspiration. For a cook, food always equates comfort for whoever needs it at the moment, and snacks play the part beautifully, for you can offer them at any hour of the day.

Growing up on a Midwestern farm, snacks and drinks meant one thing in July—Haymaker's Lunch! For us young fry, too small to be in the fields, but big enough to elbow around the picnic table, these upscale spreads of snacks and drinks were dreamed of in winter, anticipated in spring, and remembered happily in the fall. It was then that Mom got her purse, drove to the little store in town, and bought bags of unbelievably good things.

Haymaker's Lunch usually happened on the hottest days of the year, often with a storm threatening in the west. Dad would walk out to the field and check the mown hay drying in long windrows. Sometimes we'd go, too, sliding our feet over the stubble like all barefoot farmers' children learn to do in self-defense. He'd lift a big handful of hay from one windrow, then another, inspecting it carefully. "It'll be dry enough to bale by one o'clock," he would say. "Maybe we'll get it in before it rains."

"Oh, Dad, we hope lots of neighbors will come to help!" we'd exclaim.

By one o'clock, if the rain was holding off, the champing, chomping baler would be circling the field, followed by the hayrack. And sure enough, one pickup would come driving in the lane, then another, and another. Farmers in bill caps would hurry to field or haymow, stacking the square, eighty-pound bales of hay first on the racks, then in the mow, sweating in the humid heat. We'd watch in wonder as they tossed the heavy bales, ran to refill empty thermoses, or drove the little tractor that pulled the hay fork rope.

The rain often would pass to the north as the last load was stacked safely in the barn. The men, thirsty and dirty, would come in from the hot fields and hotter haymow, rivulets of sweat tracking through the hay dust on their faces. "Rain went around us this time," they'd say, or "Nice crop of alfalfa you got, Paul," while they splashed cold water over their faces and hands at the pump. And then they'd turn to the picnic table under the sycamore, where Mom had laid out a big and beautiful spread. The Haymaker's Lunch!

Wedges of frosty watermelon, tomato slices on homemade buns, potato chips, pretzels, maybe cheese curls, big, icy bottles of soda pop (one for every man), cold Gatorade, sometimes ice cream sandwiches, and sometimes root beer floats... nothing was too good for Haymaker's Lunch. The men, laying caps aside, would fall to it, the cold soda pop first, then the snacks. They'd always eat a lot, and sometimes they'd rest awhile afterward, stretching out on the cool grass. We ringed the edges, as watchful as little vultures, hoping there'd be some left for us. Finally, one by one, they'd get back in their pickups and drive off with a "Thanks for the lunch!". Then we'd circle in. We'd sit up to the ravaged picnic table and happily eat the scraps—the last of the ice cream, the end of the pretzels, the final slice of melon.

Snacks are such a heterogeneous lot that the celiac and allergic can usually find something to eat on a well-laden party table. But if you're like me, there's something satisfying about a full plate of nibbles—the salty, the sweet, the spicy. Not to mention a tall, frosty glass of something drinkable. You'll find my favorites here, gluten-free. ♪

Snack Snippets

· Snacks are, on the whole, honest. We know by looking that while we dare not touch the nacho sauce, the tortilla chips are usually okay. Though caramel apple dip is out, the apples themselves are always in.

· For buffets, ingredient lists are a kind gesture if you have celiac guests, especially children or non-cooks. So many dear folks—some I barely know—have informed me so carefully of all the cans and can'ts on a buffet that I'll never be able to serve my allergic friends enough in return. We can't expect everyone to understand these cranky tummies of ours, but God bless those who try.

· Rethink dips. Instead of cheese and sour cream dips, try salsa, guacamole, hummus, and dressed-up refried beans (see Charbie's Guacamole, Garbanzo Dip, Wildfire Pinto Dip). And if you still need the creamy kind, explore Sour Supreme (see The Celiac's Pantry).

· You'll notice popcorn taking center stage as pretzels, flavored chips, and crackers go. Maximize this with different presentations—either sweet or savory (see Maple-Butter Popcorn, Orange and Honey Snack Mix).

· Learn to make hot cocoa or chocolate milk with a syrup base (see suggestions in Hot Cocoa). Each can custom-mix their own glass with milk or milk substitute. ♪

Sausage & Cheese Bites

{ Serve these as a substantial snack on toothpicks with dipping sauces.
Try them with gourmet mustards, both sweet and spicy. }

1 pound gluten-free sausage, mild or hot, as desired

2 cups shredded cheese or cheese substitute

1/4 cup melted butter

1 1/4 cups brown rice flour

1 tablespoon baking powder

1/2 teaspoon salt

1/2 teaspoon xanthan gum

water, as needed

dipping sauces: mustards, ketchup, barbecue sauce, etc.

Preheat oven to 350°.

In a large bowl, stir together sausage, cheese, butter, brown rice flour, baking powder, salt and xanthan gum. Mix well. Add water, a little at a time, until a soft and cohesive dough forms.

Roll into small balls and place on 10"x15" baking sheet. Bake 15 to 20 minutes, or until browned and crusty. Serve warm with choice of dipping sauce.

Herbed Garbanzo Dip

*{ This dip, hummus with variations, has come through life with my
siblings and me. Home-cooked beans taste best, but take hours and
hours to cook. I like to keep canned chickpeas on hand in case a
hummus craving strikes suddenly. I usually serve it with tortilla chips,
but it makes a tasty spread, too. }*

1/2 onion, chopped

1 clove garlic, minced or pressed

2 tablespoons olive oil

1 teaspoon dried parsley flakes

1 teaspoon dried basil

1/2 teaspoon dried oregano

salt to taste

dash cumin

juice of 1 lemon

3 cups well-cooked and mashed garbanzo beans (chickpeas)

In a large skillet, sauté onion and garlic in the oil over medium heat until
soft. Add herbs and sauté 1 minute. Add cumin, lemon juice and garbanzo
beans. Cook until heated through and well-mixed. Remove from heat, turn
into serving dish and chill.

Serve with corn chips or as a hearty sandwich spread.

Wildfire Pinto Dip

{ Here's an inexpensive, easily-stirred-together dip that makes a hearty snack with a bag of tortilla chips. }

1 1/2 cups cooked pinto beans, or 16 ounces canned beans, rinsed and drained

3/4 cup water

3 tablespoons butter or olive oil

2 tablespoons minced onion

4 to 5 teaspoons chili powder

dash of garlic powder

dash of cayenne pepper

salt to taste

3/4 cup shredded cheese or cheese substitute, optional

Combine all ingredients in medium saucepan. Heat over low heat, mashing lightly until beans are somewhat pureed. Serve hot with tortilla chips.

Charbie's Guacamole

{ Guacamole is purely individual. Mix and match, increase and decrease ingredients as you please. Most people like the tomato option, my friend adds hard-boiled eggs in a very Americanized version, and I like to increase the garlic rather above social level. (Sadly, I can't eat my guacamole before I go to prayer meeting. I just save it for a snack afterward.) }

2 large avocados
1/4 cup chopped sweet onion
2 large garlic cloves, pressed
1 tablespoon fresh lemon juice
salt to taste (about 20 shakes)
chopped tomato or salsa, if desired

Peel avocado by carefully cutting around avocado lengthwise, circling the seed (like peeling a peach). Twist apart and scoop out seed with a spoon.

If you like smooth guacamole, scoop out pulp and mash with a fork. Or, if you like it chunky, score flesh into cubes with a knife (don't cut the skin), then scoop it out with a spoon.

Place avocado in a small bowl and add remaining ingredients. Stir well. Press plastic wrap against surface and chill.

Serve guacamole with corn chips, spread it on rice cakes, or use in any recipe asking for guacamole. Serves 3 to 4.

Gardeners' Hats

{ *Invite these guests to your next garden party. These whimsical appetizers pair the sweetness of ripe vegetables with tangy sour cream. · The cucumbers can be sliced and carrots shredded up to a day ahead, but assemble just several minutes before serving.* }

1 long, thin cucumber
salt and pepper
2 1/2 cups finely grated carrot
1 tablespoon finely chopped sweet onion
1/4 cup sour cream or Sour Supreme
1 teaspoon cider vinegar
fresh or dried parsley to garnish

Wash cucumber and slice into ½" slices. With melon baller or small measuring spoon, scoop a shallow depression in the center of each slice. Arrange hollow-side-up, on a serving tray. Sprinkle with salt.

In a small bowl, toss together carrots, onions, sour cream or Sour Supreme and vinegar. Season with salt and pepper to taste. Fill cucumber slices with about 1 teaspoon mixture per slice. Sprinkle with parsley. Yields approximately 25 appetizers.

Fishermen's Hats

{ *Cucumber and salmon are always happy neighbors, and this duo is showcased here.* }

1 long, thin cucumber
salt and black pepper, to taste
2 cups cooked and flaked salmon, or 15 ounces canned salmon,
drained, with bones and skin removed
1/3 cup mayonnaise or Vegenaise
1 teaspoon fresh lemon juice
2 tablespoons finely chopped sweet onion
fresh or dried dill weed, for garnish

Wash cucumber and slice into ½" slices. With melon baller or small spoon, scoop a slight depression in center of each slice. Arrange hollow-side-up on serving tray. Sprinkle with salt.

In a small bowl, toss together salmon, mayonnaise or Vegenaise, lemon juice, and onion. Taste for seasoning, and add salt or black pepper if needed.

Spoon about 1 teaspoon mixture on each cucumber slice. Sprinkle with dill weed to garnish. Serve immediately. Yields about 25 appetizers.

Spicy Corn Crackers

{ If you find yourself with a case of nibbles, mix up a batch of these crackers. They're crispy, spicy, and salty, and they couldn't be easier to make. With all the spice variations, you're sure to find one to please. Store leftover crackers airtight, ready for the next attack of nibbles. }

1 cup yellow cornmeal

1/2 cup brown rice flour

1 teaspoon xanthan gum

1 teaspoon salt

1 teaspoon baking powder

1/2 cup water, or more as needed

1/4 cup olive oil

1/2 teaspoon Worcestershire sauce, optional

1/8 teaspoon hot pepper sauce, optional

salt for sprinkling

spices for sprinkling (optional): garlic powder, onion powder, parsley, seasoned salt, chili powder, cracked pepper or paprika

additional cornmeal, for sprinkling

Preheat oven to 350°. Grease two 10"x15" baking sheets and sprinkle with cornmeal.

In a large bowl, stir together cornmeal, brown rice flour, xanthan gum, salt and baking powder. Add water, oil, Worcestershire sauce, and hot pepper sauce all at once, stirring with a fork to make a stiff but slightly soft dough. It should hold together well. Add up to ¼ cup more water if needed.

Divide dough in half, and roll one part directly onto each baking sheet until very thin. If dough sticks to rolling pin, sprinkle with more cornmeal. Prick dough with fork and cut into strips, squares or triangles with a sharp knife or pizza cutter. Sprinkle lightly with salt, and choice of spices if desired.

Bake crackers 10 minutes or until lightly browned. Cool on racks. Store airtight.

Honey "Graham" Crackers

{ *Make an allergic child tickled pink. · These crackers are excellent keepers and travel well.* }

3/4 cup butter, softened
1/4 cup honey
1/2 cup sweetener of choice
1 tablespoon baking molasses
1 teaspoon vanilla
2 1/2 cups brown rice flour
1/2 cup potato starch
1/3 cup tapioca starch
1 teaspoon xanthan gum
1 teaspoon salt
1 teaspoon baking soda
1 teaspoon cream of tartar
pinch of ground cinnamon
water—1/2 to 3/4 cup, or as needed

Cream butter with honey, sweetener, molasses and vanilla until very light and fluffy. In a large bowl, stir together brown rice flour, potato and tapioca starches, xanthan gum, salt, baking soda, cream of tartar and cinnamon. Add to creamed mixture alternately with ½ cup water. Add up to ¼ cup more water, or enough to make a soft but not sticky dough. Wrap, flatten into a disk and refrigerate 2 hours.

Preheat oven to 325°. Roll dough on rice-floured surface to ¼" thickness. Cut into rectangles with knife or pastry or pizza cutter. Lift with pancake turner onto baking sheets. Prick with a fork, and bake 25 minutes for soft cookies, longer for crispier crackers. Cool completely before storing airtight.

Garlic Potato Skins

{ *These potato skins are for serious garlic devotees. In fact, they can deliver even more—you choose the limit. · Eat this snack just barely cooled for best crispness, and if you like potato skins "loaded", serve them with any sprinkler, dipper or drizzler you like.* }

6 large russet potatoes
2 tablespoons olive oil
2 garlic cloves, minced or pressed
salt and black pepper

Preheat oven to 400°. Grease 2 large baking sheets.

Scrub potatoes and peel thickly in long strips. Arrange skins, white sides up, on 2 prepared baking sheets. Reserve peeled potatoes for another use.

Combine oil and garlic in a small bowl. Brush skins with this mixture, then sprinkle with salt and pepper.

Bake 35 to 45 minutes, rotating pans halfway through baking time, until well browned and crispy. Serve warm.

Buttery Pan Popcorn

{ *Sunday afternoon comes, and I wait. Who will be the first to ask this time? The sun goes down, the twilight deepens. "Hey, won't you make some popcorn?" my brother begs. I've learned it's no use putting anybody off, even if I'm deep in a book. Sure, of course, absolutely, I'll make some popcorn. Yes, right now.* }

1/4 cup coconut, light olive, or vegetable oil
1 cup popcorn kernels
1 tablespoon butter
salt, to taste

In a heavy-bottomed, 4 quart saucepan with a tight-fitting lid, place the oil and three kernels of the popcorn. Turn burner on just below the highest setting. Cover and listen carefully for the three kernels to pop. Have the remaining popcorn kernels, a large spoon, a big popcorn bowl, and the butter within reach.

As soon as the three kernels pop, add the remaining popcorn and butter. Stir vigorously until butter melts and all kernels are uniformly coated with oil. Replace lid. Shake pan occasionally as popcorn pops. When popcorn begins pushing up against the lid, shake pan vigorously, and pour some of the popcorn into the waiting bowl. Continue popping, emptying as needed, until popping slows to about one every two or three seconds. Quickly pour the entire panful of popcorn into the bowl. Salt popcorn to taste and serve.

Maple-Butter Popcorn

{ Light and sweet, a little buttery, a little caramel-y, this popcorn is a crowd-pleaser. My friend often brought it to church fellowship meals and she'd take home an empty tin. It's a great way to celebrate the first maple run on a chilly March night. }

> 2/3 cup popcorn kernels
> 3/4 cup maple syrup
> 1/4 cup butter
> 1/4 teaspoon baking soda
> 1/4 teaspoon salt
> 1/2 teaspoon vanilla

Preheat oven to 250°.

Pop popcorn in air-popper. Place in a large bowl.

In a medium saucepan, combine maple syrup and butter. Bring to a boil over high heat, reduce heat, and cook 4 minutes, stirring occasionally. Add baking soda, salt, and vanilla.

Drizzle maple syrup/butter mixture over popcorn, tossing well. Turn mixture onto 2 large rimmed baking sheets.

Bake popcorn for 15 minutes, stirring often. Remove from oven, and spread on wax paper to cool. Store airtight.

Orange & Honey Snack Mix

{ This popcorn snack is cinnamony, buttery, citrusy. · The honey in this mix collects moisture after a few hours. Serve immediately after baking and store leftovers airtight. }

10 cups air-popped popcorn
1 cup salted mixed nuts
1/4 cup honey
2 tablespoons freshly squeezed orange juice
3 tablespoons butter
1 teaspoon grated orange zest
1/4 teaspoon ground cinnamon

Preheat oven to 325°. Place the popcorn and mixed nuts in a greased 9"x13" baking pan.

Place honey, orange juice, butter, orange zest, and cinnamon in a saucepan and heat, stirring, until mixture comes to a full boil. Drizzle over popcorn mixture, tossing until well coated.

Bake 20 minutes, stirring every 5 minutes, until popcorn is lightly browned and crispy. Spread on waxed paper to cool. Store airtight. Makes approximately 11 cups.

Aunt Nancy's Party Mix

{ When the holidays come, everywhere Aunt Nancy goes, buckets of party mix suddenly appear. It disappears just as suddenly when the relatives come reaching. Before you know it, just spicy crumbs remain at the bottom—until the most unmannerly tips the bucket into his/her wide-open mouth. · After gluten-intolerance, I was forced to the fringes of the party, selecting a Rice Chex® here, a Corn Chex® there. Surely an entirely gluten-free snack mix was possible, but how? · I tried it one day, and found it simpler than expected. · Broken rice cakes toast to an exquisite crunch, nuts add weight, and the gluten free pretzels give interest, though the mix is acceptable without them. · Read labels: Chex® rice and corn cereal is gluten-free, but other brands may not be. }

3 cups Rice Chex®

3 cups Corn Chex®

2 cups broken rice cakes

2 cups GF pretzels, optional

2 cups roasted and salted mixed nuts, optional

4 tablespoons melted butter or olive oil

2 teaspoons Worcestershire sauce

1 teaspoon seasoned salt

1/2 teaspoon garlic powder

1 teaspoon onion powder

Preheat oven to 325°. Place cereal, rice cakes, pretzels, and nuts in a 9"x13" baking pan.

Place melted butter or olive oil, Worcestershire sauce, and seasonings in a small bowl and mix well. Drizzle over cereal mixture, tossing very well.

Bake party mix 30 minutes, stirring every 10 minutes, or until toasted and crispy. Spread on waxed paper, cool, and store airtight. Makes 10 cups

Real Fruit Gelatin Blocks

Allergic to sugar or dyes, and wondering if you'll have to live without gelatin blocks the rest of your life? Certainly not! They await you—just choose the flavor. · Children get happy over this recipe. One birthday I made gelatin blocks for my nephew instead of cake... a stacked "tower", replete with (quavering) candles. As soon as the candles were extinguished, little hands came reaching, and the three batches of gelatin blocks were gone in minutes. Really, it takes so little to make a child happy. · Add fresh fruit for dressier occasions. Try raspberries with raspberry-white grape juice, or halved seedless grapes in purple grape juice. Or go for contrast and team mulberries with white grape-peach juice. Just be an artist and experiment.

4 tablespoons plain gelatin
water, as needed
1/3 cup sweetener of choice, or stevia to taste
2 tablespoons lemon juice
12 oz. 100% juice concentrate
fresh fruit of choice, if desired

In a saucepan, sprinkle gelatin over 1 cup of water. Add sweetener and lemon juice and allow to rest 5 minutes.

Over medium heat, heat and stir mixture just until gelatin is dissolved.

In a large glass measuring cup, mix juice concentrate with enough water to make 3 cups liquid. Add to dissolved gelatin and stir. Pour into 9"x13" pan.

Sprinkle in fresh fruit, if desired, and chill until set, 1 to 2 hours. Cut into small squares and serve. Makes 24 gelatin blocks.

Fudgy Fridgies

{ This candy-like treat should satisfy any sweet tooth that comes your way. Try them from the freezer, thawed for five minutes. You'll think you're eating caramel with a crunch. }

3/4 cup honey or maple syrup

1/2 cup unsweetened baking cocoa

3 tablespoons butter

1 teaspoon vanilla extract

1/4 cup sweetener, optional

pinch salt

1/2 cup peanut butter or other nut butter

3 1/2 cups gluten free crisp rice cereal

In a medium saucepan, stir together choice of syrup, cocoa, butter, vanilla, sweetener and salt. Bring to a boil over medium-high heat, whisking well. Reduce heat and cook 2 minutes, stirring frequently.

Add peanut or other nut butter to cooked mixture and stir well. Fold in crisp rice.

Drop by heaping teaspoons on greased baking sheet. Chill. Freeze, if desired. Yields approximately 20.

Slivered Almond Toffee

{ *This toffee is rich, buttery celebration food. · I like to use an overload of nuts—up to 3 cups. There are two reasons why: No. 1. More nuts equals less sugar per square inch, and 2: More nuts make more toffee which equals more happy munchers. · The salt in this recipe is key for flavor.* }

1 cup butter, plus more for pan
2 cups slivered almonds
1 cup evaporated cane juice
2 tablespoons water
1/4 teaspoon salt

Line 9"x13" pan with heavy-duty foil. Butter foil generously. Scatter almonds into bottom of pan.

In 1 quart saucepan, place 1 cup butter, cane juice, water and salt. Place over medium heat and stir constantly until mixture comes to a boil. Sugar should be almost completely dissolved.

Increase heat to medium-high. Stirring constantly, boil to 300 degrees (hard-crack stage), or until a little dropped into cold water becomes hard and brittle.

Pour mixture immediately over almonds in pan. Allow toffee to cool slightly, then score with a knife into 1½" squares. Cool completely, break along scored lines and store airtight.

Variation:
Cashew Toffee: Substitute 1 cup raw cashews for the almonds, adding cashews directly to cooking mixture when it begins to boil. Stir carefully to prevent burning. Proceed with recipe.

Dark Chocolate Truffles

{ *These truffles are deep, dark, and mysterious. (No one will ever know the substitutions you made!) Unsweetened chocolate is unusual in truffles, but I use it in this recipe so I can choose the sweetener. Good quality chocolate matters here. · For over-the-top satisfaction, roll Mocha Truffles in ground pecans.* }

4 ounces unsweetened chocolate

1/2 cup cream cheese or Tofutti Better Than Cream Cheese

1 teaspoon vanilla extract

pinch salt

1/2 cup sweetener of choice

1 tablespoon butter

Garnish: ground pecans, unsweetened cocoa powder, or fine unsweetened coconut

In a small saucepan over very low heat, melt chocolate, stirring often.

In a small bowl, stir together cream cheese or Tofutti Better Than Cream Cheese, vanilla, salt and sweetener until sweetener is dissolved. Add chocolate and butter and beat with a mixer until thick and smooth. Cover and refrigerate 30 minutes to 1 hour, or until mixture stiffens.

Roll mixture into 1" truffles. Roll truffles in choice of garnish. Store truffles in an airtight container in the refrigerator. Bring to room temperature before serving. Makes approximately 20 truffles.

Variation:

Dark Mocha Truffles: add 1 teaspoon instant coffee powder to cream cheese or Better Than Cream Cheese before adding chocolate. Proceed with recipe.

Dark Chocolate Peppermint Truffles: add 4 to 6 drops peppermint essential oil to cream cheese or Better Than Cream Cheese mixture before adding chocolate. Proceed with recipe.

Old-Time Molasses Taffy

{ *This is a fun candy, and it's sweet, molasses-y and rich. Make it when you have plenty of time and willing little helpers—just tie back braids, butter all hands, and have a party. Do the cooking yourself, for the boiling syrup takes careful attention so it won't burn. The temperature is important—keep testing until syrup reaches exactly 258 degrees.* }

3 tablespoons butter, plus more for pan and fingers
2 cups light baking molasses
1/2 cup evaporated cane juice
1/4 teaspoon salt
1/2 teaspoon cider vinegar
1/4 teaspoon baking soda

Butter a rimmed baking sheet and chill in freezer until needed.

In a 3 or 4 quart heavy saucepan with wide bottom, stir together butter, molasses, evaporated cane juice, salt and vinegar. Place over medium heat and bring to a boil, stirring constantly. Once boiling, keep reducing heat gradually to just maintain a full boil, stirring all the time.

Cook syrup to 258°, or until a little dropped in cold water makes a hard but pliable ball. Immediately remove from heat, add baking soda (mixture will foam) and pour into prepared, chilled baking sheet. Set aside to cool.

When taffy is cool enough to handle, butter hands and a clean working surface. Have butter in reach, for you'll need more.

Gather taffy into a ball (a bench scraper or metal spatula helps) and pull taffy by stretching into a rope, doubling, twisting and stretching again. Alternate hands when doubling taffy to keep ends worked in. When taffy is too stiff to pull and lighter in color, twist into an even rope ¾" thick. Lay on greased surface and snip into 1" lengths with buttered scissors. Wrap in small squares of waxed paper, twisting ends.

Crispy Date Balls

{ These are crispy no-bake cookies, rich and sweet. Once cooled, they travel well. The amount of cereal in this recipe is variable. Each batch seems to need a different amount. You're looking for a stiff mixture sticky enough to form into balls. }

> **8 ounces whole pitted dates**
> **1/3 cup butter**
> **1 teaspoon vanilla extract**
> **1/4 to 1/2 cup sweetener of choice**
> **dash salt**
> **3 tablespoons water**
> **2 1/2 to 3 cups gluten free crisp rice cereal**

Line 10"x15" baking pan with waxed paper.

Snip dates into small pieces with scissors. Place in small saucepan. Add butter, vanilla extract, sweetener, salt, and water. Bring to a boil over medium heat, and simmer, stirring constantly, for 6 minutes.

Remove from heat. Fold in crisp rice cereal until mixture is stiff, but still slightly sticky. Cool slightly.

Roll mixture into 1" balls, and place on prepared pan to cool. Store airtight up to one week. Freeze for longer storage. Yields about 5 dozen.

Almonds Sitting Pretty

{ *You wouldn't think cream cheese and prunes would complement each other, but they do. Add a salted almond, and a wonderful little appetizer is born.* }

soft pitted prunes
cream cheese or Better Than Cream Cheese
roasted and salted whole almonds

Flatten prunes slightly, and top each with a half spoonful of cream cheese. Perch a whole almond atop each. Serve. Make as much or little as you like.

Creamy Orange Smoothie

{ This smoothie is the summer afternoon pick-me-up at our house, from toddlers with sippy cups to men with thermoses in the field. Everybody likes it so well, we sometimes make it for birthdays in lieu of ice cream. }
It brightens the corner wherever it is!

2 cups milk or milk substitute

3 tablespoons sweetener of choice, or stevia to taste

2/3 cup frozen orange juice concentrate, undiluted

1/2 teaspoon vanilla extract

6 to 8 ice cubes

In a blender, combine milk or substitute, sweetener, juice concentrate and vanilla. Add ice cubes, one at a time, until thick and smooth. Serve immediately. Makes 2 tall servings.

Hot Spiced Cider

{ This cider is bold and assertive, fragrant with warming spices. Other fruit juices give it complexity. · The optional whole spices are showy on a buffet, but you might want to omit them if you're serving this cider from a thermos to red-nosed ice skaters. }

1 gallon apple cider

3 oranges

1 teaspoon ground cinnamon

1 teaspoon ground ginger

1/2 teaspoon ground cloves

1/4 cup fresh lemon juice

1/2 cup pineapple juice

1/3 cup sweetener of choice, or stevia to taste

1/4 teaspoon salt

2 cinnamon sticks, optional

2 teaspoons whole cloves, optional

Remove 2 teaspoons zest from one orange. Juice 2 oranges, and thinly slice the third.

In a 6 quart kettle or slow cooker, combine apple cider, orange juice, orange zest, cinnamon, ginger, cloves, lemon juice, pineapple juice, sweetener, and salt. If you plan to simmer cider several hours, add cinnamon sticks and whole cloves, if desired.

Add thinly sliced oranges to cider. Bring to a simmer, reduce heat, and steep cider on low for 1 to 4 hours. If using slow cooker, heat on low 4 hours. Yields 18 (8 ounce) servings.

Hot Cocoa

{ I remember Bergy's chocolate milk—in cold glass half-gallons. Grandma used to buy it from the local dairy when we visited her in Chesapeake, and I'll never forget that chocolaty, complex sweetness sliding down my throat. · I tried hard to reinvent this chocolate milk. · I changed the temperature here from cold chocolate milk to hot cocoa, but you can make it cold if you like, by chilling the syrup and then adding cold milk. · To make either hot or cold chocolate by the glass, don't add the milk, keep the syrup refrigerated, and use 3 tablespoons syrup per cup of milk. In this way, you can make chocolate milk with milk or milk substitutes to please everybody. }

1 cup sweetener of choice

3/4 cup unsweetened baking cocoa

1/2 teaspoon xanthan gum

1/2 teaspoon salt

2 teaspoons vanilla extract

2 cups water

11 cups milk or milk substitute

In a large saucepan, whisk together sweetener of choice, cocoa, xanthan gum and salt. Add water and vanilla. Bring to a boil over medium-high heat, whisking constantly. Reduce heat slightly and boil 3 minutes.

Add milk to syrup and heat to desired serving temperature. Makes approximately 14 (8 ounce) servings.

Old-Fashioned Lemonade

{ Fresh lemons are the life of lemonade. Stevia reduces the amount of sweetener you'll need; however, you can increase or decrease it as you desire. · The sliced lemons are a pretty accent, and the rind gives a bit of pungent lemon oil to the lemonade. }

9 large lemons
1 1/4 cups sweetener of choice, more or less to taste
1 teaspoon stevia
ice
water

Juice 8½ lemons, pouring juice into glass gallon container or pitcher.

Add sweetener and stevia to juice, stirring to dissolve completely. Add ice and water to make 1 gallon.

With a sharp knife, slice remaining lemon half into paper-thin slices. Float slices on lemonade, and serve. Makes 16 (8 ounce) servings.

Twenty-Minute Iced Tea

{ *This is the kind of tea I brew when everybody's thirsty, or I suddenly remember I was asked to take beverage to a hot dog roast.* }

water

9 regular-sized tea bags (black or herb tea, as desired)

1/3 cup sweetener (more or less to taste)

3 trays ice cubes

In a medium saucepan, place one quart water. Bring to a boil over high heat. Add tea bags. Remove from heat. Cover and steep 15 minutes.

Remove tea bags. Pour tea into gallon pitcher. Add sweetener and stir until dissolved. Add water until pitcher is ⅔ full. Add ice. Add more water, if needed, to make one gallon tea. Makes 16 (8 ounce) servings.

Rosy Raspberry Wedding Punch

{ *I watched, fascinated, as my big sister stirred together this juice with that juice, then back again like a chemist. Our kitchen had turned into a lab, and the quest was punch—The Perfect Punch—for her wedding reception. "How is this? Hmmm? And that?" she asked her sisters, mom, and husband-to-be as we tasted, sampled, and sipped. This recipe is the result. · "I won't tell you if this is good," one jolly good friend said at the reception, "but I'll tell you it's my third glass." · This recipe works well with any 100% juice blend that contains raspberry. Raspberry/white grape is especially nice.* }

2 (12 ounce) cans raspberry juice concentrate
1/2 cup fresh lemon juice
1 1/2 (12 ounce) cans apple juice concentrate
1 (46 ounce) can pineapple juice
15 cups ice water

Mix all together in a 2 gallon container. Refrigerate until serving. Yields 26 (8 ounce) servings.

Homemade Root Beer Suddenly

{ I've missed root beer a lot, so this summer I decided to reinvent it, naturally. I first tried the homemade brewed kind, tried it time and again with varying amounts of yeast, sweetener and sunshine. But whatever the technique, I couldn't get past the yeasty flavor. · Meanwhile, I discovered this unexpected version. It's simple, goes together in a hurry, and happily accepts any sweetener you choose. }

1/3 cup sweetener of choice, or as desired
1 level teaspoon root beer extract
1/4 teaspoon vanilla extract
1 quart chilled seltzer water

In a small pitcher or quart jar, place sweetener and root beer extract. Add seltzer water slowly down side of pitcher or jar. Stir briskly to dissolve sweetener. Serve immediately. Makes 4 (8 ounce) servings.

"Juice Pop"

{ *For the special times in life when you just "can't exist" without soda pop.* }

1 (12 ounce) can 100% juice concentrate, any flavor
1 1/2 cups cold water
3 cups seltzer water
ice

Place juice concentrate in a 2 quart pitcher. Add water and stir until concentrate is dissolved. Just before serving, add seltzer water and ice as desired. Serve immediately. Makes 7 to 8 (8 ounce) servings.

Summer Slushy Cubes

{ *Ah, slushy cubes! "The thing is," my little sister announces, "is that we should keep slushy cubes in the freezer at all times." I shake my head and say, "Isn't that a little, well, extravagant?" But then I drink one glassful, then another. "You just might be right," I concede.* }

48 ounces pineapple juice (or 12 ounces pineapple juice concentrate, plus water to equal 6 cups)

6 ounces orange juice concentrate

1/2 cup fresh lemon juice

2 cups water

1 cup sweetener of choice, more or less to taste

6 bananas, optional

3 liters seltzer water

In a large bowl or pitcher, stir together pineapple juice, orange juice concentrate, lemon juice and water.

Place 2 cups of the juice mixture into blender container. Add bananas and sweetener and puree. Add mixture to remainder of juice, and stir well.

Pour juice mixture into ice cube trays or two 9"x13" baking pans. Place mixture in freezer and freeze at least 24 hours. Remove from ice cube trays, or if frozen in pans, cut into 2" cubes, and freeze cubes for long-term storage in an airtight container in the freezer.

To serve, place 5 or 6 cubes in tall glass, fill glass with seltzer water, and allow to rest 5 minutes. Serve with straws and/or long-handled spoons. Makes approximately 15 servings.

Party Ice Cubes

{ We sisters were still in braids when we made these for orchard parties. They transform even the simplest beverage (read: water) to an elegant drink. · Use purified water for crystal-clear cubes. }

purified water

garnishes as desired: grapes, berries, mint leaves, edible flowers (such as violets, pansies, rose petals, nasturtiums)

Fill ice cube tray(s) half full of water. In each compartment, place a garnish. Freeze one hour.

Fill compartments completely with water. Freeze two hours, or until completely frozen.

Serve in tall glasses with beverage.

Cinnamon-Orange Spice Tea

{ *One morning, peddling pies at Madison farmers' market, my nephews and I shivered in the wet wind off the lakes. "I know a vendor who sells really good tea," my nephew hinted. "Sure, let's get some!" I agreed with alacrity. We bought a cup apiece, and wrapped our stiff fingers around them. We inhaled the steam and sipped the deeply spiced liquid that seared its warming way down our throats. We couldn't forget it, so we tried to recreate it—unsuccessfully, until we hit cinnamon oil. · This is a great tea for winter breakfasts, with enough caffeine to jump-start the day. · Stevia presweetens this tea, but you can omit it and drink it black or sweeten it at the table. · Save the zest from your oranges, scatter on a plate to dry, and use in your tea. It will outshine any purchased dried zest. A good, sharp zester is one of my favorite baking tools.* }

> **3 tablespoons loose-leaf black tea**
> **2 tablespoons dried orange zest**
> **35 drops cinnamon oil**
> **3-inch cinnamon stick, broken into small pieces**
> **4 whole cloves**
> **1/4 teaspoon stevia, optional**

In a small bowl, mix all ingredients. Store airtight. To make a cup of hot tea, add 1 teaspoon tea to 1 cup rapidly boiling water. Cover, remove from heat, and allow to steep 5 minutes. Strain into teacup and serve. Tea mix makes about 12 cups of tea.

Brimming Bowls

The Bread Basket Is Full Again

{Breads, Rolls, Bagels, Biscuits, Muffins, Scones & Pancakes}

Classic Skillet Corn Bread with molasses

Be gentle when you touch bread.
Let it not lie

Uncared for, unwanted.

SO OFTEN BREAD IS TAKEN FOR GRANTED.

There is so much beauty in bread—

beauty of sun and soil,

beauty of patient toil.

Winds and rains have caressed it,

Christ often blessed it.

BE GENTLE

WHEN YOU TOUCH BREAD.

-Author Unknown

chapter two

The Bread Basket Is Full Again
{Breads, Rolls, Bagels, Biscuits, Muffins, Scones and Pancakes}

Perhaps somewhere in Sicily a little girl skips homeward, a basket of warm flatbread balanced on her head. Perhaps in France, a grandpa pedals his bicycle down a Paris street, long, crusty baguettes poking out of his bicycle basket. Perhaps in Israel, Sabbath lamps alight, a family pulls soft challah apart at the braid. And perhaps somewhere in America a ravenous second-grader home from school slathers a thick piece of white bread with peanut butter and jelly, then stuffs it into his mouth all at once.

Yes, we get the picture: everyone, everywhere is enjoying bread—their biggest staple, their staff of life; the brown and black and white... everyone, that is, except us. But wait—we see another scene: hungry-eyed children, an empty table—others, too, have no bread! We feel a stab of kinship—and then incredible richness. No bread? But we can sit down to a feast of beef roast with steamed new potatoes, or roast turkey with baked wild rice, or honey-baked chicken with sweet potatoes in their jackets. And if we're still not satisfied, we can nibble a square of velvety chocolate for dessert.

We must choose to give up wheat bread for life, but we're still blessed. Like it or not, we won't (can't) have it otherwise; we choose (who wouldn't choose?) life without bread over debilitating sickness.

Gluten intolerance is a 21st century disease, unknown when man first tilled the ground and ate its fruits. Man learned to mix crushed wheat with water and bake it on stones over a hot fire, and bread was born. In Joseph's time, Egypt's seven years of bumper wheat crops fed the hungry far and wide during the next seven years of famine. By then, housewives learned that uncovered dough collected wild yeast from the air, and bread went from crusty flatbread to lighter, springier loaves. They saved a little dough from each bread baking to add to the next to keep the yeast alive. From then through the ages, bread became the backbone of food cultures around the world.

So why is gluten intolerance, almost unknown before our parents' generation, so overwhelmingly prevalent today? No one has answered this question, though there are theories. Was celiac disease simply undiagnosed until now? Is it caused by genetically modified wheat, or maybe the new, high-gluten hybrids? Or, since gluten lurks in literally half the food on store shelves, are we simply overdosed?

Theories aside, one fact remains: We're celiacs, bread makes us sick, and it must go. Taking bread out of my diet was a hard thing. I wanted desperately to fill up the empty space inside me with bread for months. When Mom pulled loaves of her fragrant wheat bread from the oven, I pinched my nose and ran for my room. I avoided the bread aisle at grocery stores. I averted my eyes when a friend munched a cinnamon roll, or a big slice of pizza, or fat pretzels from a bag. Like most just-diagnosed celiacs, I was as hungry as a spring bear, and the sight of even one dried-up, discarded bread crust was like salt on an open wound. Like a celiac friend who found herself crying for a plate of noodles, I would have given a lot for one slice of bread. Wheat has been a part of us, and a part of so many generations before us, that it is thoroughly ingrained (yes, *ingrained*) into who we are. "Just keep remembering others with no bread!" becomes a mantra.

Gradually, a diet without bread became easier for me, just as it becomes easier for all celiacs. Returning health is our reward. Moving on, we learn to find other things to satisfy our appetites. When I discovered xanthan gum, then biscuits, muffins, and scones were all I needed. I felt rich, blessed, and satisfied.

But that's not the end of the story—sometimes blessings tip the scales, run over the rim of the cup, fill life until it bursts at the seams. How shall I tell about it adequately?

Bagels entered my life first. I really had no faith in the recipe, but it surprised me. The bagels weren't perfect, but they were browned and chewy, with the flavor of something I remembered, dimly...

Sensing a bend in the road, I took the blend of flours and fiddled with it. I worked with those bagels until they tasted and looked like I remembered bagels to taste and look. The day I decided to drop the soft, cake-like dough on a baking sheet, let it rise, and bake it was a good day. The resulting rolls were crusty, had a decided spring, and tasted a little more like that something...

I worked further with the recipe; I increased and decreased the water; I tried different shapes. And then, with trepidation, I spooned the dough into a loaf pan... I baked it... It was round-topped, light, and crusty... it tasted like... why, it *was* bread!

Bread! Now with our collection of muffins and quick breads, sandwich buns and yeast breads, our life is full. We can have bread for breakfast, for lunch, for any time of day. We can break apart warm French bread and spread it with garlic butter. We can cut pumpernickel thinly, toast it, and top it with ham. We can even make ourselves a fat PB & J sandwich. We have no reason to envy anyone around the globe. With the blessed of the blessed, we have bread too.

Bread Fragments

· Learn the feel of gluten-free bread dough. If you're a bread baker, you'll immediately notice a difference. Gluten-free bread dough is really more cake batter than bread dough. The best bread has the consistency of a thick, fluffy cake batter, the best rolls slightly thinner. To learn the exact consistency is key.

· Gluten-free bread freezes well. Freeze it sliced, ready to pop in the toaster for a warm-up.

· Gluten-free bread is best just cooled. Later, it can taste fresh again toasted or rewarmed.

· Flaxseed, inexpensive and good for you, does wonderful things to gluten-free, egg-free breads. You can buy it in bulk, grind your own in the blender, and store it in the freezer.

Yeast Dough Master Mix

{ *With this blend of flours, bread has returned from distant memory to the here and now. I am so thankful for it. It cooperates with all kinds of shapes, sizes and loaves, and I know there are hundreds more just waiting to be found. · I make big batches of this mix, and store it in the freezer or refrigerator. This bread comes together quickly; from mixing bowl to loaf, it takes only an hour to an hour and a half.* }

For 9 cups mix:

2 cups cornstarch

2 cups potato starch

1 3/4 cups brown rice flour

1 1/4 cups garbanzo bean (chickpea) flour

1 cup tapioca starch

1 cup sorghum flour or amaranth flour

For 36 cups mix:

8 cups cornstarch

8 cups potato starch

7 cups brown rice flour

5 cups garbanzo bean (chickpea) flour

4 cups tapioca starch

4 cups sorghum flour or amaranth flour

In a very large container, stir together all ingredients very well. Scoop mix into sturdy plastic bags, tie tightly, and freeze or refrigerate.

Brown Bread

{ Make this your basic loaf, the one you serve for everything. Frozen sliced, it rewarms beautifully in the toaster. Morning toast once again—gluten-free! }
"For all these mercies, Lord, we thank Thee!"

3 cups Yeast Dough Master Mix

1 tablespoon dry yeast

1 tablespoon xanthan gum

2 teaspoons salt

3 tablespoons ground flaxseed

1/4 cup sweetener of choice

2 tablespoons light olive or vegetable oil

2 tablespoons blackstrap molasses

1 teaspoon cider vinegar

2 teaspoons liquid lecithin

2 to 2 1/2 cups warm water

Preheat oven to 350°. Grease two 4"x8" loaf pans.

In bowl of mixer, combine mix, yeast, xanthan gum, salt, flaxseed and sweetener. Add oil, molasses, vinegar, lecithin, and 2 cups of the warm water. Beat well. Check consistency: dough should hold its shape very well, and be about the same consistency as a medium-thick cake batter. Add a little more water if needed—a total of 2¼ cups water is very close. Turn mixer on high and beat 4 minutes.

Turn batter into prepared pans. Cover with plastic wrap and allow to rise in a warm spot for about 40 minutes. Remove plastic wrap and bake 40 to 50 minutes, or until loaves are very brown, crusty, and hollow-sounding when tapped.
Do not underbake.

Remove pans and cool bread on wire rack. Serve just-baked. Toast or reheat after 12 hours. Slice and freeze for long-term storage. Yields 2 loaves.

Heidelberg "Pumpernickel" Bread

{ Plump, dark and fragrant, these loaves are a joy. They are so "rye-lessly" pumpernickel. They're rustic, yet, sliced thinly and sandwiched with shaved ham, they are somehow sophisticated. · I've never met anyone else who eats pumpernickel for breakfast, but I like it, toasted, with butter, of course. Some day I want to hollow a loaf and use it for an edible dip bowl—maybe with spinach dip, made with Sour Supreme. }

2 1/2 cups Yeast Dough Master Mix
1 tablespoon dry yeast
1 tablespoon xanthan gum
2 1/2 teaspoons salt
2 tablespoons ground flaxseed
1/4 cup unsweetened baking cocoa
1 tablespoon caraway seed
1/2 cup baking molasses
1/2 teaspoon cider vinegar
1 teaspoon liquid lecithin
3 tablespoons olive oil
1 3/4 cups warm water, or as needed
additional caraway seed for sprinkling, if desired

Preheat oven to 325°. Grease two 9" round cake pans.

In a mixer bowl, combine mix, yeast, xanthan gum, salt, flaxseed, cocoa, and caraway seed. Add molasses, vinegar, lecithin, and oil. Add 1¾ cups warm water, mix well, and check consistency: batter should resemble thick cake batter. A spoon should almost stand upright in batter, and it should be stretchy rather than soft. Add up to ⅓ cup more water, if needed, to reach this consistency. Turn mixer to high and beat 4 minutes.

Divide batter evenly between prepared pans, piling dough into high, 6" diameter mounds. Allow to rise for 30 to 45 minutes. Sprinkle loaves with caraway seed, if desired. Bake loaves for 45 to 60 minutes, until crusty, firm, and hollow-sounding when tapped. Cool before serving. Serve within 12 hours, or toast to reheat. Makes 2 loaves.

Crusty French Bread

{ These loaves are so crusty-crisp on the outside, so springy inside, and so skinny and long (read: so normal), they excite me. Baking them is exciting, too. You spray the risen loaves and put them in the hot oven, and they steam and sizzle, and get hard, toothsome crusts as all good little baguettes do. · This bread begs to go picnicking. I haven't yet packed a basket with a bunch of grapes, a bar of chocolate, butter, and a loaf of this bread warm from the oven, and headed off to a green hill with a friend (either book or human), but one of these days, maybe in sunny July, I'll be off. }

3 cups Yeast Dough Master Mix
1 tablespoon dry yeast
4 teaspoons xanthan gum
2 teaspoons salt
2 tablespoons sweetener of choice
2 tablespoons olive or vegetable oil
1/2 teaspoon cider vinegar
2 to 2 1/2 cups warm water
cornmeal, for sprinkling
additional water, for spraying loaves

Preheat oven to 450°. Grease two 10"x15" baking pans, and sprinkle with cornmeal.

In mixer bowl, combine mix, yeast, xanthan gum, salt, and sweetener. Mix well. Add oil, vinegar, and 2 cups of the warm water. Beat well. Check consistency: batter should be like a medium-stiff cake batter, holding its shape when spooned into a mound. Add more water if needed to achieve this consistency. Beat 4 minutes.

Spoon batter into 4 long, thin loaves, each about 2"x10", mounding batter slightly along the centers, and smoothing with spoon. Allow to rise 30 minutes.

Continued

Spray loaves well with water from a misting bottle. Bake loaves, spraying 4 more times in 4-minute intervals. Reduce heat to 425°, and bake until very browned and crusty, about 35 minutes total, switching pans if necessary so loaves brown evenly. The crusts should be completely crisp. Serve just-baked, or within 12 hours. Freeze and reheat to maintain freshness. Makes 4 loaves.

Classic Garlic Bread

{ *It's back—serve it with tomato-ey, basil-y Italian dishes as of old. You can comfortably increase the garlic to two cloves or more, depending on personal taste.* }

1 loaf Crusty French Bread
1/3 cup butter, very soft
2 teaspoons dried parsley flakes, optional
1 clove garlic, minced or pressed
salt

Preheat oven to 300°.

In a small bowl, stir together butter, parsley, and garlic. Slice French Bread diagonally into thick, ¾" slices. Spread both sides of each slice liberally with butter mixture, and sprinkle with salt. Reassemble loaf on a long piece of aluminum foil. Wrap foil tightly around loaf.

Bake bread 15 to 20 minutes, or until butter is melted, and bread well heated. Serve warm.

Sandwich Buns

{ *Eating sandwiches again, I understand why mankind is so lastingly dependent on them, so ready to think of them first of all for a quick, packable lunch. · The amount of water here is extremely important. Start with the smallest amount suggested, and add more if needed, a tablespoon at a time, to get the recommended consistency. Most of the work is simply learning to tell by look and feel when you've got the dough right.* }

3 cups Yeast Dough Master Mix
1 tablespoon dry yeast
1 tablespoon xanthan gum
2 tablespoons ground flaxseed
2 teaspoons salt
1/3 cup sweetener of choice
2 tablespoons light olive or vegetable oil
1 teaspoon liquid lecithin
1 teaspoon apple cider vinegar
2 to 2 1/2 cups warm water

Preheat oven to 350°. Grease one 11"x17" baking sheet, or two 10"x15" baking sheets.

In large mixer bowl, combine mix, yeast, xanthan gum, flaxseed, salt and sweetener. Stir well. Add oil, lecithin, vinegar and 2 cups of the water. Beat on high speed to blend well. Check consistency: mixture should hold its shape well, but be soft, like a medium cake batter. Add more water if needed to achieve this consistency. Turn mixer on high and beat 3 minutes.

With a large serving spoon, scoop batter onto prepared baking sheet(s) to make 12 mounds. Place in warm, draft-free place to rise for 20 to 30 minutes.

Continued

Bake buns for 40 to 50 minutes or until they are browned, crusty, and well done in center. To check for doneness, remove one from the oven and let cool 2 minutes. If bun doesn't shrink, it's done. Remove from pans and allow to cool on wire racks. Serve warm. Reheat or toast before serving after 12 hours. Freeze for long-term storage. Makes 12 large sandwich buns.

Honey-"Whole Wheat" Buns

{ *Not whole wheat, of course, but darker and heartier than most, these sandwich buns are for those of us who grew up on hefty, home-milled bread. · Blackstrap molasses, a surprising ingredient, gives these buns the classical "wheaty" color and earthier flavor.* }

3 cups Yeast Dough Master Mix
1 tablespoon dry yeast
1 tablespoon xanthan gum
3 tablespoons ground flaxseed
2 teaspoons salt
1/4 cup honey
2 tablespoons blackstrap molasses
2 tablespoons olive or vegetable oil
1 teaspoon liquid lecithin
1 teaspoon cider vinegar
2 to 2 1/2 cups warm water

To make buns, follow directions for Sandwich Buns, adding honey and molasses with liquids.

Rustic Onion Buns

{ Onion buns have a long and exciting history among the Kennell sisters, and it was my delight to recreate them gluten-free. They shine sandwiched with ham and cheese. }

3/4 cup chopped onion

3 tablespoons butter or light olive or vegetable oil

3 cups Yeast Dough Master Mix

1 tablespoon dry yeast

1 tablespoon xanthan gum

2 tablespoons ground flaxseed

2 teaspoons salt

1/3 cup sweetener of choice

1 teaspoon liquid lecithin

1 teaspoon cider vinegar

2 to 2 1/2 cups warm water

Preheat oven to 350°. Grease one 11"x17" or two 10"x15" baking pan(s).

In a small skillet, sauté onions in butter or oil until translucent, about 5 minutes. Set aside to cool.

In a large mixer bowl, combine mix, yeast, xanthan gum, flaxseed, salt and sweetener of choice. Reserve 3 tablespoons onion mixture, and add remaining to dry ingredients along with lecithin, vinegar and 2 cups of the water. Beat well. Check consistency. Batter should hold its shape, but be very soft, like a medium cake batter. Add more water as needed to achieve consistency. Beat at high speed 3 minutes.

With a large serving spoon, scoop batter onto prepared baking sheet(s) into 12 mounds. Spoon 1 teaspoon reserved sautéed onion on top of each bun.

Allow buns to rise 30 minutes. Bake 35 to 45 minutes, or until buns are browned and crusty and do not shrink when removed from oven. Remove to wire racks and serve warm. Toast or reheat after 12 hours. Freeze for long-term storage. Yields 12 buns.

Garlic-Rosemary Buns

{ Rosemary, I think, is just as much about fragrance as taste. Garlic is its natural companion. Perhaps earthy garlic anchors rosemary's tall-pines piquancy. · Just-made, these rolls (with plenty of butter), can ride in a backpack or grace a candlelit dinner with equal éclat. }

1 recipe Sandwich Bun batter (see index)
2 teaspoons dried rosemary
2 large cloves of garlic, minced or pressed
extra-virgin olive oil, or light olive oil
additional dried rosemary, for sprinkling

Grease two 10"x15" baking pans. Preheat oven to 350°.

Prepare Sandwich Bun batter according to recipe. When batter has been beaten, add the 2 teaspoons rosemary and the minced garlic. Mix well.

Drop batter by heaping tablespoons onto prepared pan, making mounds about 2½" in diameter. Drizzle each roll with olive oil and sprinkle with rosemary. Allow rolls to rise 30 to 45 minutes, or until doubled.

Bake rolls 25 to 35 minutes, or until rolls are browned, crusty, and do not shrink when removed from oven. Serve just warm or cooled. After 12 hours, freeze for freshness, toasting before serving. Makes about 18 to 20 rolls.

Pocket Ham & Cheese Buns

{ Here's my version of the classic plowman's lunch. Tuck a wrapped bun in your pocket or purse and you're set for whatever life holds—plowing or otherwise. }

1 recipe Sandwich Bun or Onion Bun batter (see index)
2 cups cubed fully cooked ham
2 cups cubed cheese or cheese substitute
light olive oil, for drizzling
sesame seeds, for sprinkling

Preheat oven to 325°. Grease two 10"x15" baking pans.

Prepare bun batter as directed in recipe. Drop half of the batter by heaping tablespoons about 5" apart on prepared baking sheet. Spread each thinly to about 3" in diameter.

Sprinkle each circle of dough with ham and cheese, dividing evenly. Drop remaining batter by heaping tablespoons over ham and cheese. Spread batter to cover most of ham and cheese cubes. The ham and cheese doesn't need to be completely covered. Drizzle each bun with olive oil and sprinkle with sesame seeds.

Allow buns to rise 30 to 45 minutes or until doubled. Bake buns 35 to 45 minutes, or until browned, crusty, and cheese is melting. Serve warm or within 12 hours. Freeze and reheat for freshness. Makes about 15 buns.

Pizza Crust

{ This crust bakes light, browns beautifully, and, if prebaked, holds its texture well under toppings. · Water is the crucial ingredient here—too much and your crust will be soggy, too little and it will have a stiff bread-like texture. Notice carefully how it spreads in the pan—it should spread smoothly under the spatula but with noticeable resistance. It's worth mixing again to add a little more water or rice flour, if needed. You'll get the knack of it! · The three minutes of beating are essential for an elastic texture. }

> 1/2 cup arrowroot powder or cornstarch
>
> 1/2 cup tapioca starch
>
> 1 cup garbanzo or garbanzo-fava bean flour
>
> 1 cup brown rice flour
>
> 1 tablespoon xanthan gum
>
> 2 tablespoons sweetener of choice, optional
>
> 1 1/2 teaspoons salt
>
> 4 teaspoons dry yeast
>
> 1 1/2 cups warm water, or more as needed
>
> 3 tablespoons olive oil
>
> 1/2 teaspoon cider vinegar

Combine arrowroot powder, tapioca starch, bean and rice flours, xanthan gum, sweetener, salt, and yeast in a large bowl of a standing mixer.

Stir together warm water, oil, and vinegar and add to dry ingredients. Beat with mixer 3 minutes until smooth and elastic, testing consistency during first minute of beating. Consistency should be a soft dough, much like a stiff cake batter. Add up to ¼ cup more warm water to achieve this.

Proceed with desired recipe.

Garlic-Mozzarella Focaccia

{ This playful bread goes well with many things. Try it solo for a snack, with a green salad for lunch, or in the bread basket at dinner. · My sister thinks this is an astronomical amount of garlic. Make one of the focaccia variations if you'd rather, though I like garlic in all of them. }

1 recipe **Pizza Crust** dough
4 garlic cloves, pressed or finely minced
2 tablespoons olive oil
2 cups finely shredded mozzarella cheese or cheese substitute

Preheat oven to 475°.

Spread dough thinly on 2 greased 10"x15" pans (a free-form shape is fine). Allow to rise in a draft-free place 15 minutes.

Combine garlic with oil and brush over focaccia. Sprinkle with cheese.

Bake focaccia 15 minutes, rotating pans once. Bake 5 to 10 minutes longer, if necesary, until browned and puffy. Cut into triangles or irregular pieces and serve warm. Makes about 30 servings.

Variations:

Garlic and Olive Focaccia: After brushing dough with oil/garlic mixture, sprinkle with 1 cup thinly sliced black olives, then cheese, and bake.

Garlic and Ham Focaccia: After brushing dough with oil/garlic mixture, and before sprinkling with cheese, scatter with 2 cups fully cooked ham, diced, plus a little onion if you like, and bake.

Continued

Caramelized Onion Focaccia: Omit garlic and heat the oil in a large frying pan. Slice 1 large onion, thinly, and fry over medium-low heat until onion browns and begins to caramelizes, about 20 minutes. Spread over dough, and bake, with or without the cheese.

Pepperoni and Parmesan Focaccia: Omit or reduce the amount of garlic. Brush dough with the oil and sprinkle with pepperoni slices and a generous sprinkling of Parmesan cheese or Parmesan substitute. Omit shredded cheese. Bake.

Really, Truly Bagels

{ *Really, Truly Bagels are really, truly bagels. They are fat and brown with holes in their middles, and when you bite them, they pull away with a toothsome chew. Eat them with cream cheese for breakfast, sandwich them with ham for lunch, serve them warm with soup for supper. · Boiling is the secret to bagel's chew. Evaporated cane juice added to the boiling water gives a shiny brown crust. · Keep a cache of split Really, Truly Bagels in the freezer—like all bagels, they reheat beautifully in the toaster.* }

2/3 cup brown rice flour

1/3 cup garbanzo or garbanzo-fava flour

2/3 cup potato starch

2/3 cup cornstarch

1/3 cup tapioca starch

1 cup sorghum or amaranth flour

1 1/2 teaspoon salt

2 teaspoons ground flaxseed

1 tablespoon xanthan gum

1 tablespoon dry yeast

2 tablespoons sweetener of choice

2 tablespoons olive oil

1 teaspoon cider vinegar

1 1/4 cups warm water, or more as needed

additional brown rice flour, for shaping bagels

additional water, for boiling bagels

1 tablespoon evaporated cane juice, for boiling bagels

Mix flours, starches, salt, flaxseed, xanthan gum, yeast, and sweetener in a mixer bowl. Stir together oil, vinegar and warm water and add to dry

Continued

ingredients. Beat at high speed for 3 minutes. Check consistency after first minute of beating, and add a little more water if needed to make a soft dough like a cake batter, but stiff enough to hold its shape when spooned.

Preheat oven to 375°. Grease 2 or 3 large baking sheets.

Using a soup spoon, scoop out large spoonfuls of batter onto a plate of rice flour. Shape into a smooth round, then shape hole with your fingers. Place on prepared baking sheets to rise about 10 minutes.

Fill a large, wide saucepan with water and add the 1 tablespoon evaporated cane juice. Bring to a boil. In batches of three or four, drop bagels into water and boil 2 minutes, turning once. With slotted spoon, remove bagels back to the same baking sheets. Sometimes excess flour on the bagels will thicken the water; if this happens, empty pan and reheat fresh water with additional evaporated cane juice.

Bake bagels 25 to 30 minutes or until they are deeply browned all over. Serve warm, within 12 hours, or reheated in toaster.

Variations:
Poppy Seed Bagels: Sprinkle bagels just before baking with poppy seeds.

Garlic-Rosemary Bagels: Add 2 cloves minced garlic to bagel dough before shaping. Sprinkle bagels with rosemary leaves before baking.

Cinnamon-Raisin Bagels: Add 1 cup raisins to bagel batter before shaping, then just before baking, sprinkle with cinnamon or cinnamon-sugar.

Classic Skillet Cornbread

Cornbread has many personalities. Southerners like it, Mom says, slathered with butter and molasses. Westerners eat it with chili— either atop or on the side. And Midwesterners often turn it into dessert, dousing it with sweetened berries and drowning it with the ever-ready milk pitcher. Comparing, I find the differences lie in the ratio of cornmeal to flour and the amount of sweetening. Adjust the sweetener in this recipe to suit your personal culture. · I make this recipe with fine cornmeal. If you use a coarser grind, the batter will be slightly wetter, almost "runny", but will thicken to normal consistency if you allow it to rest 10 minutes before baking.

1 cup finely ground yellow cornmeal

1 cup brown rice flour

1/2 teaspoon xanthan gum

3/4 teaspoon salt

2 tablespoons sweetener of choice, more or less as desired

1 tablespoon baking powder

1/3 cup unsweetened applesauce

1/4 cup melted butter

1 1/2 cups water, or more as needed

Preheat oven to 375°. Place butter in a 9" round iron skillet, baking pan or pie pan. Place pan in oven to melt butter.

Stir together cornmeal, flour, xanthan gum, salt, sweetener, and baking powder in a large bowl. Remove melted butter from oven, swirl it to coat sides of pan, then add it to the dry ingredients along with the applesauce and 1½ cups of water. Stir just to moisten dry ingredients. Add enough water to make a batter that will slide easily from a spoon, mounding only slightly. Pour into the prepared pan.

Bake cornbread for 20 to 30 minutes or until browned and crusty. Serve warm.

Classic Everyday Biscuits

{ This recipe is a springboard that can be taken just about anywhere.
· A cousin on a wheat-free diet uses these biscuits for bread. She's
made some interesting discoveries with them. Once she was called
away, and the dough had to rest unbaked in the pan. "This won't work,"
she thought, but baked them anyway. They were the lightest, softest
biscuits ever, and now she always lets the dough rest at least an hour.
I haven't tried this, but I give you her suggestion, in case you'd like to. }

> **2 1/2 cups brown rice flour**
> **1/2 teaspoon xanthan gum**
> **1/2 teaspoon salt**
> **1 tablespoon baking powder**
> **1 tablespoon sweetener of choice**
> **1/3 cup butter, slightly softened**
> **1 1/2 cups cold milk, milk substitute, or water**
> **additional milk or milk substitute for brushing, if desired**

Preheat oven to 400°.

In a large bowl, stir together flour, xanthan gum, salt, baking powder, and
sweetener. Cut in butter with a pastry blender or your fingers until only
small lumps remain. Toss mixture with just enough of the water or milk to
make a dough slightly stiffer than a batter but still very sticky. Add more
milk if dough seems too stiff.

Turn dough out onto a rice-floured surface and knead 10 to 12 turns. Pat out
to 1" thickness and cut into circles. Place on large ungreased baking sheet.
Brush with milk or milk substitute if desired.

Bake biscuits 20 to 25 minutes or until nicely browned. Serve warm with
butter and honey.

Green Onion-Cheese Biscuits

{ *Here is a little biscuit so hearty that, paired with green salad, it can stand in for supper all by itself. Serve warm with lots of butter.* }

2 1/2 cups brown rice flour
1 tablespoon baking powder
1/2 teaspoon baking soda
1/2 teaspoon xanthan gum
1 tablespoon sweetener of choice
1/2 teaspoon salt
1/3 cup cold butter
3/4 cup sliced green onion
1 cup grated cheese or cheese substitute
1 1/2 cups cold milk, milk substitute, or water
additional milk or milk substitute, for brushing

Preheat oven to 400°. Grease a large baking sheet.

In a large bowl, stir together brown rice flour, baking powder, baking soda, xanthan gum, sweetener, and salt. Cut in butter until only small pea-sized lumps remain. Toss in onions and cheese.

Add milk or milk substitute to mixture, tossing just until mixture forms a very soft dough. Turn dough out onto a rice-floured surface and knead 8 times. Pat dough out into a circle 1" thick and cut biscuits with a round cutter. Place biscuits on prepared baking sheet. Brush with milk or milk substitute.

Bake biscuits 20 to 25 minutes or until they are nicely browned. Serve warm with butter.

Cinnamon-Raisin Biscuits

Cinnamon-Raisin Biscuits shine brightest at breakfast. Serve them warm with butter. If your family rises with the roosters, mix the dry ingredients the night before. They can bake in the time it takes to brew a pot of peppermint tea.

- **2 1/2 cups brown rice flour**
- **1 tablespoon baking powder**
- **1/2 teaspoon xanthan gum**
- **1/2 teaspoon baking soda**
- **1/2 teaspoon salt**
- **3 tablespoons sweetener of choice**
- **1 teaspoon ground cinnamon**
- **1/3 cup cold butter**
- **1 1/2 cups cold milk, milk substitute, or water**
- **1 cup raisins**
- **additional milk or milk substitute, for brushing**
- **evaporated cane juice, for sprinkling**

Preheat oven to 400°.

In a large bowl, stir together the brown rice flour, baking powder, xanthan gum, baking soda, salt, sweetener and cinnamon. Cut in butter until only small pea-sized lumps remain. Toss with milk or milk substitute, adding just enough to make a dough stiffer than a batter, but still very sticky. Stir just until dough comes together into a ball. Fold in raisins.

Turn dough out onto a rice-floured surface and knead 8 turns. Pat dough out into a 1" thick circle. Cut out biscuits with a round cutter. Place biscuits on a large baking sheet. Brush biscuits with additional milk or milk substitute and sprinkle with evaporated cane juice.

Bake biscuits 20 to 25 minutes or until nicely browned. Serve warm with butter.

Corn Drop Biscuits

{ I made these simple biscuits a lot before the advent of Sandwich Buns. Crusty, flat, and flavorful, they still make delicious sandwiches, especially when served warm. · I use finely ground cornmeal in this recipe. If you use coarser cornmeal, allow batter to stand 10 minutes before baking. The amount of liquid is very important here: too much, and the biscuits will run together, too little, and they will mound and be crumbly instead of crisp. How the batter spreads on the pan is the test—it should flatten and spread slowly. Use more brown rice flour or water to correct consistency. }

1 cup cornmeal

1 cup brown rice flour

1 teaspoon xanthan gum

2 teaspoons baking powder

1/2 teaspoon baking soda

1 teaspoon salt

1 cup buttermilk (or milk substitute with 1 teaspoon cider vinegar), or more as needed

1/3 cup light olive oil or vegetable oil

Preheat oven to 400°.

Stir together cornmeal, brown rice flour, xanthan gum, baking powder, baking soda and salt. Add buttermilk or substitute and oil. Mix well. Check consistency, and add more liquid, if needed, until batter will run off the edge of spoon.

Grease a large baking sheet (or two 10"x15") and drop batter by tablespoons a few inches apart. Batter should spread a little, making round, flat biscuits. Add more liquid if necessary.

Bake biscuits about 20 minutes or until edges are browned and centers are firm. Serve warm immediately, or store airtight and serve toasted.

Makes about 12 biscuits.

Sweet Potato-Buttermilk Biscuits

{ Sweet potatoes add a full, rounded flavor to basic buttermilk biscuits.
They're at top best served warm with butter and honey, and/or paired }
with a pot of hearty soup.

> **1 3/4 cup brown rice flour**
> **1/2 teaspoon xanthan gum**
> **3/4 teaspoon salt**
> **2 tablespoons evaporated cane juice**
> **2 1/2 teaspoons baking powder**
> **1/2 teaspoon baking soda**
> **1/3 cup cold butter**
> **3/4 cup cooked, mashed sweet potatoes**
> **1/2 cup buttermilk (or milk substitute, plus 1 tablespoon cider vinegar), or more as needed**

Preheat oven to 400°.

In a large bowl, stir together flour, xanthan gum, salt, evaporated cane juice, baking powder and baking soda. Cut butter into small pieces and toss with the dry ingredients.

Add sweet potato and buttermilk or substitute to the mixture. Stir just until moistened, adding just enough liquid to make a soft, sticky dough, up to ¾ cup total.

Turn dough out onto a rice-floured surface and knead 5 to 6 turns. Pat out to 1" thickness and cut with 2" round cutter (or pat into a rectangle and use a sharp knife to cut into 2" squares). Place 2" apart on a large baking sheet. If you like, brush with extra milk or substitute.

Bake for 20 minutes or until biscuits are a golden brown. Serve warm.
Makes 8 or 9 biscuits.

Classic Everyday Muffins

{ *Eat these muffins warm (with butter, of course) and you'll wish breakfast could last all day. The secret to their moistness is the unexpected addition of jam in the dough. · Batter consistency is very important in muffins. When you drop it into muffin tins, the batter should slide off the spoon in large blobs. It should be soft and light. Stiff batter makes crumbly muffins, and runny batter makes sunken-center muffins— though it's better to err on the runny side. Always, always, whatever you do, avoid the crumbly muffin!* }

> 1 1/2 cups brown rice flour
>
> 2 teaspoons baking powder
>
> 1/2 teaspoon salt
>
> 1/2 teaspoon baking soda
>
> 2 tablespoons sweetener of choice
>
> 1/2 teaspoon xanthan gum
>
> 1 cup milk or water, or more if needed
>
> 3 tablespoons unsweetened apricot jam or other light-colored jam of choice
>
> 1/4 cup light olive or vegetable oil

Preheat oven to 400°.

Stir together flour, baking powder, salt, baking soda, sweetener and xanthan gum. In a separate bowl, stir together liquid, jam, and oil.

Add liquids to dry ingredients, stirring just to mix. Add a bit more water, if needed, to make a soft batter. Drop into 8 greased muffin cups.

Bake muffins for 15 to 20 minutes or until browned and springy. Serve warm with butter and more jam. Makes 8 muffins.

Apple-Cinnamon Muffins

{ Apple and cinnamon are an enduring pair, and muffins host them well.
Serve them on chilly fall mornings, warm, with apple butter. }

1 1/2 cups brown rice flour

2 teaspoons baking powder

1/2 teaspoon salt

1/4 teaspoon baking soda

2 tablespoons sweetener

1/2 teaspoon xanthan gum

1 teaspoon ground cinnamon

1 1/4 cups milk or water, or more as needed

3 tablespoons unsweetened applesauce

1/4 cup light olive or vegetable oil

1 cup cored and chopped red apple

Preheat oven to 400°. Grease 10 muffin cups.

In a medium-sized bowl, stir together the brown rice flour, baking powder, salt, baking soda, sweetener, xanthan gum and cinnamon. In a separate bowl, stir together milk or water, applesauce, and oil.

Add liquids to flour mixture, stirring just to mix. Fold in chopped apple. Drop dough into prepared muffin tin.

Bake muffins for 15 to 20 minutes or until they are lightly browned and springy in the centers. Serve warm. Makes 10 muffins.

Pumpkin Pecan-Streusel Muffins

{ Here's an elite muffin. Dressy with the autumnal pairing of pumpkin and pecans, they stay soft and moist. They're a natural for company bread baskets. }

1 1/2 cups brown rice flour

2 teaspoons baking powder

1/2 teaspoon baking soda

1/2 teaspoon salt

1/2 teaspoon xanthan gum

3 tablespoons sweetener of choice

2 teaspoons ground cinnamon

1/4 teaspoon ground ginger

1 1/4 cups milk or milk substitute, or more as needed

1 teaspoon apple cider vinegar

1/2 cup cooked, pureed pumpkin

1/4 cup light olive or vegetable oil

3 tablespoons evaporated cane juice

2 tablespoons chopped pecans

2 teaspoons melted butter

Preheat oven to 400°. Grease 8 muffin cups.

In a large bowl, stir together the brown rice flour, baking powder, baking soda, salt, xanthan gum, sweetener, and spices. In another bowl, stir together the milk or substitute, vinegar, pumpkin, and oil. Add to dry ingredients, stirring just until moistened. Test consistency: dough should drop off the end of the spoon in large, fluffy spoonfuls. Add more milk or substitute if dough is too stiff. Drop dough into the prepared muffin pan.

For the streusel, in a small bowl combine the evaporated cane juice, pecans and melted butter. Sprinkle streusel over dough in muffin pan.

Bake muffins 15 to 20 minutes, or until they spring back in centers when lightly touched. Serve warm with butter. Makes 8 muffins.

Wild Berry-Sour Cream Scones

{ *The summer my nephew Benjamin was born was a good year for wild berries. Benjie, a round-faced cotton top, had eyes like blueberries himself. He was hospitalized four times the first months of his life, and in the middle of coping with monitors, oxygen tubes and counting breaths-per-minute, we found time occasionally to break away and go on calming forays to the berry patch. My sister and I developed these scones together. Her family loved them with hot tea for breakfast. · Now Benjie, sturdy and still white-blond, likes to toddle along with us out to the mulberry tree. · You can use any jam in this recipe. I made it once with orange marmalade and it was exceptionally nice. These scones are rich, but don't think of eating them without butter.* }

3 cups brown rice flour

1/2 teaspoon salt

1/2 teaspoon xanthan gum

2 teaspoons baking powder

1/2 teaspoon baking soda

3 tablespoons sweetener of choice

1/2 cup butter, slightly softened

1 1/2 cups fresh berries of choice

3 tablespoons unsweetened apricot jam

1 cup sour cream or Sour Supreme

1/4 cup cold milk, milk substitute, or water, or more as needed

evaporated cane juice for sprinkling

Preheat oven to 375°.

In a large bowl, stir together flour, salt, xanthan gum, baking powder, baking soda, and sweetener. Cut in butter until only small lumps remain. Add berries and toss.

Continued

In a small bowl, stir together the jam, sour cream or substitute and the cold milk or water. Toss into dry ingredients just until combined. If dough is stiff, add up to ¼ cup more milk or water, but don't overmix. Dough should come together nicely, with a sticky but not batter-like consistency.

Divide dough in half. Pat both halves onto a large greased baking sheet into 1" thick circles. Cut each into six wedges. Move wedges slightly apart on cookie sheet. Sprinkle with evaporated cane juice.

Bake scones 25 minutes or until browned and springy. Serve warm with butter, honey and jam. Makes 12 scones.

Banana-Walnut bread

{ Bananas give sweetness, depth and moisture to most gluten-free baked goods, and this quick bread is a classic example. · Walnuts are optional in this recipe, but delightful against the soft, tender bread. }

3 cups brown rice flour

3/4 to 1 cup evaporated cane juice

1 teaspoon salt

1 1/2 teaspoons xanthan gum

1 1/2 teaspoons baking soda

1 cup broken walnuts

6 ripe bananas

1 cup olive or vegetable oil

1 1/4 cups milk, milk substitute or water, or more if needed

1 tablespoon apple cider vinegar

1 teaspoon vanilla extract

Preheat oven to 325°. Grease and flour two 4"x8" loaf pans.

In a large bowl, stir together rice flour, evaporated cane juice, salt, xanthan gum, and baking soda. Stir well. Add walnuts.

In a medium bowl, place peeled bananas and mash with a potato masher. Add oil, milk or substitute, vinegar and vanilla and mix well.

Add wet ingredients to dry all at once, and stir with a large rubber spatula just until flour is moistened. Batter should be soft, just holding its shape when mounded. If needed, add a little more liquid, stirring carefully.

Pour batter into prepared pans and bake 45 to 50 minutes until browned and springy in the center. Cool 20 minutes, remove pans, and finish cooling on racks. Store airtight, and freeze after 5 days. Makes 2 loaves (about 20 servings).

Pumpkin-Pecan Bread

{ Some pumpkin breads are high and firm, others soft and cake-like. This is a cake-like version. It's a good keeper and tastes best the second day. }

1 cup cooked, pureed pumpkin

2/3 cup evaporated cane juice

1 tablespoon baking molasses or maple syrup

1/4 cup light olive or vegetable oil

1 cup buttermilk, or milk substitute plus 2 tablespoons cider vinegar

1 1/2 cups brown rice flour

1 1/4 teaspoons ground cinnamon

1/2 teaspoon xanthan gum

1 teaspoon baking powder

1 teaspoon baking soda

1/2 teaspoon salt

1 tablespoon ground flaxseed

1 cup chopped pecans

Preheat oven to 350°. Grease and flour one 4"x8" loaf pan.

In a large bowl, whisk together pumpkin, evaporated cane juice, molasses or maple syrup, oil, and buttermilk or substitute. In a separate bowl, combine flour, cinnamon, xanthan gum, baking powder, baking soda, salt, and flaxseed. Add to liquids all at once, and stir just to combine. Fold in pecans.

Bake loaf 45 to 50 minutes, or until bread tests done in center of loaf. Allow to cool 10 minutes in pan, then remove and cool completely on wire rack. Makes 1 loaf.

Marbled Orange-Chocolate Bread

Orange and chocolate do good things for each other in this quick-bread now company-bread. Serve it to your most discerning guests.

1 1/2 cups brown rice flour
1/2 cup sweetener of choice
1 tablespoon baking powder
1/2 teaspoon baking soda
1/2 teaspoon xanthan gum
3/4 teaspoon salt
1 cup fresh orange juice
1/2 cup water, or up to 1 cup, as needed
1/4 cup unsweetened applesauce
1/2 cup melted butter
1/4 cup unsweetened baking cocoa
2 teaspoons grated orange peel
Orange Glaze, if desired (see index)

Preheat oven to 350°. Grease 4"x8" loaf pan.

In a large bowl, stir together brown rice flour, sweetener, baking powder, baking soda, xanthan gum, and salt. Add orange juice, ½ cup of the water, applesauce, and melted butter, stirring well to make a soft but spoonable batter. Add more water as needed.

Divide batter in half. To one portion add the cocoa, mixing well. To the other, add the grated orange rind. Spoon large spoonfuls of chocolate and orange batter alternately into prepared pan. Run a knife through batter several times to marble.

Bake loaf for 55 to 60 minutes, or until bread draws away from sides of pan and springs back when touched lightly in center. Allow to cool 10 minutes. Remove from pan and brush Orange Glaze over loaf, if desired. Serve warm or cooled, within 24 hours. Slice and freeze to maintain freshness. Makes 1 loaf.

Featherlight Flax & Bran Pancakes

{ These pancakes fry up light and tasty. They showcase good-for-you flaxseed and rice bran. Add more of each if you like—and more water to compensate, if needed. }

light olive or coconut oil, for frying
1 3/4 cups brown rice flour
1/4 cup cornstarch
2 teaspoons baking soda
1/2 teaspoon xanthan gum
1/2 teaspoon salt
1 tablespoon sweetener of choice
2 tablespoons rice bran
1 tablespoon ground flaxseed
1/4 cup light olive or vegetable oil
3 tablespoons cider vinegar
1 2/3 to 2 cups water
maple syrup, butter, apple butter or jam, to serve

Heat a skillet over medium heat. Oil lightly.

In a large bowl whisk together brown rice flour, cornstarch, baking soda, xanthan gum, salt, sweetener, rice bran and flaxseed. Add oil, vinegar and 1⅔ cups water and stir to mix well.

Spoon a pancake onto heated skillet. Batter should puff and rise, flowing outward slightly. If pancake is too thick, and doesn't fry properly in the center, add water up to 2 cups total. Fry pancakes, oiling skillet as needed.

Serve pancakes warm with choice of syrups, butters, or jams.

Rustic Cornmeal Pancakes

{ This is a well-thumbed recipe. We stir it up for all occasions, and serve it with maple syrup for breakfast or molasses alongside a chili supper. · If you use coarse cornmeal, allow batter to rest 10 minutes before correcting consistency and frying. }

light olive oil or coconut oil, for frying

1 cup yellow cornmeal

1 1/2 cups brown rice flour

1 teaspoon xanthan gum

1 teaspoon salt

1 tablespoon baking powder

2 tablespoons evaporated cane juice

1/2 cup olive oil or vegetable oil

2 cups warm water, or more as needed

butter, molasses, honey, maple syrup or jam, for serving

Heat griddle over medium heat. Generously grease with oil.

In a large mixing bowl, stir together cornmeal, brown rice flour, xanthan gum, salt, baking powder, and evaporated cane juice. Add oil and water and whisk well. Add more water, if needed, to form a soft batter that just holds its shape. Allow batter to stand 5 minutes.

Fry a pancake on heated skillet. Pancake should be soft, not dry or thick. Thin batter with more water if needed. Fry remaining pancakes. Serve with butter and choice of syrup or jam.

Gingerbread Waffles

{ *Fragrant and rich, these waffles are more dessert than breakfast. I like the texture best after they've been kept warm on an oven rack.* }

2/3 cup mild baking molasses
1/3 cup butter, melted
1 1/2 cups milk or milk substitute
2 tablespoons apple cider vinegar
2 cups brown rice flour
1/2 teaspoon xanthan gum
1/2 teaspoon baking soda
2 teaspoons baking powder
2 teaspoons ground cinnamon
1/2 teaspoon ground ginger
1/4 teaspoon ground cloves
3/4 teaspoon salt

Preheat waffle iron. In a large bowl, stir together molasses and butter. Add the milk and vinegar.

In a separate bowl, whisk together the brown rice flour, xanthan gum, baking soda, baking powder, cinnamon, ginger, cloves, and salt. Add to molasses mixture, stirring just until combined.

Bake waffles on heated iron until they are golden brown. Remove to warm oven rack until ready to serve. Serve with butter and fresh fruit, if desired. Makes about three quadruple waffles.

Pan-Fried Cornmeal Mush

{ *Every Christmas our family traveled 1,000 long miles to visit Grandpa and Grandma Hobbs in faraway Chesapeake. Coastal Virginia seemed as foreign as China to us Midwestern farm girls. We could hardly believe the groves of majestic long-needle pines, the sandy yards edged by ditches, and the ocean which looked as enormous as the world, even though we saw them every year. Then there was the food. Breakfasts were best of all, and Grandma, every year exclaiming how much we ate, served us Apple Jacks, big round oranges, and plates of fried mush with pancake syrup.* }

15 cups water, divided
4 teaspoons salt
4 cups yellow cornmeal
light olive or vegetable oil, for frying
brown rice flour, for dredging
butter, honey, maple syrup or apple butter, for serving

In a large saucepan or stockpot, place 11 cups of the water and salt. Bring to a boil over high heat.

In a medium mixing bowl, stir together remaining 4 cups cold water and the cornmeal until smooth. Add to boiling water, whisking constantly. Cook until mixture is thick and smooth. Reduce heat to low, cover and allow to simmer 30 minutes.

Pour mixture into five 4"x8" loaf pans. Allow to cool completely. Cover with plastic wrap and refrigerate overnight.

In a large (preferably cast-iron) skillet, heat enough of the oil to generously coat skillet. Turn mush out of pan onto a cutting board. Cut with a serrated knife into ½" slices. Dredge each slice well with brown rice flour. Lay slices in heated skillet, and fry until golden and crisp, about 10 minutes, turning once. Serve hot with butter, honey, maple syrup or apple butter.

Hearty Maple Cold Cereal

{ This is the classic cold cereal with which Amish and Mennonite families all over the United States start summer mornings. I'm happy to find this good old tradition is possible gluten-free. · This version is only lightly sweetened. Increase the evaporated cane juice, if you prefer. }

6 cups brown rice flour

3/4 cup evaporated cane juice

1 1/2 teaspoon salt

1 1/2 teaspoon baking soda

1 teaspoon xanthan gum

1 teaspoon vanilla extract

1/2 teaspoon maple extract

3 to 4 cups buttermilk (or milk substitute or water with 1/4 cup cider vinegar)

1/4 cup molasses or maple syrup

1/2 cup butter, melted, or light olive or vegetable oil

Preheat oven to 325°. Grease 9"x13" baking pan.

In a large mixing bowl, stir together brown rice flour, evaporated cane juice, salt, baking soda, and xanthan gum. Add extracts, 3 cups buttermilk or substitute, molasses or maple syrup and butter or oil. Beat well. Check consistency: batter should be a medium-thick consistency that holds its shape well but is not too stiff to be easily beaten with a spoon. Add more liquid as needed to achieve proper consistency.

Spoon batter into prepared pan. Bake 50 to 60 minutes, or until cake is firm, crusty, and well done in center. Allow to cool completely. Wrap and allow to rest at least 12 hours.

Preheat oven to 300°. Crumble "cake" into medium-fine crumbs. Spread into two rimmed 10"x15" baking pans. Bake 1½ to 2 hours, stirring occasionally, until crumbs are a deep brown, dried completely, and crisp. Cool completely. Store airtight. Freeze after 1 month.

Serve with milk or milk substitute, honey and/or fresh fruit.

Crunchy Corn Cold Cereal

{ *It's so handy to have a jar of this cold cereal in your pantry. It's heartier and crunchier than the classic maple cold cereal, and a little sweeter, though not overly sweet. You can add more sweetener, or pass the honey bowl at the table and each can sweeten their own, custom-style.* }

1 1/2 cups yellow cornmeal

1 3/4 cups brown rice flour

1/4 cup tapioca starch

1/2 to 3/4 cup sweetener of choice

1 1/2 teaspoons baking soda

1 teaspoon salt

1/2 cup light olive or vegetable oil

2 teaspoons vanilla extract

1/2 cup baking molasses

2 cups water, or more if needed

1 teaspoon cider vinegar

Preheat oven to 325°. Grease 9"x13" baking pan.

In a large bowl, combine cornmeal, brown rice flour, tapioca starch, sweetener, baking soda and salt. Stir well.

Add oil, vanilla, molasses, water and vinegar to dry ingredients. Stir just until combined. Batter should hold its shape well, but not be too thick to be difficult to stir. Add more water as needed in small amounts, stirring carefully.

Spoon batter into prepared pan. Bake 35 to 45 minutes, or until cake is browned and is springy in center. Allow to cool. Cover and let rest 24 hours.

Preheat oven to 300°. Crumble corn cake into small crumbs, scattering them into two large, rimmed baking pans. Bake 1 to 1½ hours, stirring every 15 minutes, or until lightly browned, crisp, and dried. Allow to cool. Store airtight. Freeze for long-term storage.

Beauties of the Table
{Green, Vegetable, Gelatin & Fruit Salads,
with a Few Salad Dressings}

Layered Lettuce Salad with Garbanzo Beans

In our springtime,

EVERY DAY HAS ITS HIDDEN GROWTHS IN THE MIND,

as it has in the earth when the little folded blades

ARE GETTING READY TO PIERCE THE GROUND.

–George Eliot

chapter three

Beauties of the Table
{Green, Vegetable, Gelatin and Fruit Salads, with a Few Salad Dressings}

Mom's garden, planted over an old cow pasture, is the jewel of our farm. There amid banks of flowers she coaxes the onions to grow big, the carrots crisp and sweet, and zucchini to produce with alarming profusion. She potters around in it happily in all weathers—she burns the skin off her nose, gets doused by rains, gets "cricks" in her back during bean season. She loves it—just like her granddaddy before her, who cultivated the sandy soil of coastal Virginia.

Early spring and late fall, Mom grows her greens—cabbage, spinach, and lettuce of all hues and shapes. It's the lettuce we really anticipate. In February, when life has been green-less too long, we hungrily dream of it. In March, when maple taps drip, snow melts, and mud churns to our boot tops, the thought of coming green is like light at the end of a miry tunnel. In April, anemic yards turn brilliant green (seemingly overnight). In May, lettuce peeks up in the garden, celadon green against black soil. We eye it eagerly, willing the broadening leaves to grow big enough to drizzle with a dab of dressing. Then it's June, and the garden bursts at the seams with bushels and bags and wheelbarrows of lettuce. We give it away, sometimes we sell it, and salads dominate the menu. We munch like bunnies through lacy Oak Leaf lettuce, polka-dotted Freckles, and little butterheads sweet and "buttery". We understand why Peter Rabbit risked his hide to nibble spring greens.

Vegetables and fruits win every tabletop beauty contest. I'm astonished every summer at their intensity—golden carrots, magenta cabbage, olive broccoli. Tossing this vibrancy together into a salad is as thrilling as splashing paint on a canvas.

One bowl of salad can be strictly vegetable or include everything from the food pyramid. It can be a simple plate of crisped, cold greens, or a well-rounded meal. Salad is the most creative dish on the planet, and fixed up or down, it can go anywhere, for any occasion. Fortunately for us celiacs, salads have always been us. Why should we complain of our "can't-haves" when the darling of the dinner table has never let us down?

Salad dressing, the little drizzle that gilds the lily, is another matter. Laden with every allergen you can imagine (and some you can't), you can sift through every brand on grocery shelves before finding one that fits your diet. Try this: make your own! Homemade salad dressings are a cinch, and the best way in the world to get your omega-3s. Unrefined olive, grapeseed and safflower oil star in dressing, and since it's not heated, your omegas are delivered intact.

Last spring, with trepidation, I purchased a salad spinner. I have a strange attraction/fear approach to new kitchen gadgets—I find them risky, but irresistible. How do I know if they'll become a happy part of life (like my garlic press or citrus zester) or be a complete fiasco—like the ice crusher? I eyed salad spinners a long time before investing. I read about them skeptically— the claims seemed inflated. Could greens really go from dripping wet to completely dry in 15 seconds flat? Space was another issue—try tucking a salad spinner in the utensil drawer! Mostly (though I'm not one to mind personality quirks), I found the way they acted a little peculiar.

Finally, weary of salad-bowl puddles, I toted one home. With the first spin, I was convinced. We used that salad spinner almost every day last spring, and it hibernates nicely in the cellar, waiting for next year. Now maybe someday I'll get brave enough to buy a "lettuce knife"; lettuce cut with this wonderful knife (they say) keeps fresh for days.

Enter gelatin salads. We've always been fascinated by gelatin—from the time we can peek up over the edge of the table, they've drawn us. We look at the clear-as-glass bowls quivering at eye level, and we wonder how the peach slices and pineapple bits stay hung in mid-air.

Flavored gelatin is becoming antique. Grocers introduced it well over 100 years ago, to instant acclaim. American cooks took the idea and ran with it (as American cooks will do), a fog of recipes fluttering in their wake. Search a few cookbooks (especially 1950s era) and you'll understand what I mean. Besides delicious fruit salads and desserts, you'll find recipes that reveal what fun these cooks had in the race. They range from the strange (avocado and strawberries in lemon-lime gelatin) to the appalling (ham, cheese and veggies in orange gelatin, or "barbecue" gelatin cubes, served in shrimp-grapefruit salad). They even crafted a "new" tuna salad: tuna, olives and pimento in a ring of brilliant lime gelatin.

I pass over these recipes with a smile. Call me a purist, but I prefer vegetables in vegetable salad and fruit in fruit. I don't serve strawberries with spinach, or grapes in chicken salad, though other cooks do, to compliments. My serve-the-savory-with-savory propensity is odd, I suppose, since I like my salad dressing sweet. Taste is a capricious thing—call on another 1950s gem, roast duck glazed with orange gelatin, as witness!

Flavored gelatin is acceptable with celiacs, but there's another way to make America's favorite quivery salad. Before flavored gelatin, our great-great-grandmothers used another kind—unflavored. With fruit juice, this gelatin goes places, too.

I've had a good time inventing fruit-juice/unflavored gelatin salads. (See my big collection!) I find the latitude of flavors fascinating. Too, I find the thought of feeding my friends and family dye-less, sugar-less gelatins a happy one. Keep two items on hand (unflavored gelatin, and 100% fruit juice concentrate) and you're set to go. I've found unflavored gelatin can make anything flavored gelatin can—from dressy creations to homey gelatin with fruit. I use it, also, in Glazed Strawberry Pie and a Mennonite classic, Danish Dessert. Perhaps I've run away with gelatin, too.

Salads, in all their diversity, are always the beauties of the table. Let them be the fixture of the menu as the sun warms the earth and the green comes back. Serve them with abandon—they're good for you! ♪

Salad Shreds

· Good salad spinners are as powerful as they claim. Use them judiciously. Iceberg, for instance, is almost indestructible, while thin-leafed greens need only a few careful spins to dry without bruising. You want greens dry if serving immediately, but allow a few drops of water on the leaves if storing. Bag uncut greens and store refrigerated.

· You can use any kind of fruit juice for gelatin salads. Just keep three things at your fingertips—lemon juice, sweetener, and a tasting spoon. Each juice or juice combination will need a slightly different ratio of tart to sweet. Stir, add, taste, taste again, and you'll find it.

· Gelatin salads are easy when you have a good-tasting juice plus this ratio in your mind: 2 cups juice to 1 tablespoon gelatin. Looking for a firmer, gelatin block consistency? Simply double the gelatin, bringing the ratio up to 2 cups juice to 2 tablespoons gelatin.

· Do you like gelatin dressed for a party? There is always the standby of an ermine coat of whipped cream or a polka-dotted scarf of marshmallows. But if these things are off-limits, try Creamy Topping for Gelatins. Or make Fluffy Layered Peach Salad or Sweet Strawberry Salad, in which you beat some of the gelatin to a creamy, light consistency before cloaking the salad. ♪

Taco Salad, Kennell Style

{ *If there's a favorite dish at our house, it's taco salad. It appears at birthdays, attends family gatherings, and becomes a permanent fixture when the garden overflows with spring lettuce. Leftovers can mysteriously disappear. Mysteriously, until you catch someone eating a bowl of taco salad for breakfast.* · }

1 pound ground beef

1 yellow onion, chopped

4 cups cooked beans, pinto, small red, black, or a mixture, rinsed and drained

1 tablespoon gluten free Taco Seasoning, or to taste

1/4 cup water

salt and black pepper

1 head romaine, leaf or butterhead lettuce, torn into bite-size pieces

1 (12 ounce) bag gluten free tortilla chips

1 sweet onion, sliced thinly

2 tomatoes, chopped, optional

ripe olives, sliced, optional

shredded cheese or cheese substitute, optional

salad dressing of choice

Brown ground beef in a skillet with chopped yellow onion. Add beans, water and taco seasoning. Season with salt and black pepper. Bring to a simmer while preparing other ingredients. Taste, and add more taco seasoning, if desired.

Place lettuce, chips, onion, tomatoes, olives, and cheese in serving bowls. Everyone builds their own salad at the table, with dressing drizzled over all.

Layered Lettuce Salad
with Garbanzo Beans

{ An old classic takes on new personality with the addition of garbanzo beans. Not only do they give dimension, but extra protein which turns this salad into a satisfying main dish. Add muffins, biscuits or scones, and it can carry supper. }

9 cups torn lettuce, leaf or iceberg, or a mixture

small bunch of green onions, sliced

2 cups peas, fresh or frozen

1/2 cup chopped green pepper

1 1/2 cups cooked garbanzo beans, rinsed and drained

1/2 cup sour cream or Sour Supreme

1 1/2 cups mayonnaise or Vegenaise

2 tablespoons sweetener of choice

2 tablespoons apple cider vinegar

salt and black pepper

1 cup shredded cheese or cheese substitute

1/2 pound bacon, fried and crumbled

Layer lettuce, onion, peas, green pepper and garbanzo beans in salad bowl in order given.

In a small bowl, combine sour cream or substitute and mayonnaise or Vegenaise. Add sweetener, then slowly whisk in vinegar until smooth and creamy. Season to taste with salt and black pepper. Spread evenly over salad.

Sprinkle salad with cheese or substitute and crumbled bacon. Chill salad well (overnight if possible). Toss just before serving.

Cauliflower & Lettuce Salad

{ I learned to know this salad at a friend's wedding, and went home to see if I could make it myself. The ingredients alone are uncomplicated enough, but together make a marriage. · It's well suited to events, for it can be made in quantity the day before, then rest patiently in the refrigerator until you're ready to toss and serve. }

1 head iceberg lettuce, torn into bite-size pieces

1 head cauliflower, in small florets

1/2 to 1 sweet onion, finely chopped

2 cups mayonnaise or Vegenaise

2 tablespoons sweetener of choice

1 pound bacon, fried and crumbled

1 cup shredded cheese or cheese substitute, optional

In a 5 quart salad bowl, layer lettuce, cauliflower and onion. Spread mayonnaise or Vegenaise over all, sealing to edges. Sprinkle sweetener over mayonnaise. Sprinkle bacon, then cheese over all. Cover and refrigerate, overnight if possible. Toss and serve. Makes approximately 20 (¾ cup) servings.

Green Pea & Cauliflower Salad

{ Sweet and tender peas contrast crunchy cauliflower. · This is a do-ahead salad: acceptable eaten immediately, but truly at its best after a 24-hour nap in the refrigerator. }

1/2 head iceberg or romaine lettuce, torn into bite-size pieces

1/2 head cauliflower, in small florets

2 cups peas, fresh or frozen

1/2 cup chopped sweet onion

1 1/2 cups mayonnaise or Vegenaise

salt

2 tablespoons sweetener of choice

3 tablespoons fried and crumbled bacon, or gluten free bacon bits

In 2 quart salad bowl, layer lettuce, cauliflower, peas, and onion. Spread mayonnaise or Vegenaise over all, sealing to edges. Sprinkle with salt, sweetener and bacon.

Cover tightly. Chill several hours, or overnight. Toss to serve.
Makes 8 to 10 servings.

Sweet & Sour Coleslaw

{ We have an ongoing debate at our house on the merits of different coleslaw dressings. Which is best—creamy or vinaigrette? · This is my vinaigrette version, and I especially like it served with fried fish. }

3/4 head of cabbage, shredded

1 medium carrot, peeled and shredded

1/2 sweet onion, chopped

1/2 green pepper, chopped, optional

3/4 cup apple cider vinegar

1 cup sweetener of choice

3 tablespoons water

1 teaspoon salt

1 teaspoon dry mustard

In a large bowl, toss together cabbage, carrot, onion, and green pepper.

In a small saucepan, stir together vinegar, sweetener, water, salt, and mustard. Bring to a boil and boil 2 minutes. Pour hot over cabbage and toss. Chill several hours before serving.

Mom's Potato Salad

This fourth-generation potato salad has gone where most potato salads don't go. I remember it particularly at my sister's wedding: assembling it around our table, its place of honor beside the multicolor vegetable tray, and the friends and neighbors remembering it afterward. It followed Denise to her new home, and now she makes it for her own little boys. · Two secrets: shred the potatoes to allow them to absorb more dressing, and make it one or two days before serving (leftovers are better than first time around).

2 quarts cooked, peeled and shredded potatoes
1/2 cup finely chopped celery
1/2 cup finely chopped sweet or green onion
parsley, fresh or dried, a good sprinkling
pickle relish, according to personal taste
2 cups mayonnaise or Vegenaise
3 tablespoons cider vinegar
1/4 cup sweetener of choice
2 tablespoons yellow mustard
salt and black pepper, to taste

Place potatoes in a large bowl. Add onion, celery, parsley, and pickle relish.

In a separate bowl, whisk together mayonnaise or Vegenaise, vinegar, sweetener, and mustard. Season well with salt and black pepper. Toss well into potato mixture. Analyze texture and taste. Add more mayonnaise if it needs it, or more salt and pepper.

Wrap or cover tightly and chill, several hours, or preferably overnight. Correct seasoning again before serving. Makes 18 servings.

Pink Beet & Potato Salad

{ From a cousin in Costa Rica comes this extraordinary version of potato salad. · Beets tint the dressing an amazing pink, but the sweet, earthy taste of beet against potato is just as amazing. }

4 large potatoes

2 large or 4 small red beets

4 tablespoons sweetener of choice

3 tablespoons apple cider vinegar

salt and black pepper

1 cup minced sweet onion

2 cups mayonnaise or Vegenaise

In a large saucepan, place scrubbed potatoes and red beets. Cover with cold water. Bring to a boil over high heat, cover and simmer 40 minutes or until vegetables are tender. Remove potatoes first if necessary. Drain.

Allow vegetables to cool to lukewarm. Beets may be cooled to lukewarm in ice-water bath. Peel potatoes and beets and cut into small dice. While vegetables are still warm, toss with sweetener, vinegar, and a generous sprinkle of salt and pepper.

When vegetables are completely cooled, stir in onion and mayonnaise or Vegenaise. Cover tightly and refrigerate overnight. Adjust seasoning before serving. Makes 8 to 10 servings.

Double Apple Salad

Bits of red-skinned apples peek from this amber-golden salad. It's not just doubly apple, but can double as dessert. · If you don't have cider, use apple juice concentrate, reconstituted with a little less water than directed.

2 tablespoons unflavored gelatin

3 3/4 cups apple cider, divided

3 tablespoons lemon juice

3 tablespoons sweetener, more or less as desired (or stevia to taste)

1/4 teaspoon salt, optional

3 1/2 to 4 cups cored and chopped red apples

1/2 cup chopped walnuts

Sprinkle gelatin over 1 cup cider in a small saucepan. Allow to rest five minutes. Add sweetener, lemon juice, and salt. Heat gently over low heat just until dissolved.

Pour gelatin mixture into serving bowl. Add remaining cider gradually. Chill until syrupy.

Fold apples into cider mixture. Sprinkle walnuts on top of salad. Allow to chill until completely set.

Blueberry-Pineapple Salad

{ Celebrate high summer with this beautiful taste combination. Molded, it makes a statement on any menu. In fact, it's great for breakfast. }

1 tablespoon plus 1 teaspoon unflavored gelatin

1 3/4 cups pineapple juice

2 tablespoons lemon juice

3 tablespoons sweetener of choice, or stevia to taste

2 cups fresh blueberries

1 diced banana

Sprinkle gelatin over ½ cup pineapple juice in saucepan. Allow to rest 5 minutes. Add lemon juice and sweetener and heat gently just until dissolved.

Stir remaining pineapple juice into gelatin. Chill until gelatin is syrupy. Fold in fruits. For a molded salad, pour into a serving bowl or lightly oiled 2 cup mold and chill until firm. Dip mold briefly in hot water and unmold on a plate. If you want a salad in a bowl, pour gelatin mixture into a serving bowl and chill until firm.

Cherry & Apple Gelatin Salad

{ *This is a child-friendly salad. It needs a long chilling time to fully set.* }

3 tablespoons unflavored gelatin
1 cup water
1/4 cup sweetener of choice, or to taste
1 tablespoon lemon juice, or to taste
1 quart canned pitted sweet cherries
2 cups unsweetened applesauce
6 ounces 100% white grape-raspberry juice concentrate
water, as needed

Sprinkle gelatin over 1 cup water in a medium saucepan.
Allow to rest 5 minutes.

Add sweetener and lemon juice to gelatin mixture and heat gently,
stirring just to dissolve.

Drain cherries, reserving juice. Slice cherries in half.

In a liquid measuring cup, stir together juice concentrate, reserved cherry
juice, and gelatin. Add water to equal five cups liquid. Taste for lemon/
sweetener ratio. Stir in applesauce and cherries. Pour into 2 quart serving
bowl and chill, preferably overnight. Makes 16 servings.

Pineapple-Orange Gelatin Salad

{ *This summer salad perks wilted appetites on the most sweltering days.*
With a touch more sweetener, it can stand in as a light dessert. }

1 tablespoon plain gelatin

**3 tablespoons sweetener of choice, more or less to taste
(or stevia to taste)**

1 cup water

1/4 cup orange juice concentrate

**1 (20 ounce) can pineapple chunks or tidbits
water, as needed**

2 oranges, peeled and diced

1 or 2 bananas, sliced

Combine gelatin and sweetener with 1 cup water in small saucepan.
Allow to rest 5 minutes. Heat gently just to dissolve gelatin.

Drain pineapple, reserving juice. Add water to the juice to make 1¼ cups
liquid. Add to gelatin mixture. Add juice concentrate. Chill until gelatin
begins to thicken.

Fold 1 cup of the pineapple chunks or tidbits, oranges, and bananas
into gelatin. Pour into 1 quart serving bowl and chill several hours until
completely set. Makes 8 servings.

Quick Peach Gelatin Salad

{ *This is a basic quickie you can stir up 30 minutes before dinner with an assortment of fruit and fruit juices. I give the peach version, because it is really very good.* }

- **2 tablespoons unflavored gelatin**
- **1 cup water**
- **2 tablespoons lemon juice**
- **1/3 cup sweetener of choice (or stevia to taste)**
- **12 ounces 100% white grape/peach juice concentrate**
  water, as needed
- **4 cups frozen peaches, slightly thawed and broken apart**

Sprinkle gelatin over 1 cup water in small saucepan. Add lemon juice and sweetener and allow to rest 5 minutes. Heat gently to dissolve.

In a large measuring cup, combine juice concentrate with water to make a total of 3 cups liquid. Pour into large serving bowl. Add dissolved gelatin mixture.

Add peaches to gelatin. Stir until gelatin just thickens. Chill to set completely, 15 to 20 minutes. Makes 14 (½ cup) servings.

Apple Gelatin Salad For A Crowd

{ A childhood classic reborn. Shredded apples always do wonderful things for gelatin salads. · Cut the recipe in half, if you like, but you might wish you hadn't. }

4 tablespoons unflavored gelatin

2 cups water

1/2 cup sweetener of choice (or stevia to taste)

2 tablespoons lemon juice

pinch salt

2 (12 ounce) cans red 100% juice concentrate

water, as needed

4 to 6 red apples, washed, cored, and shredded (with or without skins)

In a small saucepan, sprinkle gelatin over 2 cups water. Add sweetener, lemon juice, and salt. Allow to rest 5 minutes. Heat gently to dissolve.

Add water to juice concentrate to equal 6 cups liquid. Place gelatin in a large serving bowl, and gradually add juice mixture. Add shredded apples. Chill, stirring occasionally until set to evenly disperse apples. Chill, overnight if possible. Makes 20 (½ cup) servings.

Creamy Lime Salad

{ *Honeydew melon in lime salad? Yes!* · *For a dessert, use up to ½ cup sweetener.* · *For very best results, use fully ripened honeydew and fresh lime juice.* }

1/2 cup raw cashews
2/3 cup boiling water
1/3 cup freshly squeezed lime juice
1 small or 1/2 large honeydew melon, or as needed
3 tablespoons unflavored gelatin
1/4 cup sweetener of choice, or to taste
thin slices of lime for garnish, optional

Place cashews into blender container. Add boiling water and blend on high for 2 minutes. Check consistency, and if still grainy, blend longer until texture is completely creamy. Add lime juice. Pour into a small metal bowl and place in freezer to quick-chill.

Peel and seed honeydew and cut into chunks. Blend in blender, using enough to make 3 cups puree. Pour ½ cup of the puree into a small saucepan and sprinkle gelatin on top. Allow to soften 5 minutes. Add sweetener and heat gently just until completely dissolved.

Blend honeydew puree and cashew mixture together in blender. Slowly add gelatin mixture. Blend several minutes. Taste and add more sweetener or lime juice if needed.

Pour into a glass bowl or lightly oiled 1 quart mold. Chill several hours or until set. To serve molded salad, dip mold briefly in hot water and invert onto serving plate. Garnish salad with lime slices if desired.

Fluffy Layered Peach Salad

{ *Since going dairy-free, I've often hankered after that cloud-like something on my gelatins. I bewailed this until the day I read in an old pamphlet about whipping gelatin to a fluffy consistency. Experimenting, I found xanthan gum gives the whipped layer even more fluff. It all came together in this gelatin salad, and my clouds almost thrilled me to tears. · Garnished with slim peach slices, this salad is dressed to go.* }

3 tablespoons unflavored gelatin

1 cup water

1/4 cup sweetener of choice

pinch salt

1 (12 ounce) can 100% white grape-peach juice concentrate

1 quart canned peaches, drained, reserving juice

water, as needed

sliced bananas and orange sections, optional

1/2 teaspoon xanthan gum

peach slices or orange segments for garnish, if desired

In a small saucepan, sprinkle gelatin over 1 cup water. Add sweetener and salt, and allow to rest 5 minutes. Heat gently, stirring just to dissolve.

Pour mixture into 2 or 3 quart serving bowl.

In a liquid measuring cup, place reserved peach juice, juice concentrate, and enough water to equal 5 cups liquid. Add gradually to gelatin mixture and stir well. Remove 2 cups of the mixture, place in mixer bowl, and chill in refrigerator.

Add drained peaches, oranges, and bananas (if using) to mixture in serving bowl. Place in refrigerator and stir often as it congeals.

Continued

When the 2 cups of gelatin in mixer bowl is set but still jiggly, add xanthan gum and beat with a standing mixer for 6 to 10 minutes, or until mixture is fluffy, is almost tripled in volume, and stands in peaks when beaters are lifted.

Pile beaten gelatin on gelatin in serving bowl. Chill until completely set. Garnish with peach slices or orange segments, if desired. Makes 16 servings.

Sweet Strawberry Salad

{ *Pink fluffy stuff—really, how sweet! I knew this salad would delight nieces of mine, and I wasn't disappointed. I'm still partial to pink gelatin myself.* }

2 1/2 tablespoons unflavored gelatin

1 cup water

1/2 cup sweetener of choice

pinch salt

1 tablespoon lemon juice

9 ounces (3/4 of 12 ounce can) 100% white grape-raspberry juice concentrate

2 cups crushed strawberries, partially thawed if frozen, unsweetened or very lightly sweetened

water, as needed

1/2 teaspoon xanthan gum

In a small saucepan, place 1 cup water. Sprinkle gelatin over water, and allow to rest 5 minutes. Add sweetener, salt, and lemon juice and heat gently just to dissolve, stirring constantly. Pour mixture into 2 quart serving bowl. Add juice concentrate, 2 cups water and strawberries. Remove 2 cups of the mixture and place into large mixer bowl. Refrigerate both mixtures just until set.

Add xanthan gum to gelatin in mixer bowl. Beat on high speed 6 to 10 minutes or until mixture has tripled in volume and stands in peaks. Pile beaten mixture over gelatin in serving bowl. Refrigerate until completely set, about 2 hours. Makes 8 to 10 servings.

Purple Grape Salad

{ This orchid-colored gelatin salad looks complex, but it's a simple blend of unusual ingredients. · Children like the color, and you can dress it up or down for any occasion. }

3 tablespoons unflavored gelatin

2 1/2 cups water, divided

1/2 cup raw cashews

1/2 cup boiling water

1 (12 ounce) can unsweetened grape juice concentrate

1 tablespoon lemon juice, if needed

sweetener of choice to taste

whole green seedless grapes and mint leaves for garnish, optional

Sprinkle gelatin over 1 cup water in a small saucepan. Allow to rest 5 minutes, then heat gently just to dissolve. Cool to lukewarm.

Place cashews in blender and grind to a fine powder. Add boiling water and blend 2 minutes. Add the juice concentrate and blend another 2 minutes. Add remaining 1½ cups water and blend briefly. Add gelatin. Taste, and add lemon juice and sweetener if needed.

Pour mixture into serving bowl. Chill until set. Garnish salad as desired with whole grapes and mint.

Grandma Kennell's Cranberry Salad

{ From Grandma's handwritten recipe book comes this central feature of every family feast. Maybe Dad remembers when she started making it, but I certainly don't. It was just always there. }

12 ounces cranberries, fresh or frozen, sorted and rinsed

1 1/4 cups water, divided

3/4 cup sweetener of choice, more or less as desired

1 tablespoon unflavored gelatin

1/2 cup crushed pineapple, well-drained

1/2 cup seedless grapes, halved

whipped cream or whipped topping, optional

Combine gelatin with ¼ cup of the water in a small bowl. Set aside until needed.

Place cranberries, the 1 cup of remaining water, and sweetener in a saucepan. Bring to a boil and cook, covered, until cranberries "pop". Press cranberries through a sieve into a large bowl. Add softened gelatin and stir to dissolve.

Allow mixture to cool and partially set, then fold in pineapple and grapes. Pour into a serving bowl and refrigerate until well set, up to 24 hours. Garnish with whipped cream or whipped topping, if desired.

Pineapple & Coconut Salad

{ *I make this salad with memories of a tiny kitchen in Phoenix and sunny February days. With fruits of all kinds at our fingertips, my friend and I mixed and matched a rainbow of fruits in salad after salad.* }

- 1 (20 ounce) can chunk pineapple
- 2 tablespoons cornstarch
- 3 tablespoons sweetener of choice (or stevia to taste)
- 1 1/2 tablespoons lemon juice
- 1/2 cup shredded unsweetened coconut
- 1 cup raisins
- 2 bananas, sliced
- 1/2 to 1 cup walnut pieces

Drain pineapple. Pour juice in a saucepan. Stir cornstarch, sweetener, and lemon juice into juice and bring to a boil, whisking until smooth and bubbly. Remove from heat and stir in coconut and raisins immediately. Allow to cool.

Fold bananas, walnuts, and pineapple chunks into mixture. Turn into a serving bowl and chill until serving.

Variation:

Rainbow Pineapple and Coconut Salad: Omit raisins and walnuts, and with the pineapple chunks fold in your choice of fruits. A few suggestions: strawberries, raspberries, blueberries, or kiwi.

Sour Cream & Grape Salad

{ Grapes and sour cream sing harmoniously in this salad, a first-cousin-once-removed to Waldorf salad. You can play with the ingredients, adding or subtracting as you like. · Serve this creamy salad in sherbet glasses. }

> 1 (20 ounce) can chunk pineapple
> 2 tablespoons cornstarch
> 1 tablespoon fresh lemon juice
> 3 tablespoons sweetener of choice
> 1 cup sour cream or Sour Supreme
> 1 cup red grapes

Drain pineapple, placing juice in a saucepan, and reserving chunks. Stir cornstarch, lemon juice, and sweetener into juice and bring to a boil, whisking, until thickened and bubbly. Cool.

Fold sour cream or Sour Supreme, pineapple chunks and grapes into cooled mixture and chill until serving.

Creamy Topping For Gelatin Salads

{ *This rich, lightly tart topping can turn a plain gelatin salad into company fare.* }

1 1/2 tablespoons unflavored gelatin

1 cup water

2 cups crushed pineapple, drained, with juice reserved

1/4 cup frozen white grape juice concentrate

1/2 cup sweetener of choice

1/4 cup cornstarch

1 tablespoon freshly squeezed lemon juice

3/4 cup sour cream or Sour Supreme

1/4 cup mayonnaise or Vegenaise

Sprinkle gelatin over water in medium saucepan. Allow to rest 5 minutes. Add 1 cup reserved pineapple juice and grape juice concentrate, cornstarch, sweetener, and lemon juice. Place over high heat and bring to a boil, whisking well, until smooth and thickened.

Cool gelatin mixture. Add sour cream or Sour Supreme, crushed pineapple and mayonnaise or Vegenaise. Spread over gelatin salad. Chill. Makes enough to cover one large or two small gelatin salads generously.

Honey-Mustard Salad Dressing

{ *This is my all-purpose, must-have salad dressing. It's wonderful on taco salad, but good with any other greens on the menu. During lettuce season, it's a good thing to keep tucked in the refrigerator. · Would you like to try brilliant lime-green dressing? Use 5 green onions (with tops) for the yellow onion. · The touch of mayonnaise or Vegenaise here keeps the dressing emulsified.* }

1/3 cup honey
1/4 cup cider vinegar
1 teaspoon salt
3 tablespoons yellow mustard
1/2 teaspoon mayonnaise or Vegenaise, optional
1/2 cup yellow onion, sliced
1 cup olive oil, room temperature
parsley, fresh or dried

Place honey, vinegar, salt, mustard, mayonnaise or Vegenaise, and onion in blender container. Blend until pureed. While blender is running, slowly drizzle in oil, blending until thick and creamy. Add a sprinkle of parsley for color. Chill leftovers, airtight, for up to a week. Makes about 2 cups dressing.

All-American French Dressing

{ If you've grown up with this classic, tomato-ey dressing, here it is again, ingredient-controlled. · This dressing dominates one side of the family in our "French and Onion War", which means it has to appear wherever Onion-Mustard is. }

1 cup light olive or vegetable oil, room temperature

1 cup ketchup, room temperature, or nearly so

1/4 cup cider vinegar

1/3 cup sweetener of choice

large slice of onion, or 3 green onions

1 teaspoon salt

1 teaspoon paprika

Combine all ingredients in blender. Blend one minute, or until fully emulsified. Chill airtight, and use within one week. Makes approximately 2½ cups dressing.

Creamy Ranch Dressing

{ *This herby, creamy dressing can go so many places. Use it in place of mayo in chicken salad. Spread it in sandwiches. Use less of the soured milk and turn it into a classic veggie dip. It's exciting to have ranch dressing back in the menu.* }

1/2 cup milk or substitute
2 teaspoons cider vinegar
1/2 cup mayonnaise or Vegenaise
1/4 cup sour cream or Sour Supreme
3 green onions, sliced thinly
1 clove garlic, minced
2 tablespoons finely minced bell pepper
1 tablespoon chopped fresh parsley or 1 teaspoon dried
1 teaspoon fresh lemon juice
salt and black pepper

In a small bowl, stir together the vinegar and milk or substitute. Allow to rest five minutes.

In a medium bowl, stir together the mayonnaise or Vegenaise and sour cream or Sour Supreme. Stir in enough of the soured milk or substitute to make a medium-thick consistency. You may need to add more as dressing thickens.

Stir in onion, garlic, bell pepper, parsley and lemon juice. Add salt and black pepper to taste. Refrigerate until well chilled. Makes about 1¼ cups.

Hasty, Tasty Lunches & Suppers
{Soups, Stew, Chili & Sandwiches}

Chicken, Mushroom, & Wild Rice Soup

Good cooks offer pleasure readily...

content with the ringing of spoons on

old soup bowls

and the view down the table of heads

BOWED OVER HOT SUPPERS.

–Christopher Kimball

chapter four

Hasty, Tasty Lunches and Suppers
{Soups, Stew, Chili and Sandwiches}

It's thirty below zero, and the wind is brisk, knifing through layers of clothing the instant we step outside. We pull scarves over our faces, attempting to cover every inch of skin, yet straining to see the buckets, feed bunks, and calves huddled together in their sheds and hutches. The cold is like a monster with killing strength, and every lungful burns its way through nostrils and windpipe. We scoop out extra measures of grain, toss down straw to give the animals a comfy place to sleep, then gratefully wade through the snow back to the house. We open the door and something incredibly warm and savory hits our noses. What can it be? We fumble our way to the kitchen and lift the kettle lid. Steaming fragrance bursts into our faces, thawing our frozen cheeks and warming our insides from nose to toes. Soup! Hearty, bubbly soup! We down a few bowls of it, then, comforted, we cozy up in cushy blankets, our toes on the registers. How incredible that such a simple thing as soup can almost compensate for a bitter Midwest winter!

Though soup is natural for farm suppers, it adapts to many situations happily. Beef and vegetable hitchhikes with folks to work in thermoses on frosty mornings, chili is offered at delis and filling stations all over America, and more refined versions (maybe clarified chicken stock or shrimp bisque) attend many-course dinners. As unassuming as soup can be, it finds its way into every class and serves prince or peasant with equal aptitude.

Soup can be a catch-all of leftovers, or a careful balance of ingredients. It can be broth-based, tomato-based or dairy-based, and ingredients run the gamut. Because of this changing, always-something-new characteristic, allergic celiacs can usually find a soup that works for them. And, happily, if you can't find a recipe, soup can always be improvised.

Enter sandwiches, America's quintessential fast-food, our go-to lunch on everyday days, our easy-to-grab meal on wash days or picnic days. But what's in our normal, white-bread-and-bologna-and-cheese sandwich? Gluten, dairy, egg (yes, all three!), and so, for the allergic celiac, they must go. Someone who's carried sandwiches since first grade can find this a major shift.

Gluten-free sandwiches remind me of sunshine and pink roses. I'll tell you why: My first sandwich after 10 years of sandwich-less-ness happened in June several years ago. I remember it was June, partly because... well, who can forget a sunny June Sunday? and partly because we were celebrating my oldest sister and husband's anniversary.

We decided naively to recreate their wedding menu. They'd served stacks of sandwiches on homemade buns, a kaleidoscope of raw veggies with dip in hollowed purple cabbages, potato salad from Mom's special recipe, and vanilla-iced chocolate cake with ice cream. And peppermints, dispersed by little white-aproned cousins (why peppermints, exactly?... let's just say peppermints figured hugely in their relationship).

It was a simple menu, and should have been simple to redo. But since their wedding day, gluten, egg, and milk intolerances have entered our midst. These (as they often do!) turned simple into complicated—very complicated.

What would we have left if all these allergens were removed from the menu? I took a look. I scratched the sandwiches, the potato salad. I crossed off the chocolate cake, the ice cream. And (thinking of my hypoglycemic brother-in-law) said good-bye to even the peppermints. Would we have to reduce the wedding feast to nothing but vegetables—vegetables without dip?

Now vegetables are wonderful, but they could hardly carry the feast alone. I'd have to regroup; pull together other options. I'd found Vegenaise, which was a start—it would give us back potato salad and sandwich spread (if we had something to spread it on!). Gluten-free chocolate cake had already come back—to our eternal gratefulness. Starting with these, could we try the feast after all?

"Listen, you don't have to do this—it's going to be a terrible amount of work!" my sister said. Now a mom of four, she's learned to budget time and trim the unnecessary to make room for the necessary.

"But I *want* to do it," I insisted. If I was a mother of boys, maybe I wouldn't try "impossible" things, either. (But...some things are born in us.) "Just let me think about it, and do some planning."

First, I knew we needed double menus. Still unsure of my footing in gluten-free cooking, I didn't want to subject everyone to the ills of a few. I began preparing "normal" food, still thinking...

Regular chocolate cake, gluten-free chocolate cake...potato salad with mayonnaise, potato salad with Vegenaise... it was coming together.

"This wouldn't be hard," I said to myself, "if it weren't for those sandwiches!" Celiac disease takes us where we never imagined going. Here I was, wondering for days how to make a sandwich!

We could build our sandwiches on rice cakes or corn tortillas. Both are adequate substitutes. Why, after ten years of self-denial, was I asking for yeast-raised sandwich buns? As I stamped out wheat rolls with Mom's signature tuna-can cutter, I wondered if I needed to reaccept the celiac issue.

Then, Eureka! I remembered bagels. In the last several months, a rather odd recipe for bagels had produced bagels, after a fashion. They were a little flat, a little doughy, a little lopsided. It was taste that saved the recipe—a flour blend strangely like wheat. Could I?...

The morning of the celebration, I mixed a batch of bagel dough. I dropped spoonfuls on baking sheets in roll shapes, let them rise into high, soft mounds, baked them until browned and crusty...and the rest is history. Yes, I won't forget that day, when, surrounded by family and June sunshine, I tasted that first tentative bite of soft roll against creamy Vegenaise, spicy salami and soy cheese. Just a substitute? I could happily carry this for all life's lunch-box days. ♪

Soup and Sandwich Snatches

·Chili bars are easy-do company meals. Since the flavor of chili improves on mellowing, you can make most of the meal ahead of time. Offer Mexican-style add-ins: black olives, sweet onion, cheese or sour cream (if permissible), guacamole, pickled jalapeno. You can offer a basket of multicolored tortilla chips, or warm cornbread with butter. Something fruity and cooling makes a nice dessert, like Frosty Fruit Sherbet with shortbread.

·Soup pairs beautifully with bread. Try Hearty Peasant Soup with Crusty French Bread, White Bean and Ham Soup with Heidelberg Pumpernickel, or Thanksgiving Evening Turkey Soup with Pumpkin Pecan-Streusel Muffins.

·If you make gluten free buns fresh, they'll be fine in the lunch box until noon. If you use frozen or day-old buns, take a toaster to work or school. Pack the sandwich components and heat buns right before lunch. Since both warm together, hot ham and cheese or sloppy joe sandwiches work well. Sandwich buns will accept any filling or topper, and go open-faced or "hatted" with equal talent.

·Corn tortillas must be heated or toasted just before eating. Again, pack them separately, and heat on the spot. Try corn tortillas with refried beans, ham and sweet relish, or (does this sound strange?) wrapped around the hot dogs with ketchup and onion.

·Rice cakes are best just out of the bag. They wilt within five minutes after touching the rest of the sandwich. Build your sandwich right before eating. Rice cakes are especially nice with creamy salad-type sandwiches (think tuna, salmon, or chicken salad), or in a PB & J.

Comfort Chicken-Rice Soup

{ *This is a wonderful way to make one chicken serve a family, comfortably. I like the large amount of celery, and the small amount of rice, which will just barely thicken the soup.* }

1 (3-pound) chicken, cut in pieces, or 4 chicken leg quarters
1 or 2 bay leaves
1 large onion, sliced
1 garlic clove, peeled
salt and pepper
6 quarts water
5 carrots, sliced
5 celery stalks, sliced
1 large onion, chopped
1/2 cup uncooked brown rice

Place chicken, bay leaves, sliced onion, garlic, a moderate amount of salt and pepper, and water into soup pot. Bring to a boil and simmer until chicken is tender, about 1 hour. Remove chicken and strain broth.

Return broth to soup pot. Add carrots, celery, onion and rice to broth, return to a boil, and simmer until rice and vegetables are tender.

Remove chicken meat from skin and bones, dice meat and add to soup. Taste and adjust seasoning. Heat through and serve.

White Bean & Ham Soup

{ Here's homey comfort, fast. Unlike a lot of bean soups, which can take half the day to make, this one starts with cooked beans and is simmered only until the flavors blend. }

2 tablespoons butter

2 carrots, finely diced

1 onion, finely chopped

1 1/2 cups cubed, fully cooked ham

2 1/2 cups water

3 to 4 cups white beans, well-cooked and slightly soft

1 bay leaf

salt and pepper

Heat butter in soup pot and sauté carrots and onions until softened. Add ham. Add water, beans and seasonings. Simmer to heat through and blend flavors. Taste and adjust seasonings. Remove bay leaf and serve.

Note: If cooked beans are firm, you may want to mash half the beans before adding to the soup.

Creamy Sausage & Potato Soup

{ This robust, fully seasoned soup is my answer for dairy-free potato soup, but it's a soup in its own right. · It's spicy and warming, an ideal winter night comfort food. }

2 quarts chicken broth

4 cups diced potatoes

2 carrots, shredded or finely sliced

1 large onion, chopped

1/2 to 1 pound mild gluten free sausage

2 tablespoons brown rice flour

salt and pepper, to taste

In a soup pot, bring broth, potatoes and carrots to a boil. Cover and simmer until tender.

Meanwhile, brown sausage and onion in a skillet. Set aside.

Transfer half of cooked vegetables to a blender, adding enough cooking liquid to blend well. Add rice flour. Return to soup pot. Add browned sausage and mix well. Taste for seasoning and heat through. Serve.

Autumn Harvest Soup

{ Here's a meal in a bowl, so robust you'd almost call it chili. The hodgepodge mix of beans and rice makes it warming and satisfying. }

1 pound combination of dried yellow and/or green split peas, lentils, brown rice and/or wild rice

2 quarts water

1 pound ground beef

1 yellow onion, chopped

2 cups sliced carrots

2 cups sliced celery

2 cups sliced cabbage

1 to 1 1/2 quarts whole canned tomatoes, tomato juice, or beef broth or stock

Place pea/lentil/rice mixture in a large soup pot. Add water and bring to a boil. Simmer one hour.

Brown ground beef with onion in skillet. Add to soup pot, deglazing skillet with some of the simmering liquid.

Add vegetables and beef stock or tomatoes. Simmer one additional hour.

Season to taste with salt and pepper. Serve.

Hearty Peasant Soup

{ *Last winter my almost-twin cousin and I spent a rare few days together. To celebrate, we invented this dressed-up soup. We both love to cook, and we added, sampled and sipped until the results met our criteria. · We served our soup with a salad of lettuce, avocado and tomato, and freshly-baked tortilla chips.* }

1 pound gluten free mild bulk Italian sausage

2 medium onions, chopped

6 garlic cloves, minced or pressed

1 pound boneless, skinless chicken breast, cut into 1" cubes

4 cups cooked beans: cannelli, small red, black, or a mixture

2 1/2 quarts chicken broth (or 1 1/2 quarts chicken broth and 1 quart canned chunk tomatoes)

1 teaspoon dried basil or 1 tablespoon minced fresh basil

1 teaspoon dried oregano or 1 tablespoon minced fresh oregano

6 cups chopped fresh spinach

salt and pepper, to taste

In a stew pot, brown sausage, breaking apart into large chunks. Add onions and garlic and sauté until onions are limp. Add chicken breast, and sauté until chicken is no longer pink.

Add beans, chicken broth, basil and oregano to stew pot and bring soup to a boil. Reduce heat and simmer 15 minutes, or until chicken is tender.

Just before serving, add spinach. Allow spinach to wilt several minutes, correct seasoning, and serve.

Chicken, Mushroom, & Wild Rice Soup

Silky mushrooms and earthy wild rice take chicken soup to lofty heights here. It's a nice "company soup", though I've eaten the leftovers for a quick, by-myself breakfast. If you are the accomplished cook who keeps quality stocks in your freezer at all times, this soup can come together very quickly.

1 pound boneless, skinless chicken breast halves
2 tablespoons light olive oil
1 1/2 cups chopped onion
1/2 cup chopped carrot
8 ounces white button mushrooms, sliced
2 quarts chicken stock or well-flavored chicken broth
1/2 cup uncooked wild rice (or wild/brown mix)
salt and pepper, to taste

Heat oil in a large saucepan or heavy stockpot over high heat. Lightly brown chicken. Remove, reduce heat to medium, and add onions, mushrooms, and carrot. Sauté lidded, about 8 minutes, or until mushrooms release juice. Stir occasionally and do not over brown. Add stock and rice. Simmer slowly 45 minutes. Cut chicken into ½" cubes. Add to soup and simmer an additional 15 minutes. Correct seasoning and serve.

Thanksgiving Evening Turkey Soup

{ Here's the Frugal Housewife's Soup. First it utilizes the turkey bones to make stock, then leftovers to make a soup. If the family is still hanging around, tie aprons on everybody and put them to work. The aunts or uncles can pick the bones, the teens chop veggies, and the tots stir the heating soup—all in time to "Now Thank We All Our God." }

bones from one roasted turkey, picked completely clean, meat reserved

4 quarts water

2 cloves garlic, halved

3 large onions, chopped

3 stalks celery, sliced

3 carrots, sliced

any leftover gravy, gluten-free

2 to 3 cups leftover mashed potatoes, dairy-free

1/3 cup butter

leftover roasted turkey, diced

salt and pepper, to taste

Place bones in a large stockpot with water. Add garlic, bring to a boil over high heat, reduce heat to a gentle simmer, and simmer for about 2 hours.

Strain stock, discarding bones, and returning stock to pot. Bring stock to a boil and add onions, celery, and carrots. Simmer until vegetables are very tender, about 30 to 40 minutes.

Place potatoes and butter in a medium saucepan. Remove 1 cup of the hot soup and add. Warm potatoes, mashing well, until completely heated and smooth, and butter is melted. Add to simmering soup.

Add turkey meat to soup. Heat through and correct seasoning. Serve hot.

Mom's Beef Stew

{ One whiff, and everybody knows they've come home. Beef stew is Mom's signature dish: visitors are delighted with it, married sisters miss it, and when I taste it, I realize I've forgotten how good it is. · Mom doesn't make it very often, for it's a long-simmered stew, but when she does, we know it's going to be an occasion (if nothing else, beef stew will make it one). · Mom likes to serve her stew with fresh rolls and apple butter. }

olive oil, for browning beef

2 pounds stew beef, cut into 1" cubes

1/4 cup brown rice flour

salt and pepper, as desired

1 medium onion, sliced

1 garlic clove, minced

1 bay leaf

1/2 teaspoon Worcestershire sauce

1/2 teaspoon sweetener of choice

5 cups water, or more as needed

3 large potatoes, peeled and cut into large chunks

4 large carrots, peeled and cut into large slices

5 onions, cut into large chunks

3 stalks celery, cut into large slices

In a large stew pot, heat enough olive oil to just coat bottom of pan over medium-high heat. Toss beef with brown rice flour and place in single layer in heated pot. Brown meat on all sides, seasoning with salt and pepper. You may need to brown beef in batches.

Add onion, garlic, bay leaf, Worcestershire sauce, sweetener and water to browned meat. Bring to a boil, cover, and reduce heat to a steady simmer. Simmer beef 2 hours.

Add vegetables to stew and bring stew back to a simmer. Simmer 30 minutes or until vegetables are tender. Correct seasonings. Serve hot.

Farm Auction Chili

{ Should I include this recipe? Each cook has their favorite version of chili, I know. But I think I will, because it's mine, and because just looking at it makes me feel so thankful inside. · I invented it when asked to provide the lunch stand for a farm auction. · I don't frequent farm auctions, and I wasn't sure what to serve. What do farmers eat at auctions? How many would come? How many would buy lunch? For a sale in snowy/sunny April, should chili be an option? I wrote yards of lists. I prayed. I revised, then re-revised menus. · The sale day was chilly and the farmers ate, then ate again. They forked in slices of pie, drank cups of coffee, and scarfed down many sandwiches, but warming chili was the hot item. · This is a thick, moderately spicy chili; spices and tomatoes are variable. }

2 pounds ground beef

1 onion, chopped

1 green pepper, chopped

2 cloves garlic, minced or pressed

4 cups cooked pinto beans, black beans, red beans, or a mixture

6 cups tomato juice

4 cups canned whole tomatoes

2 tablespoons chili powder

2 teaspoons ground cumin

1/4 teaspoon ground cayenne pepper

1 tablespoon brown sugar

salt and pepper, to taste

In a large saucepan or soup pot, place ground beef, onion, green pepper, and garlic. Brown beef well over medium-high heat. Add beans, tomato juice, tomatoes, chili powder, cumin, cayenne pepper, and sugar. Bring to a boil, reduce heat, and simmer at least 30 minutes before serving. Correct seasoning, adding salt and pepper as desired. Serve hot. Makes 16 (1 cup) servings.

Dilled Salmon Salad Sandwiches

{ Teamed with warm Sandwich Buns, salmon salad is one of my favorite suppers. Try it on a sultry evening with fresh cucumber and iced tea. }

2 (15 ounce) cans pink salmon, drained, with skin and large bones removed

3/4 cup mayonnaise or Vegenaise

1 tablespoon freshly squeezed lemon juice

2 tablespoons snipped fresh dillweed, or 2 teaspoons dried dillweed

salt and pepper

2 teaspoons prepared mustard

1/2 cup sliced green onion

Sandwich Buns, Corn Drop Biscuits (see index), or rice cakes

Place salmon in a medium bowl and flake into large chunks.

Add remaining ingredients to salmon and toss lightly. Serve immediately or cover and chill until serving. Serve on buns, biscuits, or rice cakes.

Beef Salad Sandwiches

{ *Here's a quick, rib-sticking sandwich that utilizes leftover beef. Plan ahead and roast aplenty, then have these sandwiches later in the week. · You can substitute other mustards for yellow.* }

leftover roasted or boiled beef, minced to make 1 cup

1/2 cup chopped sweet onion

5 tablespoons mayonnaise or Vegenaise

2 tablespoons sweet pickle relish

2 teaspoons yellow mustard

Sandwich Buns, Corn Drop Biscuits (see index) or rice cakes, to serve

Stir all ingredients in a small bowl, mixing well. Cover and refrigerate. Serve chilled on Sandwich Buns, Corn Drop Biscuits, or rice cakes.

Spicy Beef Gyros

{ *Spicy beef and cooling cucumber sauce are folded into tortillas in this Greek "sandwich" gone gluten-free. My sister and I put together this recipe for a memorable Grecian meal, and served the gyros with cheeses, assorted olives, green salad and fresh lemonade. · Check the label on the soy sauce to make sure it is made from soybeans instead of wheat. · Slice the beef while it is partially frozen to make the task easier.* }

1 yellow onion, peeled

2 garlic cloves, peeled

2 tablespoons sweetener of choice

1 tablespoon ground mustard

1/2 teaspoon ground ginger

1 teaspoon black pepper

1/4 teaspoon ground red pepper

1/2 cup gluten free soy sauce

1/2 cup water

2 1/2 pounds beef, sliced in 1/4" thick strips across the grain

olive oil, for frying

1 cup water, for finishing beef

corn tortillas, for serving

sliced sweet onion, for serving

tomato, for serving, optional

Cucumber Sauce:

2 cups plain yogurt, soy yogurt, or Sour Supreme

1 small cucumber, seeded and chopped

salt to taste

Continued

Place onion, garlic, sweetener, mustard, ginger, black and red pepper, soy sauce and water in blender and blend well. Pour into a large glass or stainless steel bowl and add beef strips, tossing well to coat. Allow to marinate 1 to 2 hours in the refrigerator.

Drain beef well. Coat frying pan with oil and heat over medium heat. Lay a layer of beef strips in pan. Fry until nicely browned. Repeat with remaining beef, placing fried beef in a casserole dish as you go. Pour water over beef and bake at 300° for 1 hour or so until tender.

For cucumber sauce, stir together all ingredients just before serving. Warm tortillas. Serve beef strips wrapped in tortillas with tomato, onion and Cucumber Sauce.

Falafel In Tortillas

{ Garbanzo bean patties, fried until golden, wrap with cucumber and sour cream into a classic Mediterranean Sandwich. Serve with cured olives and Old-Fashioned Lemonade. }

3 cups garbanzo beans
1/2 cup chopped onion
1/4 cup brown rice flour
pinch xanthan gum
1 teaspoon dried parsley
1 teaspoon ground cumin
2 cloves garlic, minced or pressed
salt and pepper, to taste
light olive or vegetable oil, for frying
sour cream or substitute, for serving
sliced cucumber and sweet onion, for serving
warm corn tortillas, for serving

Drain garbanzo beans, reserving liquid. In a large bowl, combine beans with chopped onion, rice flour, xanthan gum, parsley, cumin, and garlic in blender or food processor. Blend well. Check consistency. Bean puree should be soft and slightly moist. Add a little of the reserved bean liquid if puree seems dry.

Heat a large skillet over medium heat. Add 2 tablespoons oil to the skillet and heat. Divide mixture into 12 balls and flatten slightly. Fry falafel 2 or 3 minutes per side, or until browned and crusty.

Serve falafel in warmed corn tortillas with sour cream, cucumber and onion.

The Full Dinner Plate

{Meats, Main Dishes, Casseroles, Savory Pies & Side Dishes}

Spice-Rubbed Roasted Turkey

I thank the Lord my Maker

For all His gifts to me;

For making me partaker

OF BOUNTIES RICH AND FREE;

For father and for mother,

Who give me clothes and food,

For sister and for brother,

And all the kind and good.

–Thomas MacKellar

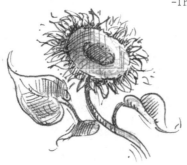

chapter five

The Full Dinner Plate
{Meats, Main Dishes, Casseroles, Savory Pies & Side Dishes}

Whenever I pull a turkey from the oven, my mind always goes back...

It's Thanksgiving morning, and the sun bathes the stubbled prairie. It peeks at the hay crammed to the rafters in the haymow. It reflects brightly off grain bins obese with corn and oats and beans. It sends shafts of light into the cellar windows and touches shelves heavy with home-canned goods. It reaches into our bedroom window and splashes our faces. We jump up in excitement—who sleeps in on Thanksgiving Day?

We gulp down our breakfasts with one big question: Did our Ohio cousins get to Grandpa's yet? We are going to find out. The ground is frosty—oops, we'll need shoes. Are there any from last spring that still fit our brown, calloused feet? We find big sister's pair and impatiently pull them on. Now to the barn! Through the old horse stalls, up the ladder to the hayloft! The bales are stacked like an Everest, and we are brave mountain climbers. Up, up we go, to the oak-pegged rafters at the peak. The bales almost touch the hay fork track at the very top, and we do chin-ups and balance on our iron tightrope. Careful, now—grab here, now there! More chin-ups, and we scramble up into the cupola. Fat spiders scuttle into webs, and startled pigeons flap away on creaking wings.

Our ancient barn still retains one sign of decaying beauty, a cupola. We dare not lean on the rickety walls, and so many ventilation slats are missing that we can see far and wide across the level prairie. It's by turns an observation point, a watchtower, a crow's-nest, and that's why we're here on this frosty and bright Thanksgiving morning.

We peer intently to the west, where Grandpa Kennells live in a little one-and-a-half-story house. We blink our eyes and peer again (oh, for a ship captain's telescope!)—and then we see it! A big green van parked by Grandpa's back door.

"They're here! They're here!" We scamper down twice as fast as we went up, gladly risking our necks. What else matters, anyway, on this November day?

"Mom, Mom, can we walk up to Grandpa's? They're here!" we plead. After an agony of waiting on this sister to find her stockings and that sister her sweater, we march up the arrow-straight road to Grandpa's in our Sunday best. When we hit the yard, cousins burst upon us in noisy meeting. We're ecstatic to see each other—it's been a whole three months! Arms linked, we try to fit into the house.

At the door, fragrant steam hits us in the face. We smell Grandma's turkey, roasting long and slow since early morning. And we see Grandpa in the living room, setting up tables. "Roy! We'll never fit in there!" Grandma exclaims from the kitchen, where she scurries about, deep in her special stuffing. Grandpa grins his twinkly grin at us, and unfolds another card table.

Uncles smile benignly over cups of coffee at the kitchen table. Aunts bestow motherly hugs all around. "Roy, there's second cousins coming now. Let's just eat cafeteria-style in the kitchen like always. Roy?" Grandma worries. Grandpa unfolds more chairs, then yet another card table. "I say, bring me some more tablecloths, Grandma," he says.

It's a quarter to ten now, and we pack into vans and head off to church to hear the 100th Psalm. "Enter into His gates with thanksgiving, and into His courts with praise: be thankful unto Him, and bless His name." Our minds slow, and we relax into quiet worship as the words wash over us.

Once back at Grandpa's, preparations accelerate. Anticipation heightens. Cars line the lane, cousins converge from all areas, and tummies rumble in all corners of the house. Grandma ties on a fresh apron, crinkling with starch, and things get serious.

"Roy, I know the children will get stains on the carpet!" she says. She pulls the turkey from the oven and two aunts begin carving. A cousin-once-removed makes gravy in the roaster. We girls hang over everything. Uncles and boy cousins are constantly underfoot. They snitch one too many times, and...

"Anybody who doesn't want a job better get out of the kitchen!" shrills an aunt. The boys drop back, but we girls decide to pay the price.

The kitchen emanates good smells, layer upon layer like rich tapestry. In the living room Grandpa carefully counts and recounts, then sets up more chairs. We girls do little things: put "oleo" on a plate, cut pumpkin pies into eighths, and—oh, joy!—spread whipped cream on the cranberry salads. Grandma makes lots of cranberry salad, and there are four or five of us on the job: one to do, and three to lick surreptitious snitches. We finish with astonishing swirls and peaks.

Everything is finally baked or roasted or boiled or stewed to satisfaction. Even Grandma is summoned to the living room. We gather around the extended and re-extended table to find a place for everyone, down to the smallest cousin and second cousin and first cousin once-removed. Some of us even have china.

Grandpa sits at the head and looks down the lengthy rows of faces. "I say, let's sing a verse of "I Thank the Lord My Maker." There's a catch in his mellow voice.

Voices rise to fill the little house to bursting. All the Kennells are enthusiastic singers, tunefully or otherwise. We count our blessings as we sing, remembering each steaming bowl of food and every face on each side of the table.

Gluten-intolerance is no respecter of persons, or family traditions for that matter. It barges right into those togetherness times and we see the greater part of the Thanksgiving feast disappear before our eyes.

I set out last November to beat this unwelcome imposter. We would have our Thanksgiving, I vowed, even with gluten-intolerance among us. All of us—yes, all—would have full plates that day.

It would be Thanksgiving just for our immediate family. Cousins have grown and hollowed out other homes in the wider world. There's an aching void where Grandpa's twinkly smile and Grandma's serving hands used to be. It would be beginning new traditions, but I asked my sisters and families to come home for Thanksgiving. We were blessed, despite empty chairs and the gluten free monster.

"Don't bring anything," I told them. "Just get here." I tried to sound generous, but I had an ulterior motive: I really wanted the cooking all to myself. I planned it for weeks.

I decided to try an all-new way to roast the turkey; first brined, then roasted very hot. I know it would have scandalized Grandma, and it took a leap of faith for even my adventurous soul. The stuffing, too, was a seismic shift. Instead of Grandma's traditional dried white bread, I used gluten free cornbread and wild rice. One of my sisters was horrified to see me toss four cloves of minced garlic with the butternut squash. And the chai tea following dessert was eyed with suspicion—somehow it smacked of exotic, far-from-Midwest places.

But I think the Lord was looking out for me—as He so often does. One of the sweetest blessings that day was watching my gluten-intolerant nephews carry loaded plates from the buffet. And I knew my efforts had passed a discriminate test when my non-gluten free sister went back for more stuffing, when several more squabbled for the remaining cranberry salad, and one brother-in-law got the leftover turkey out of the fridge later in the day and (with some assistance) *ate all of it.*

I live that plateful of edibles over and over. It's proof to me that, just as hearts can heal and stretch and grow, so can traditions live on, despite gluten-intolerance. ♪

Main Dish Miscellany

·Main dishes are masters at deception. Unlike an honest loaf of wheat bread, casseroles cleverly hide gluten, egg, or milk—often all three. We evict wheat from gravies, to turn and find it hiding in scalloped potatoes. We must rethink most of our casseroles, meatloaf, meatballs, even soups and stews.

·Read every ingredient on every label. Watch cream soups (all but a few brands contain cream and wheat flour), gravy mixes and soy sauce.

·Cream soups have been casserole standbys since Grandma's day, and we may feel lost without them. Explore Onion White Sauce as a substitute. In beef casseroles, rich beef gravies are excellent. Try this: when browning the beef, brown it well to get a good "fond" across the bottom of the pan. A pat of butter will hasten this, plus add richness. Toss a few tablespoons of brown rice flour with the browned beef (use 2 tablespoons per cup of liquid), and add liquid (broth is nice, though well-browned meat can stand up to water).

Stir the gravy briskly as it comes to a boil, season highly, and proceed with your casserole.

·If you dredge meat with flour before browning (such as round steak, beef stew, chicken and rice), try rice flour. Use about 1 cup per 2 pounds of meat, mixed with ½ teaspoon xanthan gum and liberal seasoning. Some fried dredgings benefit from a little cornmeal for crunch (see "Fish Fry" and "Oven-Fried Chicken").

·Revive the classic idea of picnic chicken. Americans rely largely on wheat and egg in packed lunches, but well-made chicken drumsticks can outshine them all. Include dipping sauce(s), and don't forget a big stack of napkins.

·Once you find gluten-free pastry doable, use savory pies to perk menus. They're also picnic-happy. ♪

Sunday Dinner Beef Roast

{ We pile home from church, renewed spiritually, but in body as hungry as bears. We catch whiffs of it from the yard, we scent it stronger on the porch, but when we open the door the full aroma of this roast comes out to greet us. We grip our middles and scramble to get that roast on the table posthaste. And when it arrives, in brown, rich slices, it's wonderful to see there'll be enough for everyone, plus second and third helpings. · This roast will take 3 hours to bake. If we put it in the oven just when we slip out the door, it is ready when we return at 12:30 or 1:00. You might need to adjust the oven temperature to accommodate your schedule. }

1 center cut or top round beef roast (approximately 4 pounds), thawed if frozen
1 1/2 teaspoons seasoned salt
1 teaspoon garlic powder
1/2 teaspoon onion powder
1/2 teaspoon red pepper, optional
1/4 cup cold butter, diced
1/2 cup water

Preheat oven to 350°.

Place roast in roasting pan. Stir together seasoned salt, garlic powder, onion powder and red pepper in a small bowl. Rub roast with spices and dot with butter. Pour water into roasting pan.

Roast, uncovered, for 3 hours. Remove roast to cutting board and let stand 15 minutes before carving.

Make gravy according to the recipe Gravy from Roast (see index). Keep warm.

Cut roast into 1/2" slices across the grain. Serve with the gravy.

Spice-Rubbed Roasted Turkey

{ Moist and tender from the brine, seasoned with warm and mellow spices, this turkey is worth every step of the way. · Begin this recipe three days before serving, seven if the turkey is frozen. · By no means do you have to wait until a holiday to make this turkey—anytime you need a large roast for serving a crowd, or freezing for later use, this recipe will do very nicely. }

1 (13 pound) turkey
2 cups table salt
2 gallons cold water
3 tablespoons mustard powder
2 tablespoons ground cumin
3 tablespoons paprika
2 tablespoons dried thyme
2 teaspoons ground ginger
1 tablespoon olive oil

If turkey is frozen, remove from freezer to refrigerator at least seven days before you plan to serve it. Three days before serving, combine salt and water in a clean five-gallon bucket, stirring well to dissolve. Immerse turkey and refrigerate 48 hours or until the day before you plan to roast it. Drain and rinse turkey, then pat dry inside and out. Air dry 30 minutes.

Mix mustard powder, cumin, paprika, thyme, and ginger. Combine 1 tablespoon of this mixture with the olive oil in a small bowl. With fingers, separate skin from breast and work moistened spice rub under skin. Be careful to not break skin. Rub 2 tablespoons dry rub inside cavity of turkey, and the remaining over the outside. Refrigerate, uncovered, 24 hours or until ready to roast the following day.

Continued

Three and a half hours before serving time, preheat oven to 400°. Place turkey breast-side-down in uncovered roasting pan on rack.

Roast turkey 45 minutes. Rotate turkey onto one side. Roast additional 15 minutes. Rotate turkey to opposite side and roast another 15 minutes.

Flip turkey breast-side-up and roast about 1 hour longer. When done, a meat thermometer in thickest part of breast will register 170°. Remove turkey from oven and lift it from roasting pan onto a rimmed cookie sheet. Allow to rest 30 minutes before carving.

While turkey is resting, make gravy (see index for Gravy from Roast recipe).

Carve turkey and serve with gravy.

Roasted Brined Chicken

{ *I discovered the merits of brining with this recipe, and I've happily used it many times since. Brining is really all about flavor: a soak in salt water will season chicken to the bone. But there is another merit, I discovered: brined chicken is marvelously juicy. Because of this, you can roast it uncovered at high temperatures, producing a browned and crackly skin, without drying the meat. · Be sure the salt in the brine is completely dissolved before immersing chickens, and roast chickens until they are really done. Don't let nicely browned skin fool you—use the fork test and wiggle the thigh bone to be safe. · Here's a suggestion: even if you have a small family, make the full recipe, for there's nothing like having leftover roast chicken in the refrigerator.* }

2 whole chickens

For Brine:
1 cup table salt
1 1/2 cups evaporated cane juice
4 garlic cloves
1/2 cup lemon juice
1 gallon water

In a large plastic container, stir together brine ingredients until salt is completely dissolved. Immerse chickens. Cover and let rest in a cool place overnight or up to 24 hours.

Two hours before serving, preheat oven to 400°. Remove chickens from brine and place in a large roaster with rack (or 10"x15" rimmed baking sheet with rack set inside).

Roast, uncovered, for approximately 1 hour and 15 minutes. If pan juices threaten to scorch, pour about 1/2 cup water into broiler pan.

Continued

Chickens are done when thighs easily rotate in sockets, and juices run clear when skin is pierced.

Remove chickens from pans to platter. Allow to rest 15 minutes before carving.

Meanwhile, follow recipe for Gravy from Roast (see index) to make gravy from pan juices. Carve chicken and serve with gravy.

Oven-Fried Chicken

{ *This recipe goes places. It starred at a seminar dinner for 30, is often served as part of a hot, filling meal for the bakery girls up the road, and has appeared on the menu at home time and again. · Oven-Fried Chicken begs to be served with mashed potatoes, gravy, and sweet new peas.* }

5 pounds young chicken pieces, or chicken quarters, cut into thighs and drumsticks
1/2 cup butter, melted
1 cup brown rice flour
1 cup yellow cornmeal
1/2 teaspoon xanthan gum
2 teaspoons seasoned salt
1/4 teaspoon pepper
1 teaspoon garlic salt

Preheat oven to 375°.

In a small skillet, melt butter. Stir together flour, cornmeal, xanthan gum and seasonings in a shallow dish. Line 10"x15" baking pan with aluminum foil.

Rinse chicken pieces. Roll each in butter, then in flour mixture. Lay in prepared pan, spacing an inch or two apart. Drizzle any remaining butter over all.

Bake 45 to 60 minutes, or until chicken is fork-tender and coating is browned and crusty. Serve hot.

Honey-Barbecued Chicken

{ *This is one of our favorite ways with chicken. It bakes up browned, saucy, and tender. It's especially good with boiled rice and a green salad. · Honey-Barbecued Chicken is an ideal way to feed a crowd—especially if you have access to a convection oven. Know your group; once I doubled this recipe, and it served 13 adults (predominantly women) and three children, comfortably. Thirteen men could easily do away with three batches. A few tips: Have chicken pieces oven-ready in the refrigerator. Use extra-wide, heavy-duty foil to line baking sheets. Preheat convection oven well beforehand. Place chicken into oven exactly 45 minutes before you sit down to eat. Warm platters, and keep foil nearby to tent chicken. Place stacks of extra napkins on the table.* }

5 pounds chicken pieces, or chicken quarters, cut into thighs and drumsticks

salt and black pepper, to taste

1/2 cup melted butter

1/2 cup honey

1/4 cup yellow mustard

1 additional teaspoon salt

1 1/2 teaspoons onion powder

Preheat oven to 425°. Rinse chicken pieces. Line two large rimmed baking sheets with aluminum foil. Lay chicken on sheets, skin sides up. Sprinkle generously with salt and black pepper. Bake 15 minutes.

Meanwhile, stir together butter, honey, mustard, 1 teaspoon salt, and onion powder. Brush chicken with sauce. Bake 5 minutes. Brush with sauce again. Bake 5 more minutes and check smaller chicken pieces, removing if done. (When pierced with a fork, juice should run clear.) Keep warm on a platter until all chicken is baked. Makes approximately 14 servings.

Spicy Picnic Thighs & Drumsticks

{ Chicken is the quintessential picnic food, and this recipe is my favorite. It's delectable cold, but you can serve this chicken at any temperature, from a silver platter or a wicker picnic basket. Notice you'll need to start preparing it a day ahead. }

5 pounds chicken thighs and drumsticks
2 tablespoons salt
3 tablespoons evaporated cane juice
2 tablespoons chili powder
1 tablespoon paprika
1 teaspoon black pepper
1/2 teaspoon garlic powder
1/8 teaspoon red pepper

Line broiler pan or two rimmed baking sheets with aluminium foil. Position broiler rack in broiler pan, or cooling rack on baking sheets.

Rinse chicken and cut several slashes in the skin of each piece. Combine spices in a small bowl. Coat chicken well with spices. Lay chicken pieces on prepared rack. Refrigerate, uncovered, 12 to 24 hours.

Preheat oven to 425°. Roast chicken (on rack, uncovered) for 25 minutes. Raise heat to 500° and roast another 10 minutes. Check chicken for doneness: when pierced, juices should run clear. If not, roast 5 minutes longer. Remove from oven.

Serve hot or cold. Makes approximately 14 servings.

Quick Chili Chicken

{ Here is impulsive chicken, the kind you make after you look at the clock and realize dinnertime is almost here. · For an impromptu picnic, pop this chicken in the oven, stash some napkins and a few nibbles in a basket, tuck in the finished chicken, and be off in half an hour. · No amounts are given: count on 2 or 3 pieces of chicken per person, and season with as much of the chili powder and salt as you like. }

chicken pieces or chicken legs and thighs, completely thawed if frozen
light olive oil
chili powder
salt

Preheat oven to 400°. Line a large rimmed baking sheet with foil.

Rub chicken pieces with olive oil, then sprinkle lightly with chili powder and generously with salt.

Lay chicken on prepared baking sheet. Bake 30 to 40 minutes or until juices run clear when pierced with knife.

Serve hot or cold.

Cornmeal-Crusted Fried Fish

{ *Great-Grandaddy Hobbs, a Virginian, liked to fish, Mom recounts. "He was a drawbridge operator on the Chesapeake-Albemarle Canal. On his time off, he'd tune up his fishing boat—Grandmother always packed him a lunch in a black frying pan—and go fishing on the canal or Back Bay. He'd bring home buckets of fish. And oh, those fish fries we had on the beach!" · Of course, fresh fish is by far the best in this recipe, but you can use frozen fish fillets if you're an inlander, like Mom now is. · Fried fish is wonderful on warm Sandwich Buns, served with tartar sauce, rings of sweet onion, and Sweet and Sour Coleslaw (see index).* }

1 1/2 pounds white fish fillets (whiting or pollock are nice), completely thawed if frozen
2/3 cup brown rice flour
1/3 cup yellow cornmeal
1/4 teaspoon xanthan gum
1 teaspoon seasoned salt
dash of garlic salt
black pepper, to taste
3 tablespoons coconut oil or vegetable oil, plus more as needed

Tartar Sauce:
1 cup mayonnaise or Vegenaise
1/4 cup sweet pickle relish
1 teaspoon fresh lemon juice
salt and pepper, to taste

In a shallow dish, stir together the brown rice flour, cornmeal, xanthan gum, seasoned salt, garlic salt and pepper. Heat oil in a large cast-iron skillet until almost smoking.

Cut fish fillets in half, and coat with cornmeal mixture. Fry in hot skillet over medium heat until browned and the meat flakes easily with a fork in the thickest part of the fillets, turning once. Lay on a paper-towel-lined platter and keep warm until serving.

Green Bean-Potato-Beef Casserole

{ This simple casserole is "home food": the kind that makes people scramble for leftovers or dream about when gone from home. · This recipe can be doubled, tripled, quadrupled; the only limit is your oven size. With larger casseroles, you'll need to add to the baking time accordingly—a huge casserole might take 2½ hours. }

2 pounds ground beef
1 yellow onion, chopped
6 to 8 potatoes, shredded
salt and black pepper, to taste
3 cups beef broth
4 tablespoons brown rice flour or cornstarch
1/4 cup cold water
1 quart canned or frozen green beans

Preheat oven to 350°. Grease a large casserole.

Brown ground beef with onion in a large skillet. Brown well to make a good fond across the bottom of the skillet, being careful not to burn. Layer potatoes in prepared casserole. Season generously with salt and pepper and toss. Layer browned ground beef over potatoes.

In the same skillet used for browning beef, heat beef broth, stirring to remove any browned bits from bottom of skillet. Bring to a simmer. Stir together brown rice flour or cornstarch and water in a small bowl until lump-free and slowly add to simmering broth, stirring briskly. When thickened and bubbly, remove from heat, taste for salt and pepper, then pour over casserole. Scatter green beans over beef.

Cover and bake for 1 to 11/2 hours, or until potatoes are very tender. Makes approximately 8 servings.

Chili & Cornbread Bake

{ In this casserole, the popular chili/cornbread duo is united in one dish. I like to make it on blizzardy winter evenings when brave chore-folk need something warm and hearty to thaw them out. }

Filling:
- **1 pound ground beef**
- **1/2 cup chopped yellow onion**
- **2 (1 pound) cans gluten free baked beans**
- **salt and pepper, to taste**
- **1 cup beef broth or water**

Cornbread Topping:
- **1/4 cup butter**
- **1 cup brown rice flour**
- **1 cup yellow cornmeal**
- **1 tablespoon baking powder**
- **1/2 teaspoon salt**
- **1/2 teaspoon xanthan gum**
- **1 tablespoon sweetener of choice**
- **1 1/2 cups water, or as needed**

Preheat oven to 400°.

For filling, brown ground beef with onion in a large skillet. Add remaining filling ingredients. Taste for salt and pepper. Simmer until heated through.

Meanwhile, prepare topping. Place butter in a 9"x13" baking pan and place in oven to melt. Stir together brown rice flour, cornmeal, baking powder, salt, xanthan gum, and sweetener. Add melted butter and water. Batter should be soft, but able to hold its shape. Add more water if needed.

Pour beans into prepared pan. Drop cornbread batter into mounds over chili. Bake until well-browned and bubbly, about 25 minutes. Makes 8 servings.

Chicken Over Rice

{ *This is a simple combination of ingredients which gives big results. I think the secret is browning the chicken, which then richly flavors the rice and vegetables as they bake. · Use your favorite rice—Jasmine brown rice has a nut-like flavor that pairs well with the chicken. · Mom grows celery in her garden, and the leafy, pungent ribs do wonderful things to this casserole.* }

6 pieces chicken, thawed if frozen, and rinsed
rice flour, for dredging
coconut, light olive, or vegetable oil, for frying
seasoned salt, for seasoning chicken
2 cups brown rice
1 cup chopped celery
1 1/2 cups chopped yellow onion
2 teaspoons salt
small pinch dried oregano
4 1/2 cups water

Preheat oven to 350°. Grease shallow casserole or 9"x13" baking pan.

Heat a large skillet over medium-high. Add oil to coat bottom of pan.

In a shallow bowl, place rice flour. Dredge chicken pieces in flour, shake off excess, and lay pieces skin-side-down in hot skillet. Fry for 5 minutes, turning once, or just until skin is nicely browned. Chicken will not be fully cooked. Remove chicken to a plate, and brown remaining chicken pieces, adding more oil to skillet if necessary.

Layer rice in prepared casserole. Sprinkle evenly with celery, onion, salt, and oregano. Position chicken in single layer over rice. Pour water over all. Do not stir.

Cover casserole and bake 11/2 to 13/4 hours or until chicken is very tender and rice is well done. Yields 6 servings.

Thanksgiving Casserole

{ *Here you have it: all the flavors of the feast together on a fork. · If you have plenty of leftovers from Thanksgiving, use them in this casserole, using leftover gravy as the second layer, stuffing as the third, and mashed potatoes as the fourth. · We've prepared this (multiplied by 8, in an 18 quart roaster) for 50 people. My aunt gave me the idea; she said for fellowship meals in their church, the ladies brought the separate layers, and put them together on the spot. The whole casserole heated nicely during worship.* }

2 to 3 cups cooked and cubed turkey, chicken or ham
3 cups chicken, turkey or ham broth
3 tablespoons cornstarch
3 tablespoons brown rice flour
3 cups crumbled Classic Cornbread (see index)
1 cup cooked brown/wild rice mix
8 ounces fresh or canned mushrooms
1/3 cup chopped yellow onion
1/3 cup chopped celery
1/2 cup finely chopped carrot
3 1/2 cups peeled and cubed potatoes
2 tablespoons butter
1/4 cup sour cream or Sour Supreme
salt and black pepper

Preheat oven to 325°.

First layer: In a greased 2 quart roaster, place cooked turkey, chicken or ham.

Second layer: Make gravy by whisking broth, cornstarch, and brown rice flour in a saucepan, and bringing to a boil over high heat, whisking until smooth. Boil 3 minutes. Salt and pepper to taste. Pour half of this over meat and reserve remainder.

Continued

The Full Dinner Plate :155:

Third layer: Cut cornbread into small cubes. Stir in cooked rice. In a small skillet, heat 1/3 cup butter. Add celery, onion and carrot. Sauté until tender. Add mushrooms and sauté just until limp. Toss sautéed mixture into cornbread/rice mixture. Salt and pepper generously. Layer over meat, packing lightly.

Fourth layer: Place potatoes in saucepan. Cover with cold water. Salt generously, cover and bring to a boil over high heat. Simmer 20 minutes or until potatoes are very tender. Drain. Mash potatoes with 2 tablespoons butter, sour cream or Sour Supreme, and salt and pepper to taste. Mixture will be stiffer than most mashed potatoes. Spread over stuffing layer, forming a slight depression in center.

Fifth layer: Pour remaining gravy over all.

Cover casserole and bake 45 to 60 minutes or until bubbly and well-heated.

Ham-Under-The-Clouds

{ *Serve this to your family on a chilly, rainy day and tell them to cheer up, because a cloudy day can be a good day, anyway. · One hint: Make the potatoes very stiff; don't be tempted to add more sour cream and butter while mashing them. As the casserole heats, the potatoes will absorb some of the gravy.* }

3 quarts peeled and diced potatoes
water, as needed
1/2 cup butter, divided
1/2 cup sour cream or Sour Supreme
2 tablespoons additional butter or light olive oil
3 cups cubed fully cooked ham
1 onion, chopped
1/4 cup brown rice flour
2 cups water
salt and pepper

Preheat oven to 375°.

Place potatoes in a large saucepan. Add water to cover. Salt generously. Cover and bring to a boil over high heat. Lower heat and simmer 20 minutes, or until potatoes are very tender.

Meanwhile, in a large skillet, melt the 2 tablespoons butter or olive oil over medium-high heat. Add ham and onion and sauté to brown slightly. Add flour, stirring well to coat. Add water and bring to a boil, stirring vigorously to make a smooth, medium-thick gravy. Taste for salt and pepper.

Pour ham mixture into large, greased roaster. Cover to keep warm.

Drain potatoes and mash with 1/4 cup of the butter and the sour cream or Sour Supreme. Taste for salt and pepper. Potatoes will be thicker than for most mashed potatoes.

Spread potatoes over ham. Dot with remaining butter. Cover tightly and bake 20 to 30 minutes or until completely hot and gravy is bubbly.

Gourmet Chicken & Broccoli Casserole

{ *Holding its own in any buffet or basket dinner, this is a special occasion dish. The water chestnuts are optional, but they add a delightful crunch. · Don't overbake this casserole for the sake of the delicate broccoli. · If you use Sour Supreme, perk it first with a teaspoon of fresh lemon juice.* }

2 cups cooked and cubed chicken breast
1 large head broccoli, cut into florets
8 ounces sliced water chestnuts, optional
3 1/2 cups chicken broth
1/2 cup brown rice flour
1/2 cup water
1/4 cup sour cream or Sour Supreme
1/2 cup mayonnaise or Vegenaise
salt and pepper, to taste
2 1/2 cups crushed potato chips, gluten free crackers, or cornflakes
2 tablespoons butter or olive oil
3/4 cup slivered almonds, optional

Preheat oven to 375°. Grease 2 quart casserole or 9"x13" baking pan.

Blanch broccoli one minute in a pot of boiling water, then plunge into an ice-water bath. Drain. Combine broccoli, chicken, and water chestnuts, if using, in prepared pan or casserole.

In a saucepan, bring chicken broth to a boil over high heat. Stir together brown rice flour and water until lump-free. Add slowly to boiling broth, whisking well, until broth is just thickened. You might not need all the rice flour. Remove from heat and stir in sour cream or substitute and mayonnaise or Vegenaise.

Stir broth mixture into chicken/broccoli mixture. Taste for salt and pepper.

Continued

In a medium bowl, stir together crumbs, butter or oil and almonds. Scatter mixture over casserole.

Bake 20 to 30 minutes, or until sauce is bubbly and almonds well toasted. Makes about 6 servings.

Scalloped Potatoes & Ham

{ *This is an easy do-ahead dish. If you make the white sauce and cook the potatoes ahead of time, it comes together effortlessly. · A little butter over all makes a nicely browned surface.* }

> **2 1/4 pounds potatoes, cooked or uncooked**
> **salt and black pepper, to taste**
> **1 recipe Creamy Onion White Sauce (see index)**
> **2 cups cubed fully cooked ham**
> **1/4 cup butter**

Preheat oven to 400°. Grease a 9"x13" baking pan or casserole.

Peel potatoes. Grate coarsely into prepared casserole. Salt and pepper generously. Stir in ham and sauce.

Dot surface with butter. If using raw potatoes, bake 45 minutes covered, then 15 minutes uncovered. If using cooked potatoes, bake uncovered 30 minutes, or until hot and browned.

Creamy Chicken-etti

{ Fresh mushrooms and sour cream or Sour Supreme make this casserole rich and comforting. · Because the noodles are cooked twice, be sure to boil them until just under al dente. · A green salad is nice with this. }

2 tablespoons butter or light olive oil
1 yellow onion, chopped
1 celery rib, thinly sliced
1/4 cup chopped green pepper
8 ounces fresh mushrooms, sliced
8 ounces gluten free spaghetti noodles
2 cups cubed, cooked chicken
4 cups chicken broth
1/2 cup brown rice flour
1/2 cup cold water
1/2 cup sour cream or Sour Supreme
salt and black pepper, to taste

Preheat oven to 350°. Grease a casserole dish.

In a skillet, sauté onion, celery and pepper in butter or oil until tender. Add mushrooms and sauté just until softened. Remove from heat.

Cook spaghetti in a large pot of salted water until softened but not completely cooked. Drain and place in prepared casserole.

Toss sautéed vegetables and cooked chicken with spaghetti noodles.

Heat broth in a saucepan to a rolling boil. Mix rice flour and cold water, stirring well. Whisk into broth, using just enough to make a thin sauce. Simmer 2 minutes. Whisk in sour cream or substitute if using. Stir sauce into mixture in casserole. Taste for seasoning. Cover and bake 30 minutes, or until heated through.

Potato Puff Casserole

{ *This is special occasion food—especially served with Cauliflower and Lettuce Salad. · Some potato puff brands contain gluten. Read labels carefully.* }

2 pounds ground beef
1 large yellow onion, chopped
1 tablespoon butter or olive oil
1/4 cup brown rice flour
2 to 2 1/2 cups water
3 cups peas, fresh or frozen
salt, pepper and seasoned salt
2 cups shredded cheese or cheese substitute, optional
2 (1 pound) packages frozen gluten free potato puffs

Preheat oven to 350°. Grease a large casserole or lidded roaster.

Brown beef with onion in a large, heavy skillet. Add butter or oil, browning well to form a good fond across bottom of skillet. Do not burn. Add flour, tossing well to coat. Add water and stir over high heat until thickened and bubbly. Add peas. Season to taste.

Turn mixture into prepared casserole dish. Cover with shredded cheese or cheese substitute if desired. Scatter potato puffs over all.

Cover casserole and bake 45 minutes. Uncover and bake until potato puffs are nicely browned. Serve hot.

Aunt Ruth's Chicken Stir-Fry

{ *My sisters and I reached the end of our 1,100-mile journey on a gorgeous spring evening. We had come to Virginia to attend a conference, and the sun was slanting gold across the Shenandoah Valley. Aunt Ruth was tending an iron skillet. "You all come in and teach me how to make stir-fry!" she said, hugging us all around. Together we added, stirred and tasted. Then, bug-eyed, we watched our artist aunt arrange the stir-fry on a platter: the rice mounded in the center, the stir-fry circling it. · The next evening, after a long day of learning, my sisters wanted ice cream, but I begged for leftover stir-fry. · Be sure to check soy sauce labels for wheat.* }

1/2 cup sliced onion
3/4 cup sliced celery
3/4 cup thinly sliced green pepper
3/4 cup thinly sliced red pepper
1/2 cup thinly sliced carrots
2 tablespoons oil
1 cup thinly sliced chicken breast
1/2 cup water
2 tablespoons cornstarch
1/4 cup gluten free soy sauce, or more if needed
4 cups hot rice, for serving

Prepare vegetables and keep close at hand. In a small bowl, stir together water, cornstarch, and soy sauce. Set aside.

In a large skillet or wok, heat oil over medium-high heat. Add chicken breast and fry, stirring, until no longer pink. Add onion, and sauté briefly. Add remaining vegetables and sauté just until crisp-tender.

Pour soy sauce mixture over stir-fry, stirring quickly until thickened and bubbly. Taste for seasoning, adding more soy sauce if needed. Serve stir-fry over warm rice. Serves 4.

Crusty Bean Bake

{ *This is a long-suffering recipe. It has endured variations, changes and omissions, and it just comes through, time and again. We've served it to company, at a birthday meal, for many summer suppers. · This recipe is best in a deep pan, rather than a flat, larger one (think casserole-style versus pizza-style), and best of all served with a green salad with ranch dressing (see index).* }

2 tablespoons light olive or vegetable oil
1 yellow onion, chopped
1 clove garlic, minced or pressed
4 cups cooked black or pinto beans, undrained
water, if needed
2 teaspoons chili powder
salt and black pepper, to taste
hot pepper sauce
1/2 cup cornmeal
1/2 cup brown rice flour
1/4 teaspoon xanthan gum
1/2 teaspoon salt
2 teaspoons baking powder
2 tablespoons butter, melted
3/4 cup water, or as needed
cheese or cheese substitute, optional

Preheat oven to 375°. Grease a casserole dish or 9"x13" baking pan.

In a large skillet, heat oil. Add onion and garlic and sauté 5 minutes. Add beans. If beans don't have enough liquid to cover, add water as needed. Bring to a boil and add chili powder, salt, black pepper, and hot sauce. Simmer while preparing crust.

Continued

In a medium bowl, stir together cornmeal, flour, xanthan gum, baking powder, and salt. Add melted butter and water to make a soft batter. With back of spoon, spread thinly across bottom and partly up sides of prepared pan.

Carefully pour hot bean mixture into crust. Bake 25 to 35 minutes or until crust is browned and filling is bubbly. Top with cheese, if desired, and allow to melt. Serve hot.

Curry Rice Skillet Supper

{ *My sister invented this one-dish meal to feed the voracious little-boy appetites at her house. It meets the prerequisites: filling, tasty, and fast enough to get to the table in a hurry. They like it with green salad.* }

1 pound ground beef
1 medium yellow onion, chopped
2 ribs celery, chopped
2 carrots, peeled and chopped
2 1/2 cups long-grain white rice
2 1/2 teaspoons salt
2 teaspoons gluten free beef broth base
1 teaspoon curry powder
1 teaspoon onion powder
5 1/2 cups water
parsley for garnish

Brown beef with onion in a large, heavy skillet over medium-high heat. Add celery and carrot and fry 2 minutes. Add rice and spices and fry another 2 minutes, stirring.

Add water to skillet, increase heat to high, and bring to a boil. Stir to loosen browned bits at bottom of skillet. Reduce heat to low and simmer, covered, for 25 minutes.

Stir well and serve hot.

Chicken Veggie Pie

{ Make this main-dish pie on a cool spring evening when the peepers are singing. Add to the menu some baby greens and Rhubarb-Blueberry Tapioca for dessert. Serve with a big spoon—tender chicken in gravy, loaded with bright veggies, under a flaky crust—richness! }

Classic Butter Pie Crust dough for one double-crust pie (see index)
1 cup finely cubed potatoes
1 cup sliced carrots
1/2 cup sliced celery
1/2 cup chopped onion
1/2 cup peas, fresh or frozen
2 cups cooked and cubed chicken meat
1 garlic clove, minced or pressed, optional
2 1/2 cups chicken broth
3 tablespoons rice flour
3 tablespoons cornstarch
salt, pepper and dried parsley

Preheat oven to 400°. Roll and fit bottom crust into a deep-dish 9" pie pan.

Place potatoes, carrots, celery and onion in a saucepan. Add water to cover, and salt well. Bring to a boil. Cover, reduce heat and simmer 10 to 12 minutes, or just until vegetables are tender. Remove from heat and drain. Toss with chicken meat, peas, and garlic in a large bowl.

In the same saucepan, bring broth to a boil over high heat. In a small bowl, stir together flour and cornstarch with just enough water to moisten. Whisk into boiling broth, adding enough to make a medium gravy. Season with salt, pepper and parsley.

Continued

Pour broth over chicken and vegetable mixture, and toss. Taste again for seasoning, and turn into pastry-lined pie pan. Roll top crust to 10" circle. Moisten edge of top crust with wet pastry brush. Position top crust, trim edge to 1/2", then turn edge under. Flute to seal. Vent top crust with sharp knife. Sprinkle lightly with salt.

Bake 35 to 45 minutes or until crust is browned and gravy is bubbly. Serve hot.

Beef & Onion Pie

{ Meat pies entered my life in beautiful Quebec. Our friends served us fascinating food—salads, soups, multiple meats and rich desserts in five- and six-course meals. Meat pies kept reappearing, and when I make this recipe, it floods me with memories of pastoral valleys, church spires, and hosts who urged us in French to eat more than was humanly possible. · This pie can be served as a simple lunch or supper, or with a full-course dinner. }

Classic Butter Pie Crust dough for 1 double-crust pie (see index)
1 pound lean ground beef
1 recipe Creamy Onion White Sauce (see index)
salt and pepper to taste
salt for sprinkling

Preheat oven to 425°.

Roll and fit bottom crust into 9" pie pan.

In a large skillet, brown beef well. Stir in enough Onion White Sauce to make a thick "gravy" consistency (you may not need all the sauce). Heat through. Salt and pepper to taste.

Turn beef mixture into prepared pastry-lined pan. Roll top crust to 10" circle. Moisten edge of bottom crust with wet pastry brush. Position top crust, trim edges to 1/2", then turn edge under even with pie pan. Flute as desired to seal. Vent top crust with a sharp knife and sprinkle lightly with salt.

Bake pie 30 minutes or until crust is well browned, top and bottom. Remove from oven and serve hot. Yields 8 servings.

Incredible Edible Pizza

{ *It's back! The only difficult thing about this recipe is choosing the toppings—and that won't be hard if you've been dreaming of pizza for 10 years. · If you use pizza sauce, spread it thinly to help keep crust crisp. · To really recreate past times, serve with "Juice-Pop" or "Root Beer, Suddenly" (see index).* }

1 recipe Pizza Crust (see index)
cornmeal, for sprinkling
olive oil, for drizzling
choice of toppings: pizza sauce, browned gluten-free sausage, browned ground beef, gluten-free pepperoni slices, sliced mushrooms, sliced black olives, chopped sweet onion, chopped or sliced green pepper, as and if desired
cheese or cheese substitute, grated

Preheat oven to 400°.

Grease two 12" pizza pans and sprinkle with cornmeal. Spread half of pizza dough in each, spreading evenly and building up edges slightly. Allow to rise 20 minutes.

Brush dough lightly with olive oil. Prebake crusts 10 minutes, rotating pans once. Remove from oven and add toppings.

Bake pizzas, rotating pans, for 10 to 15 minutes. Sprinkle pizzas with cheese. Bake 5 to 10 minutes longer until cheese is melted and bottoms of crusts are crisp and very well-browned.

Cut pizzas and serve immediately.

Loaded Tostadas

{ This is a playful main dish you can make on the spot for few or many.
· The toppings are strictly a matter of choice, so tostadas are ideal
in a pick-and-choose buffet. Supply forks and a big stack of napkins.
· Here's the fun thing about tostadas: when you're eating them with a
fork, you think maybe your fingers would be simpler, and when you use
your fingers, a fork seems so much easier, after all. }

Tostadas:
corn tortillas (2 or 3 per person)
coconut, light olive or vegetable oil, for frying

Toppings:
thick chili and/or
hot refried beans and/or
hot boiled rice
sliced sweet onion
shredded lettuce
grated cheese or substitute
sour cream or Sour Supreme
chopped tomatoes or salsa
black olives, sliced
guacamole

In a large skillet, heat 1/4" oil until hot but not smoking. Fry corn tortillas
one at a time until crisp, turning once. Drain on paper towels and keep
warm in oven until all are fried. Serve warm. To serve, place tostada on plate
and pile with any or all of the toppings suggested.

Boston Baked Beans

{ *A pot of baked beans is one of our favorite dishes, and so I decided it was time to learn to make them myself—beginning with dry beans. This was the result, and here are two tricks I learned along the way: Use the right kind of molasses, and don't double the recipe. · I like baked beans sweet. If you're unsure of the sugar content here, try reserving some of the evaporated cane juice until the beans are baked, then adding to your personal taste when you adjust the seasoning before serving.* }

1 pound dried pea beans
1/2 cup mild baking molasses, divided
1/4 cup evaporated cane juice
8 slices bacon
1 yellow onion
9 cups water
1 teaspoon salt, or more if needed
2 teaspoons yellow mustard
1 teaspoon cider vinegar
black pepper

Preheat oven to 300°.

Pick beans over and rinse. Set aside.

In a Dutch oven with oven-proof lid, fry bacon over medium heat until crisp. Remove bacon to plate, cool and crumble. Chop onion, add to bacon fat, and sauté until tender.

Add bacon, beans, evaporated cane juice, water, salt, and mustard to Dutch oven. Add all but 2 tablespoons of the molasses. Reserve remaining molasses.

Cover Dutch oven tightly and bake beans, stirring once in a while, for 4 hours. Remove lid. Continue baking beans until liquid is thickened and beans are soft, about 11/2 hours longer. Add remaining molasses and the vinegar. Add additional salt and black pepper, if desired. Serve hot.

Zucchini-Carrot Fritters

{ On hot summer evenings when cicadas are humming and zucchini plants producing at high speed, mix up a batch of these fritters. With tomato slices and glasses of icy tea, they can carry supper all by themselves. }

light olive or vegetable oil, for frying
2 small zucchini, finely shredded
1 small onion, chopped
1 large carrot, finely shredded
1 garlic clove, minced or pressed
1/2 teaspoon salt
1/2 teaspoon xanthan gum
3/4 cup brown rice flour
1/2 teaspoon baking powder
water, as needed
sour cream or Sour Supreme, to serve, optional

Heat a large cast-iron skillet over medium heat with enough oil to just cover bottom of pan.

In a large bowl, toss together zucchini, onion, carrot, garlic, salt, xanthan gum, brown rice flour and baking powder. Check consistency, and add a little water if necessary to moisten vegetables.

Drop fritter batter by heaping teaspoons into hot skillet and fry until well-browned, turning once. Serve warm with sour cream or Sour Supreme, if desired.

Cornbread-Wild Rice Stuffing

{ *Is "stuffing" an incorrect name for a stuffing not stuffed in a turkey?
Maybe. But we'll call it stuffing, anyway, because it's stuffed with
hearty wild rice, cornbread and mushrooms. · Since there are a lot
of steps involved, try baking cornbread, sautéing vegetables, and
cooking both rice and giblets several days ahead. Then, on a rushed
Thanksgiving morning, it will come together quickly. · Sometime I'd
like to try sausage in this stuffing.* }

> 1 recipe Classic Cornbread (see index)
> 1 3/4 cups brown rice and wild rice, mixed
> 8 1/2 cups chicken broth
> 1 1/2 teaspoon salt
> turkey neck, heart and gizzard (liver discarded)
> 4 ounces fresh button mushrooms, sliced
> 2 yellow onions, chopped
> 2 stalks celery, sliced
> 1/2 cup butter
> salt and pepper

Preheat oven to 350°.

Crumble cornbread and set aside.

Place brown and wild rice, 3 1/2 cups of the broth and 1 1/2 teaspoon salt in a medium saucepan. Bring to a boil, cover, and simmer 25 to 30 minutes.

In a small saucepan, place giblets. Cover with water and sprinkle with salt. Bring to a boil, cover, and simmer until tender, about 45 minutes. Cool in liquid, then remove meat from bones, dice meat in small pieces, and reserve.

Continued

Sauté mushrooms, onions, and celery in butter until tender. In a large bowl, toss together cornbread, rice, giblet meat, and vegetables. Add the balance of the broth, or enough to make a rather wet consistency. Salt and pepper to taste.

Turn mixture into a greased 2 quart casserole dish. Bake uncovered 30 to 40 minutes or until well-browned and heated through. Serve with roast turkey.

Roasted Butternut Squash

{ *Of all the beautiful heirloom squashes (and there are hundreds!) butternut remains queen. It's rewarding from the time the plants grow luxuriant in the garden to when you cut open a slim-necked squash to reveal the red-gold inside. · Roasting brings out the sweetness of most vegetables, and squash is no exception. · The amount of garlic here just faintly flavors the squash; increase it as much as you like. Roasted squash takes a lot of oven room, so be sure you have space before including it in a large dinner menu.* }

2 medium to large winter butternut squash
4 tablespoons olive oil
4 garlic cloves, minced or pressed
salt

Preheat oven to 425°.

Peel, seed and cut butternuts into 1" cubes with a sharp knife. Place in a large bowl, and toss with oil and garlic. Spread in single layer on two large baking pans. Sprinkle with salt.

Bake squash, stirring occasionally, for 45 minutes or until browned and tender. Serve at once.

Gravy From Roast

{ *Rejoice! Gravy comes gluten-free, too. Here's the secret: equal parts cornstarch and rice flour. Rice flour gives body and depth, and cornstarch adds a silky finish.* }

Remove roasted meat from pan to a rimmed baking sheet. Tent with foil to keep warm.

Check the "fond" (browned, roasted-on bits) on the roasting pan. A thick, toasty-brown fond will make the very best gravy. If fond is burned over most of the pan, don't try to make gravy with it, or it will taste burned. Just a bit of burned fond should be fine.

Add water or light broth to juices in roasting pan. The amounts really vary here; it depends on the size of the roast you made and the size of the pan. For something as big as a turkey, start with about 3 cups. For a small roast, begin with 1 1/2 cups.

Place roasting pan on stove and heat on medium-high. Use a spatula to scrape fond from the bottom of the pan as the liquid comes to a boil.

When pan is completely clean, strain liquid through a sieve into liquid measuring cup. Allow fat to come to the top, then dip off and discard as much fat as possible.

Pour liquid into a flat, wide pan—a skillet works well. Add any juices that have collected under resting roast. Taste, and add more water as necessary to bring to a desired gravy strength. It should be rich and meaty, but not overpowering. If your roast was well-seasoned, you might not need salt, but add if necessary. I like gravy with plenty of seasoning, because a little has to go such a long way on the plate. Bring liquid to a boil.

Stir together equal parts cornstarch and rice flour in a small bowl. Start with 1 tablespoon cornstarch and 1 tablespoon rice flour per cup of gravy, then a little more to be safe. Stir an equal amount of cool water into flour/starch. Stir very well to remove all the lumps (a shaker is nice for this).

Whisk a small stream of this mixture into boiling liquid until desired consistency is reached. Gravy may thicken further as it boils, so be conservative with your guess. Reduce heat and simmer gravy 10 to 15 minutes. Taste and correct seasonings. Serve piping hot. 1 cup gravy makes about 5 servings.

Creamy Onion White Sauce

{ *I unabashedly use Creamy Onion White Sauce everywhere a cream soup goes. It never lets me down. Every time I spoon the limp cooked onions into the blender, and two minutes later pour out smooth, mellow white sauce, I'm amazed at the metamorphosis. · Part of the beauty of this sauce lies in its versatility: it stars in ham and potatoes, sings in creamy soups, and adds a silky feel to casseroles. I haven't exhausted its talents.* }

1/2 cup water
2 large sweet onions, peeled and sliced
1 garlic clove, peeled and cut in half
2 tablespoons butter
2 tablespoons rice flour
salt and black pepper, to taste

In a large lidded skillet, bring water, onions, and garlic to a boil. Cover tightly and simmer 20 minutes.

Transfer onion mixture to a blender container. Blend two minutes, or until sauce is very smooth. Blend in flour and butter. Add salt and pepper to taste. Blend until thick and creamy. Use sauce immediately. Makes about 2 cups.

The Nice Slice

{Pastry, Pies, and a Tart}

Apple Pie, My Way

"...I didn't buy that tumbledown homestead of my dreams.
BUT I HAVE THE PIE,
THE FAT BEAUTIFUL PIE
cooling in the breeze, and
I think life's pretty good.
It was the pie which made that
house a dream house, after all."

 chapter six

The Nice Slice
{Pastry, Pies and a Tart}

Pies remind me, oddly, of exploring...

My sisters and I were out for a walk when we happened upon The Place. We'd glimpsed it many times from our living room window two miles away. Most locals could, in fact. It was a dense growth of trees, the only thicket for miles on the flat and plowed prairie. Sure, we were aware it was there, but we were never as close as now, standing on the edge, and peering into its dark depths. It was a neglected tangle—no one lived back the old lane that led into the heart of it. Evergreens cast murky shadows over the lane and raggedy trees held skeleton arms over it.

Should we explore? Yes! We tiptoed into the overgrown lane, edging deeper and deeper into that big, dark thicket.

"I'm scared!" I quavered.

"Nonsense!" said a sister, the bravest of us. She propelled me along, past clumps of wild rhubarb and blackberry runners that grabbed our skirts.

What was in the middle of that overgrown homestead? Nothing but a small clearing, shafts of warm sunlight, and a little tumbledown house.

My sisters rambled off, but I stood looking at that house with the caved-in roof, silvery gray siding, and the broken window with a wide windowsill.

Who had lived in this house once upon a time? How had it looked when it was used and loved? I closed my eyes and saw it painted white and clean, the porch straight and new, and on the wide windowsill I glimpsed a pie on a red-checked cloth cooling in the breeze. *I'll buy this place when I'm grown up,* I dreamed. *I'll buy it and prune the apple trees. I'll fix the porch. I'll plant blooming flowers. I'll bring life to this little house again and put a fat, steaming pie back on the windowsill.*

Pies are still the epitome of home comfort to me. They probably are for most of us. Who doesn't remember a grandmother or mother rolling pastry and fluting it with flour on her fingers? So it's interesting to look at pie's history and find that pie, compared to bread and cake, is a newcomer. In fact, dessert pies are reputedly American.

England had her "pyes"—sturdy pastry enveloping savory fillings. A favorite among the gentry was game pie, made with hot water pastry and venison brought from stag hunts in Scotland. Little sweet pastries were called tarts, and may have been brought by the Pilgrims. The few remaining pioneer women who roasted, baked and stewed for the first Harvest Feast are said to have fashioned tarts from corn flour and dried berries.

Pie, in Great-Grandmother's day, was something more refined. By then pies were being called pies, and the criteria had risen steeply. Pie crust went from sturdy hot water pastry and rustic cornmeal crust to something crisp, light and flaky. It became the benchmark of a cook, her skill measured by the quality of her pie crusts. The risks were numerous: flour wasn't consistently fine, lard was preferred cold in an era before refrigeration, and the oven could be cooperative or not. The challenge was great, but no greater, I'm convinced, than the challenge modern-day bakers face when making pie crust gluten-free.

Let me tell you how I formed this conviction. Before I tried gluten fee pie crust, I thought it would be an easy-do. Why would pie dough—the most tender of all baked goods—need gluten? Alas, my first attempts were utter failures. Puzzled, I exiled pies into the remotest corner of my brain and ordered them to stay there. But they kept returning... *Remember Grandma's blackberry pie?* I'd reminisce. *My brother-in-law's sister's apple crumb pie? Mom's coconut cream pie, the elixir of ills?* I tasted the homey goodness on my tongue until, in desperation, I looked gluten free pies in the face and accepted the challenge.

My first step was to analyze the pie crust inch by inch, crumb by crumb. What I found amazed me. Pie crust is a little nod to chemistry. When this simple mixture of flour, cold fat and water hits the hot oven, a transformation happens. The bits of cold fat steam, causing the dough to stretch into pockets and flakes, creating a tender, almost layered texture. Gluten is key, because the dough needs enough stretch—not too much, just a little—to form those tiny pillows. Who would have guessed? Apparently that's why my pie crusts weren't pie crusts—they were crackers.

What would happen if I tried another binder (like xanthan gum) in place of the gluten? I added a little, but the results were capricious. Some pie crusts were nearly successful, others decidedly not. What was I doing wrong?

One day I declared war on the cracker pie crust. "No sleep for me," said I, "until I solve this mystery." I would increase the xanthan gum; I'd decrease it. I'd use combinations of flours; I'd use single flours. I'd use lard, butter, coconut oil, palm oil, but I was going to solve it.

My first try contained a big measure of xanthan gum, and it *looked* good. In the oven, layers of crispy-looking flakes puffed and browned. My hopes puffed, too. I kept peering into the oven, feasting my eyes. *Wheat couldn't do it better*! I rejoiced... then pulled it from the oven and sampled it. Or tried to sample it. As I tugged dismally, I had to admit this new, beautiful pie crust was about as light and tender as an old shoe. Deflated, with heroic goals in the wastebasket, I went to bed, feeling bleak.

I woke up the next morning with newborn zeal. *Why did I give up so soon*? I wondered. I heated the oven and went back to work. But after five experiments, most flaky-looking, all inedible, I came to the realization that the gluten free pie crust was only getting worse. Each emerged from the oven more terrible than the last, and in sudden panic, I backed away from the rolling pin and slumped into a kitchen chair. I thought suddenly of Thomas Edison's famed trash heap, and wondered if mine would compare. It was time to pray about it—and maybe do some more brain work.

Up to that point, I was using a high ratio of xanthan gum to produce those coveted flakes. I was becoming suspicious that it was also responsible for the dreadful rubber-tire consistency. Should I reduce it? I hated to—think of the flakes! How could I tenderize those crusts?

Maybe, I thought, in a moment of inspiration, *maybe it's not the xanthan gum, but how much water is binding with it. Could I keep all the xanthan gum if I coated it with something that repels water... let's see... oil—yes!*

I jumped off the chair and grabbed the rolling pin again. Fine brown rice flour, salt, a touch of sugar for browning, xanthan gum, then just a little oil tossed well among it all. Next the cold butter, working it slightly, then ice-cold water to make a cohesive ball... I rolled it, popped it cold into the hot oven, took it out, broke off a piece, tasted, and cried some happy tears. Who would have guessed that one and one-half tablespoons of oil could change it all? Suddenly weary, I dragged off to bed for a nap, but I was so euphoric I couldn't sleep a wink. All I could think of were those flakes, browned and crispy, that had lain in tender layers on my tongue.

I didn't buy that tumbledown homestead of my dreams. But I have the pie, the fat, beautiful pie cooling in the breeze, and I think life's pretty good. It was the pie which made that house a dream house, after all. ♪

Pie Pointers

·For the very best pie crust, don't skip chilling. In a pinch, you can pop it in the freezer for a few minutes. Wrap gluten-free pie dough well when chilling; it dries quickly.

·Gluten-free pie crusts are notoriously hard to roll, but if properly made and chilled, they're doable. Some cooks roll the dough between wax paper, but I do it on a rice-floured surface, moving the dough as I roll to help prevent sticking. Keep a bench scraper or big spatula on hand to lift the rolled dough into the pan.

·To make flakes happen, pie crust must go from cold to hot very quickly. Chill dough well, and if you're making multiple crusts, keep remainder refrigerated as you work. Preheat oven well, especially when baking a single crust. At 425° (which I recommend), pie crust gets flakiest, but watch carefully. At this temperature, you have only a narrow time margin between doubtfully done and decidedly burnt.

·A single crust can trap steam in a bubble between crust and pie plate as it bakes. Before it forms in this shape, deflate it with a fork. A lot of cooks use pie weights (and you definitely can, too), but it can also prevent the puffy flakes across the bottom of the crust. I prefer saving my hard-won flakes—I'd rather stand around watchfully, fork in hand.

·For double-crust pies with a cooked filling, I like to put the filling in hot. Hot filling makes venting and fluting more difficult (try making vents in the top crust before lifting it on the pie), but pies with hot filling bake quicker, crisper, and flakier.

·You'll notice I use "perma-flo" to thicken pie fillings. Perma-flo is corn-derived, and makes crystal-clear fillings. Cornstarch is cloudy by comparison, but works as well. Perma-flo can be hard to find; I get it at bulk food stores. ♪

Classic Butter Pie Crust

{ *Welcome back, pies! With this recipe, I rediscovered old pie friends—*
apple crumb, rhubarb cream, cherry lattice... · This recipe is a delicate
balance of ingredients, and for best results, measure carefully and
don't substitute anything unless you're prepared for a month of
reinventing. I think the grind of the flour is the important factor
here—use the finest rice flour you can find. Test by rubbing a pinch
of it between your fingers—it should be only a little more grainy, if at
all, than white all-purpose wheat flour. · On warm days, remove butter
from the refrigerator just before mixing the dry ingredients. }

For 9" 1-crust pie:

1 cup brown rice flour
1/2 teaspoon xanthan gum
1 teaspoon evaporated cane juice
1/3 teaspoon salt
1 1/2 tablespoon light olive or vegetable oil
1/3 cup butter, very slightly softened, cut in 1/4" cubes
4 to 6 tablespoons ice water
additional rice flour for rolling

For 9" double-crust pie:

2 cups brown rice flour
1 teaspoon xanthan gum
2 teaspoons evaporated cane juice
2/3 teaspoon salt
3 tablespoons light olive or vegetable oil
2/3 cup butter, very slightly softened, cut in 1/4" cubes
8 to 12 tablespoons ice water
additional rice flour for rolling

Continued

In a medium mixing bowl, stir together flour, xanthan gum, evaporated cane juice and salt.

Add oil and mix very well, or until mixture resembles fine sand.

Add butter, working slightly with fingers, until only pea-size lumps remain.

Toss mixture with 4 (8) tablespoons ice water. Add more as needed just until dough comes together into a moist, but not sticky ball. Do not overmix. Divide dough into 1 (2) ball(s), flatten each into a disk shape, wrap well and refrigerate 30 minutes or up to several hours.

Remove plastic wrap and place dough on a rice-floured surface. Roll a few strokes with a rolling pin, then give dough a half-turn, adding more flour as needed to prevent sticking. Repeat until circle of dough measures 11" in diameter.

With bench scraper or pancake turner, roll dough loosely over rolling pin and lift over pie plate. Ease dough into pie pan generously, patching any rips.

For double-crust pie, trim dough even with edge of pie plate. Proceed with desired recipe to fill, roll top crust, flute and bake.

For single-crust pie, trim dough hanging over edge of pie pan to 1/2" all around. Fold overhang under itself to make crust even with the edge. Flute edge as desired.

For unbaked single-crust pie shell, proceed at this point with recipe.

For a baked single crust, prick sides and bottom of crust with a fork. Bake at 425° for about 14 minutes, watching carefully. When done, crust should be evenly browned, crispy and slightly puffed. Remove to a wire rack to cool completely. Store airtight if not using immediately.

Apple Pie, My Way

{ *Made with Granny Smiths or Jonathans, Golden Delicious or an heirloom
from a backyard orchard, apple pie is the queen pie. There's something
homey in the whole procedure: from picking rosy-cheeked apples to
watching the steam curl from the dappled, hills-and-valleys crust. · The tiny
bit of salt in the filling is key—don't omit it. · You can make a good apple pie
with most firm-fleshed apples, tart or sweet, with a little tweaking of lemon
and sweetener. Taste a slice. For tart apples, reduce or omit lemon juice,
and increase sweetener. For sweet apples, increase the lemon and decrease
sweetener. Making apple pies is as personal as a signature; no two cooks
make them exactly the same.* }

Classic Butter Pie dough for double-crust pie
5 cups peeled and thinly sliced apples
1/4 to 1/2 cup sweetener of choice
up to 2 tablespoons fresh lemon juice, optional
1 teaspoon ground cinnamon
2 tablespoons cornstarch
pinch of salt
evaporated cane juice, for sprinkling

Preheat oven to 350°. Roll and fit bottom crust into pie pan.

In a large bowl, toss apples with sweetener, lemon juice if using, cinnamon,
cornstarch, and salt. Pile apples into prepared pie crust.

Roll second crust to fit, moisten edges of bottom crust with wet pastry brush,
and position top crust. Cut edge with 1/2" overhang all around. Turn edge
under itself even with edge of pan. Flute edge as desired. Make vents in top
crust with a sharp knife. Sprinkle with evaporated cane juice.

Bake pie 45 to 55 minutes or until crust is nicely browned top and bottom and apples
test very tender when pierced with a fork. Serve warm or cold. Makes 8 servings.

Apple Crumb Pie

{ If I could compel myself to choose a favorite dessert (I can't), this might be the one. There's something about buttery crumbs against tart apple that is unmatched. · You can use less sweetener than in double-crusted apple pie because of the sweetened crumbs. And you don't need the pinch of salt, because of the salted butter in the topping. I use evaporated cane juice in the topping because it browns nicely and hints of butterscotch. · How many people does a gigantic 24-cups-of-apples Apple Crumb Pie serve? Exactly 50, we discovered one September evening beside a bonfire. It was my sister's birthday, and she thinks this might be her favorite dessert, too. The memory of that enormous pie glowing by lantern light is still a pleasure. }

Classic Butter Pie dough for single-crust pie
5 cups peeled and thinly sliced apples
1/4 cup sweetener of choice, or more if desired
up to 2 tablespoons fresh lemon juice
1 teaspoon ground cinnamon
2 tablespoons cornstarch
3/4 cup brown rice flour
1/4 cup evaporated cane juice
1/2 teaspoon xanthan gum
1/3 cup softened butter

Preheat oven to 350°. Roll and fit crust into pie pan, fluting edges.

In a large bowl, toss apples with sweetener and lemon juice to taste, ground cinnamon, and cornstarch. Pile apple mixture into prepared pastry.

In a medium bowl, stir together brown rice flour, evaporated cane juice, and xanthan gum. Cut in butter until mixture is uniformly crumbly. Scatter evenly over apples.

Bake pie until crumbs have browned evenly to dark golden color and apples test very tender when pierced with a knife, 45 to 55 minutes. Serve lukewarm or cooled. Makes 8 servings.

Cherry Lattice Pie

{ If you've ever seen red cherries against pale, creamy pie crust, you'll understand how cherry lattice pie came to be. Instead of hiding all those lovely cherries inside, a crisscross lattice lets them peep through. · This recipe uses small, tart pie cherries. Large, dark sweet cherries will produce a completely different pie. }

Classic Butter Pie dough for double-crust pie
3 cups fresh or frozen pitted pie cherries
3/4 cup water, divided
1/4 cup perma-flo or cornstarch
3/4 to 1 cup sweetener of choice
6 drops natural almond extract
evaporated cane juice, for sprinkling

Preheat oven to 400°. Roll and fit bottom crust into pie pan.

Place cherries and 1/2 cup water in medium saucepan. Cover and bring to a boil.

Shake or stir together remaining 1/4 cup water and perma-flo or cornstarch until smooth. Stir briskly into boiling cherries in a thin stream. Cook until thickened and bubbly.

Remove from heat. Add sweetener and almond extract. Pour into prepared pie shell.

Roll second portion of dough on rice-floured surface to a 10" round. Cut dough with pastry cutter or sharp knife into 3/4" wide strips. Lay strips across pie 1" apart. Repeat with strips crisscrossed in the opposite direction. Don't attempt to weave strips. Sprinkle well with evaporated cane juice.

Bake pie 15 minutes. Reduce heat to 350° and bake another 25 to 30 minutes, or until filling is bubbly and crust is well-browned. Serve warm or cold. Makes 8 servings.

Wild Blackberry Pie

Grandpa and Grandma Kennell, born and nourished on corn-and-grain farms four miles apart, were very much alike in food tastes, but here is one pie where they differed. "Grandpa," Grandma told me (almost apologetically), "thinks black raspberry pie is best, but I like blackberry." Wild blackberries, picked from savage-thorned bushes, do make delicious pies. The filling is a deep, royal purple.

Classic Butter Pie dough for double-crust pie
3 cups wild blackberries, fresh or frozen
3/4 cup water, divided
1/4 cup perma-flo or cornstarch
1 tablespoon fresh lemon juice
1/2 cup sweetener of choice, or as desired
evaporated cane juice, for sprinkling

Preheat oven to 400°. Roll and fit bottom crust into pie pan.

Place blackberries and 1/2 cup of the water in a medium saucepan. Cover and bring to a boil over medium-high heat.

Shake or stir together remaining 1/4 cup water and perma-flo or cornstarch until smooth. Add to boiling berries in a thin stream, stirring briskly. Cook until thickened and bubbly. Add sweetener and lemon juice. Pour into pastry-lined pie pan.

Roll top crust to 10" circle. Moisten edges of bottom crust with wet pastry brush. Position top crust, trim edges to 1/2" from pan all around, and turn edges under even with edge of pan. Flute as desired. Vent top crust with a sharp knife. Sprinkle generously with evaporated cane juice.

Bake pie 15 minutes, reduce temperature to 350°, and finish baking, 25 to 35 more minutes, or until filling is bubbly and crust is nicely browned. Serve warm or cold. Makes 8 servings.

Blueberry Citrus Pie

{ Mild blueberries are sparked with bright orange in this recipe. }

Classic Butter Pie dough for one double-crust pie
3 cups blueberries, fresh or frozen (do not thaw)
3 tablespoons cornstarch
1/2 cup sweetener of choice
1/4 cup fresh orange juice
1/2 teaspoon orange peel
evaporated cane juice, for sprinkling

Preheat oven to 400°. Roll and fit bottom crust into 9" pie pan.

In a large bowl, toss together blueberries, cornstarch and sweetener. Add orange juice and peel and mix well. Pile berries into prepared pastry.

Roll top crust. Moisten edges of bottom crust with pastry brush dipped in water. Position top crust and trim to 1/2" all around. Fold edges under itself even with edge of plate. Flute, cut vents in top crust, and sprinkle with evaporated cane juice.

Bake pie 15 minutes. Reduce heat to 350° and bake additional 35 to 40 minutes until juices are very bubbly and thickened in center of pie, and crust is nicely browned. Serve warm or cooled. Makes 8 servings.

Raspberry-Rhubarb Pie

*{ Here's an example of two fruits working for one pie in happy partnership.
It's a spring/summer combination, but if you don't have raspberries
and rhubarb ready at the same time, frozen fruits work nicely. }*

Classic Butter Pie dough for one double-crust pie
1 1/2 cups sliced rhubarb, fresh or frozen
1 1/2 cups red raspberries, fresh or frozen
2/3 cup sweetener of choice
3 tablespoons cornstarch
evaporated cane juice, for sprinkling

Preheat oven to 400°. Roll and fit bottom crust into pie pan.

In a large bowl, toss together fresh or frozen rhubarb and raspberries,
sweetener and cornstarch. Pile into bottom crust.

Roll top crust. Moisten edges of bottom crust with a wet pastry brush.
Position top crust, trim edges 1/2" all around, and turn edges under itself
even with pie plate. Flute as desired. Cut vents in top crust with a sharp
knife. Sprinkle generously with evaporated cane juice.

Bake pie 15 minutes. Reduce heat to 350° and bake additional 30 to 40
minutes, or until filling is bubbly in center and crust is well-browned. Do not
under bake. Serve warm or cold. Yields 8 servings.

Grandma's Peach Cream Pie

{ *It's nearing September and we're thinking about them lately. Our last hoarded jars are empty, our last box in the freezer has disappeared in smoothies. Hungrily, we make our order—seven bushels this year, instead of six. And, anticipation mounting, we dispatch the van to Michigan, where orchards flourish around the Great Lakes. It's a long, long time until the van comes back, and then we hurry to open the doors and the ambrosial smell of crates and crates of them comes to meet us in a rush. We choose the biggest, the cheekiest, the pinky-orangest, and we open our mouths wide and they enter, in big, chin-sopping mouthfuls. Ah, peaches! · Grandpa and Grandma Kennell used to bring back peaches for neighbors all around, and this is Grandma's recipe, now gluten-free. · This pie improves on chilling, and is even better the second day.* }

Classic Butter Pie dough for single-crust pie
4 cups peeled and thinly sliced fresh peaches
1 cup cream, milk or milk substitute
3 tablespoons cornstarch
1/2 cup sweetener of choice
1/4 teaspoon salt
1/2 teaspoon ground cinnamon

Preheat oven to 325°. Roll and fit pie dough into 9" pie pan.

Place sliced peaches into pie shell. In a small bowl, whisk together the cream or substitute, cornstarch, sweetener, salt, and cinnamon. Pour over peaches in crust.

Bake pie 45 to 50 minutes or until center is only slightly jiggly, and peaches test done when pricked with fork. Allow pie to cool before serving. Serve room temperature or chilled. Makes 6 to 8 servings.

Woodford County Rhubarb Cream Pie

{ Here's a thoroughly Midwestern pie. Old-time cooks make it from the time the first "pie plant" stalks shoot out of the warming soil until hot August ruins the patch. Why this open-faced, cream version instead of the two-crusted pie found in most parts of the country? All I know is it's wonderfully good—even with milk substitute instead of cream. }

1 single-crust Classic Butter Pie Crust, unbaked
1 cup cream, milk or milk substitute
1/4 cup cornstarch
2/3 cup sweetener of choice
dash salt
2 1/2 cups finely chopped rhubarb

Preheat oven to 350°.

In a small bowl, whisk together cream, milk or substitute, cornstarch, sweetener and salt. Scatter rhubarb into bottom of pie shell. Pour liquid mixture over rhubarb.

Bake pie 35 to 45 minutes or until center is set and crust nicely browned. Cool before serving. Makes 8 servings.

Canadian Raspberry Cream Pie

{ Midwestern cooks are professionals with rhubarb and peach cream pies, but I was first served the raspberry version in Ontario. It's a homey-looking pie with a dressed-up flavor. }

1 single-crust Classic Butter Pie Crust, unbaked
1 1/2 cups red raspberries, fresh or frozen
1/2 cup sweetener of choice
4 tablespoons cornstarch
1 1/4 cups cream, milk, or milk substitute
pinch of salt

Preheat oven to 375°.

Scatter berries into pie shell.

In a medium mixing bowl, combine sweetener, cornstarch, cream or substitute, and salt. Whisk well. Pour over raspberries.

Bake pie 30 to 40 minutes or until crust is browned and filling is set. Cool completely before serving. Makes 8 servings.

Unbaked Fresh Blueberry Pie

{ *I like the fresh taste of this summer pie. You can make it with frozen berries, too, which makes it quick to whip up on the spur of the moment. · The pinch of salt and the tablespoon of butter are key for flavor.* }

1 baked single-crust Classic Butter Pie Crust
4 cups fresh blueberries
1/2 cup sweetener of choice
3 tablespoons cornstarch
pinch salt
1/4 cup water
1 tablespoon fresh lemon juice
1 tablespoon butter
whipped cream to serve, optional

In a large saucepan, stir together sweetener, cornstarch, and salt very well. Add water, stirring until smooth. Add half of berries, and cook over medium heat, stirring and mashing berries constantly, until mixture is thickened and bubbly. Remove from heat.

Add lemon juice and butter to cooked berries. Allow to cool slightly, then add remaining berries. Spoon into baked pie shell. Chill at least two hours. Serve with whipped cream, if desired.

Glazed Strawberry Pan Pie

{ *What is spring without strawberry pie? Not so springy, I think. · Once the crust is baked and cooled, you can pull this dessert together quickly. Run out to the strawberry patch, and have this pie on the table within an hour. Or even faster. When I first made this pie, I had folks "starved" for strawberry pie waiting around with forks. With no time to lose, I popped the assembled pie into the freezer for a very fast chill. It was ready in about 10 minutes, just in time to "save my skin".* }

**1 recipe Shortbread Crust for Desserts (see index), baked in
9"x13" baking pan and cooled
2 cups water, divided
1 cup 100% white grape-raspberry juice concentrate, undiluted
1/4 cup perma-flo or cornstarch
1/2 to 2/3 cup sweetener of choice, or stevia to taste
2 tablespoons unflavored gelatin
fresh strawberries, about 7 cups, sliced
whipped cream or non-dairy whipped topping, if desired**

In a small bowl, sprinkle gelatin over 1/2 cup of the water. Allow to rest 5 minutes.

Stir together remaining 11/2 cups water, juice concentrate, perma-flo or cornstarch and sweetener in a saucepan. Bring to a boil, whisking constantly, until thickened. Remove from heat and add the softened gelatin mixture. Whisk to dissolve gelatin. Allow mixture to cool to lukewarm (an ice-water bath speeds this).

Heap strawberries in baked pie shell, and pour glaze over berries to cover completely. Refrigerate to set. Top with a layer of whipped cream, or a dollop on each slice, if desired. Cut in squares to serve. Makes 15 servings.

The Newest Pecan Pie

{ *I thought egg-free pecan pie impossible until I discovered this recipe. Despite untraditional preparation, it's surprisingly "pecan pie-ish". You can make one large pan pie instead of two 9" pies, using a 9"x13" baked and cooled Shortbread Crust for Desserts (see index).* }

2 baked single-crust Classic Butter Pie Crusts
1 pound whole pitted dates
4 cups water, divided
3 tablespoons cornstarch
3 tablespoons unflavored gelatin
2 tablespoons butter
6 tablespoons pure maple syrup
1 tablespoon baking molasses
1/4 teaspoon salt
1 tablespoon vanilla extract
2 cups chopped pecans

Snip dates with scissors into a small saucepan. Add 2 cups of the water and bring to a boil. Cover, lower heat, and simmer 5 minutes.

In a small bowl, stir together the cornstarch and 1 cup of the water. Add to the boiling date mixture. Cook until thick and clear.

Place remaining 1 cup water and gelatin in blender. Allow to rest 5 minutes. Add hot date mixture and blend well. Add butter, maple syrup, molasses, salt, and vanilla. Pour into a medium bowl, cover and chill until slightly set.

Meanwhile, toast pecans by scattering in a rimmed baking sheet and baking at 350° for about 10 minutes, shaking pan occasionally, and watching closely to prevent burning.

To assemble pies: Pour partially set date mixture into baked pie crusts. Scatter pecans on top, pressing slightly into mixture. Chill well and serve. Makes 16 servings.

Refrigerator Pumpkin–"Sour Cream" Pie

{ *Pumpkin pie might be as old as America, but this one's a newborn. · Pumpkin pie is a custard pie, and eggs are basic in custard pies. I've missed pumpkin pies on the occasions when they should be there... when the maples and sumac hang out blazing banners... when you bring in the pumpkin harvest—the big, the medium-sized, and the little orange ones called—yes, pie pumpkins. · I hesitated a long time to remove pumpkin pies from the custard category, but one day I leaped the chasm. Here's the result: an unbaked pie set with gelatin, creamy with "Sour Supreme". · I've never tried real sour cream in this recipe, but I suspect it would perform nicely. · Anything on top is a little superfluous. The Kennells like whipped cream with pumpkin pie, though, and just a dollop on each slice brings this fifth-cousin-once-removed closer into the family.* }

2 baked, single-crust Classic Butter Pie Crusts
4 cups cooked, pureed pumpkin
1 cup sweetener of choice
1 1/2 cups milk, soy milk or almond milk
1 teaspoon salt
2 1/2 teaspoons ground cinnamon
2 tablespoons cornstarch
2 tablespoons unflavored gelatin
1/3 cup cold water
1 cup Sour Supreme
whipped cream or non-dairy whipped topping to garnish, if desired

In a small bowl, stir together gelatin and water. Allow to soak 5 minutes.

In a large saucepan, whisk together pumpkin, sweetener, milk or substitute, salt, cinnamon and cornstarch. Cook, whisking constantly, until mixture is

Continued

hot and thickened. Remove from heat. Add gelatin mixture, stirring well to dissolve. Cool.

Fold Sour Supreme into cooled pumpkin mixture. Transfer to baked crusts and refrigerate until set, at least 2 hours. Garnish with dollops of cream or whipped topping on each slice if desired. Makes 12 to 16 servings.

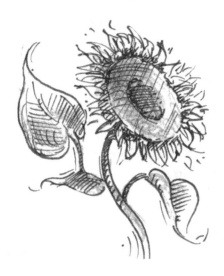

French Apple Tart

{ *Rustic and free-form, this tart somehow contrives to be elegant. · It was invented for a brother-in-law's milestone birthday. Serve it in wedges slightly warm.* }

brown rice flour, for dusting pan
Classic Butter Pie Crust dough for double-crust pie, well chilled
5 cups sliced apples
1/2 to 2/3 cup sweetener of choice
1/2 teaspoon cinnamon
1/4 teaspoon vanilla extract
evaporated cane juice, for sprinkling

Preheat oven to 400°. Grease one 12" round pizza pan and dust with brown rice flour.

Place chilled pie dough directly on prepared pan. Sprinkle dough well with rice flour, and roll with rolling pin to 1/4" thickness, and pie dough extends just over edge of pan.

In a large bowl, stir together apples, sweetener, cinnamon and vanilla. Toss well. Pile in the center of the pie dough, allowing 3" margin all around. Using a pancake turner, carefully lift edges all around to overlap apple filling by 2 or 3 inches, leaving a large area of exposed apples in center. Patch any rips in pie dough carefully.

Sprinkle crust edges with evaporated cane juice. Bake 30 minutes, reduce temperature to 350°, and finish baking for approximately another 30 minutes, or until crust is a deep golden and apples are just tender. Serve warm. Makes 10 servings.

New, True Friends

{Cookies, Shortbread, Brownies, Bars, & Biscotti}

Maple-Pecan Drop Cookies, Black-Bottom Banana Bars, Buttery Almond-Apricot Cookies, Chocolate Shortbread, Orange-Sour Cream Biscotti, Sour Cream Spritz Cookies.

 I want Benjie to come and spend the winter with me," wrote Grandmother. "I need a man-body to look after me and keep me company."

Benjie felt there was no one in all of North Carolina quite as important as Benjamin Bartholomew Barnett. And when he went to bed that night, he lay awake as long as five minutes, and as he fell asleep, it seemed to him he could...

taste the rich, waxy molasses cookies

from Grandmother's cookie jar.

–Mabel Leigh Hunt

 chapter seven

New, True Friends
{Cookies, Shortbread, Brownies, Bars and Biscotti}

Peek into a schoolboy's pocket. Search a picnic basket rattling toward the park. Peer into the depths of a big jar in the corner of Grandma's cupboard. What will you find?

Cookies, of course. Cookies have to be America's favorite dessert. We like them so well they're not just dessert—they're anytime snacks. We wrap them up and tuck them in our purses, our glove compartments, our lunch boxes. They go with us to work, to play, to school.

Just like people, cookies are a hodgepodge bunch. They are plump and jolly, dark and spicy, light and sparkly. And, like people, cookies are greatest all mixed together. After all, to some folks, a holiday family gathering isn't a family gathering unless there's a tray of assorted cookies there, too.

A cookie knows no nationality. It is found in most crannies of the earth, under the aliases of cookey, cooky, koekje, sweet cake, biscuit, etc., but a cookie, just the same. Alegria, a Mexican amaranth cookie, literally means "joy"; unexpected, but fitting. A cookie is a happy, lunch-in-the-pocket, treat-in-the-middle-of-a-big-day, here's-a-friend-in-a-hard-world treat. Mankind is on such intimate terms with cookies, in fact, that he gives them a whole lexicon of pet names. Here's a sample from three or four cookbooks: Sandies, Crickets, Jumbles, Mumbles, Hermits, Monsters, Pinwheels, Porcupines, Lizzies, Pick-Ups, Take-Alongs, Rise and Shiners, Mud Rockets, Bachelor Buttons, Jim Dandies, Joe Froggers, and Rickety Uncles.

Cookies remind us of people, places, and things. Every time I make Aunt Maggie's gingersnaps, I think of her in a gray-sided house on Chesapeake Bay, stirring together these chewy cookies with no measuring cup in sight.

Mom's refrigerator cookies make me think of a one-room school and a pink lunch box that often contained two of these thick, wheaty cookies. I loved them, even if they made me late to the playground.

Chocolate chip cookies remind me how, as a teenager, I stretched Grandma Kennell's patience to the utmost as she taught me to make them. Her criteria for the perfect chocolate chip cookie was exacting. I still remember the day her wrinkled fingers picked up a test cookie, broke it in half, and said, "It stands up nice, yet it's still chewy. See—it's about right." I had joined a new "club", and I wore the title like a badge: *Cookie Baker.*

Grandma herself was a veteran of the ranks. Almost until the day she went home to be with the Lord, she kept an ice-cream bucket of cookies in the cellar. We were aware it was there, and the chore-boy cousins, the cleaning-girl cousins, and the just-visiting cousins would make cellar-pilgrimages and return with filled tummies, mouths, and sometimes pockets.

Since Americans seem to consider cookies a major food group, celiacs can feel downright friendless without them. If we do manage to banish the lonesomeness, it returns in big waves when we watch others scarf them down with enjoyment—little boys munching happily from lunch boxes, sisters blissfully sampling Christmas trays.

The only recourse is to find a new circle of cookie friends. But cookies, some of the easiest things to make with gluten, are some of the hardest to make without, third only to bread and pie crusts. When creating gluten-free cakes, results are fairly predictable with xanthan gum and attention to liquid. Cookies are members of another camp.

Along with gluten, cookies depend heavily on sugar and eggs, and removing or reducing all three creates (you guessed it) failure. Finding solutions is like searching for the password to a new clique. It took years and the coming of xanthan gum to gather this gluten-free, egg-free, low-sugar group. But that's okay; a warm Buttery Almond-Apricot Cookie is compensation, every time. I should have named them My-New-Best-Friend Almond-Apricot Cookies. ♪

Cookie Codes

·Xanthan gum amounts are key. Xanthan gum binds with liquids—and liquid in cookies varies hugely. For instance, most shortbread has no added liquid, and xanthan gum must bond with the small amount of moisture in butter, while cake-like cookies have a very moist batter, often with up to 1 cup added liquid. That's why the ratio of xanthan gum to brown rice flour in Coconut Shortbread is 1¼ teaspoons per cup; Date-Pinwheels only ¼ teaspoon.

·Butter is *big*. It's difficult to make a tasty cookie without it. I've clung to butter tenaciously for cookies, perhaps at my expense. For those who *really* can't do butter, EarthBalance is the best substitute I've found. It should perform well in most recipes.

·Coarsely ground brown rice flour can't hide in high-butter, low-moisture cookies. Use the finest flour possible.

·More than bread or cake, gluten-free cookies are keepers. They freeze well, and some (biscotti, shortbread, and brownies) stay fresh surprisingly long at room temperature, airtight.

·For the chronically busy: try refrigerator cookies (Icebox Butter Cookies, Date Pinwheel Cookies). They fit into small slots of time. If you keep them in the refrigerator, you can slice and bake a pan of them in minutes. Make them your best trick on busy school or work mornings. ♪

Chocolate Chip-Nut Cookies

{ Sweet butter cookies, with chunks of chocolate and walnuts. Really, how real. }

2 1/2 cups brown rice flour
2 tablespoons cornstarch or tapioca starch
1/2 teaspoon salt
1 teaspoon baking soda
3/4 teaspoon xanthan gum
1 cup butter, softened
1 cup evaporated cane juice
2 teaspoons vanilla extract
2/3 cup milk or milk substitute, or more if needed
1 cup chopped walnuts or pecans
1 1/2 cups chocolate chips

Preheat oven to 350°.

Stir together brown rice flour, cornstarch or tapioca starch, salt, baking soda, and xanthan gum.

In mixer bowl, cream butter and evaporated cane juice until light. Add flour mixture alternately with milk or substitute. Add vanilla. Dough should be stiff, but still creamy. If needed, add more milk or substitute, a little at a time, until a creamy consistency is reached. Stir in nuts and chocolate chips.

Drop by teaspoon onto baking sheets. Bake 10 to 15 minutes or until browned around the edges. Allow to rest on cookie sheets for several minutes or until set. Remove to racks to cool completely.

Maple-Pecan Drop Cookies

{ Maple and pecan are complementary flavors, and here they unite in rich, buttery morsels. · Once cooled, these cookies are sturdy and packable. }

1/3 cup maple syrup
1/2 cup evaporated cane juice
1/2 cup butter, softened
1/3 cup light olive or vegetable oil
2 teaspoons vanilla extract
1 2/3 cups brown rice flour
1/3 cup tapioca starch
1/2 teaspoon salt
1 1/2 teaspoons xanthan gum
1 cup chopped pecans

Preheat oven to 350°.

Cream together maple syrup, evaporated cane juice, butter, oil, and vanilla until light and fluffy.

In a medium mixing bowl, stir together brown rice flour, tapioca starch, salt, and xanthan gum. Add to creamed mixture, stirring just to combine. Stir in pecans.

Drop cookies by heaping teaspoons on baking sheets. Bake 10 to 12 minutes or until edges start to brown. Cool several minutes before removing to wire racks to cool. Store airtight.

Date Pinwheel Cookies

{ *I never knew Great-Grandma Lena, but her industry and get-up-and-go are legendary. I've read her 1950 diary ("Monday: Made 8 star quilt blocks... Ironed all but rags and overalls. Tuesday: Made 7 star quilt blocks... Done rest of ironing."), I've tried her Sunday go-to-meetin' bonnet (it fit perfectly), and now I make her Date Pinwheels, gluten-free. Grandma Lena was famous for them, and I think you'll like these pretty cookies too.* }

Cookies:
- **1 cup butter, softened**
- **1 cup evaporated cane juice**
- **2 teaspoons vanilla extract**
- **3 1/2 cups brown rice flour**
- **1 teaspoon salt**
- **1 teaspoon baking soda**
- **1 teaspoon xanthan gum**
- **1 cup water**

Filling:
- **16 ounces whole pitted dates**
- **water, as needed**

additional brown rice flour, for rolling

Cream butter and evaporated cane juice until light and fluffy. Add vanilla extract.

In a large bowl, combine brown rice flour, salt, baking soda, and xanthan gum. Add to creamed mixture alternately with water. Beat well. Wrap dough in plastic wrap, shape into 2 disks, and chill 1 to 2 hours.

Continued

For filling, cut dates into small pieces with a scissors. Place in a saucepan, add water to almost cover dates, and bring to a boil over high heat. Reduce heat, cover, and simmer until dates are tender and pureed, about 10 minutes. Cool.

On a sheet of lightly rice-floured waxed paper, roll half of dough to make a 7"x10" rectangle. Spread half the date mixture on dough to within 1" of edges. With the help of the waxed paper and starting at a long edge, roll dough into a log shape, peeling off waxed paper as you roll. Seal long ends well. Wrap in the waxed paper, return to refrigerator and chill 1 hour, or up to several days. Repeat with remaining dough and date filling.

Preheat oven to 350°. Remove waxed paper from rolls, slice into 1/4" slices with sharp knife, lay slices on baking sheets and bake 10 to 15 minutes or until golden brown. Allow cookies to rest several minutes on cookie sheets before removing to wire rack to cool completely. Store airtight. Makes about 4 dozen cookies.

Buttery Almond-Apricot Cookies

{ Tart apricots are a pleasant foil in this butter-rich cookie. They're dense, chewy, and chunky. They're celebration cookies, happily at home on any cookie tray (gluten-free or otherwise). }

1 cup butter, softened
1 cup evaporated cane juice
2 teaspoons vanilla extract
1/4 cup water
1 3/4 cups brown rice flour
1/2 teaspoon salt
1 teaspoon xanthan gum
1 teaspoon baking soda
3 cups sliced almonds
1 cup snipped dried apricots

Preheat oven to 375°.

Cream butter and evaporated cane juice until very fluffy. Add water, beating until creamy. Add vanilla.

In a medium mixing bowl, stir together brown rice flour, salt, xanthan gum, and baking soda. Stir into creamed mixture, beating well. Stir in almonds and apricots until well-blended.

Drop dough by heaping teaspoon onto baking sheets. Bake 11 to 12 minutes, or until cookies are golden brown and puffed. Allow to set several minutes on baking sheets before removing to wire racks to cool. Store airtight.

Mocha Fudge Cookies

{ *Before she was a mother of four, my cousin baked boxes of beautiful cookies for Christmas. Frosted mocha-walnut cookies were her masterpieces. We were happy recipients in the gluten days, and missing them, I tampered with her recipe to come up with this one. They're not iced like the original, but still rich and sweet.* }

1/2 cup butter, softened
3/4 cup evaporated cane juice
1 teaspoon vanilla extract
1 1/2 cups brown rice flour
6 tablespoons unsweetened baking cocoa
1 teaspoon baking powder
1/2 teaspoon baking soda
1/2 teaspoon salt
1 teaspoon xanthan gum
1 tablespoon instant coffee granules
3/4 cup milk or milk substitute, or more as needed
1 teaspoon cider vinegar
1 cup chocolate or carob chips, sweetened or unsweetened
1/2 cup chopped walnuts

Preheat oven to 350°.

Cream butter and evaporated cane juice until light and fluffy. Add vanilla.

In a medium bowl, stir together brown rice flour, cocoa, baking powder, baking soda, salt, xanthan gum, and instant coffee granules. Add to creamed mixture alternately with milk or substitute and vinegar. Check consistency— dough should be soft, just holding its shape. Add more liquid if needed. Stir in chips and walnuts.

Drop by teaspoons onto baking sheets. Bake 15 minutes, or until puffed and firm. Remove cookies to wire racks to cool. Store airtight.

Gingerbread Men

Make these to please the little boys in your life! Ice them or sprinkle them, give them raisin buttons or chocolate chip eyes. Make them tall and skinny or chubby and jolly, thick and chewy or thin and crisp, and watch those laddies (the human ones) grin.

3 cups brown rice flour
1/4 cup sweetener of choice, optional
3/4 teaspoon baking soda
1/2 teaspoon salt
1 teaspoon xanthan gum
1 tablespoon ground cinnamon
2 teaspoons ground ginger
1/2 teaspoon ground cloves
3/4 cup butter, slightly softened
3/4 cup baking molasses
2 tablespoons water, or more as needed

In a large bowl, stir together brown rice flour, sweetener, baking soda, salt, xanthan gum, cinnamon, ginger, and cloves.

Cut butter into dry ingredients until mixture resembles sand with a few pea-sized lumps. Add molasses and water, and stir to form a soft but not too sticky dough. Add more water if needed to obtain this consistency. Wrap dough and chill 1 to 2 hours.

Preheat oven to 350°. Roll chilled dough between sheets of wax paper to 1/8" to 1/4" thick. Remove top sheet of waxed paper, cut dough with gingerbread man cutter or other desired cutter, remove to baking sheets and bake 8 to 11 minutes. Cool on wire racks.

Spicy Date Roll-Outs

{ *These are winter-evening-around-the-fire cookies, fragrant with warming spices. The sprinkling of evaporated cane juice melts in the oven to form a shiny, crackly crust.* }

1/2 cup butter, softened
1/2 cup evaporated cane juice
1/4 cup water
1 1/2 cup brown rice flour
1/2 teaspoon baking soda
1/2 teaspoon xanthan gum
1/4 teaspoon salt
1 teaspoon ground cinnamon
1/2 teaspoon ground cloves
3/4 cup finely chopped whole pitted dates
3/4 cup raisins
1/2 cup chopped walnuts
additional water, for brushing
additional evaporated cane juice, for sprinkling

Cream butter and evaporated cane juice until fluffy. Add water and beat until creamy.

In a medium mixing bowl, combine brown rice flour, baking soda, xanthan gum, salt, cinnamon, and cloves. Add to creamed mixture. Fold in dates, raisins, and nuts. Wrap dough and chill several hours.

Preheat oven to 350°. On a rice-floured surface, roll dough to 1/4" thickness. Cut with 21/2" or 3" round cookie cutter. Place rounds on greased baking sheets. Brush with water and sprinkle with evaporated cane juice. Bake cookies 10 to 12 minutes or until edges are set but centers soft and puffy. Allow cookies to cool several minutes on baking sheets before removing to wire racks to cool completely. Store airtight. Yields 2 1/2 dozen 2 1/2" cookies.

Sour Cream Spritz Cookies

{ The light touch of sour cream or Sour Supreme plays beautifully against the buttery flavor of these spritz cookies. · Dough consistency is very important in this recipe. The dough should be stiff enough to give a slight resistance when piped. Test a few cookies first. If the dough is too stiff it will prevent crisp exteriors and chewy interiors. If the dough is too soft, the cookies will flatten, with a crisp consistency all the way through. Remedy with a little more flour, or a bit more water, as needed. · I like the pastry bag method for piping the cookies. It is quick and easy to control. Along with the classic stars, you can pipe any shape you please. }

> **1 cup butter, softened**
> **3/4 cup evaporated cane juice**
> **2 tablespoons sour cream or Sour Supreme**
> **3 tablespoons water**
> **1 teaspoon vanilla extract**
> **1 3/4 cup brown rice flour**
> **3/4 teaspoon xanthan gum**
> **1/4 teaspoon salt**

Preheat oven to 375°.

Cream butter and evaporated cane juice 4 minutes or until very light and fluffy. Scrape sides of bowl with spatula and beat again. Beat in sour cream or Sour Supreme, water and vanilla. Add brown rice flour, xanthan gum, and salt.

Place cookie dough in cookie press or a large pastry bag with a very large open-ended star tip. Press or pipe cookies into 11/2" stars on ungreased baking sheets.

Bake cookies 11 to 15 minutes, or until edges are golden brown. Allow cookies to cool a few minutes on sheets before removing to wire racks to cool completely.

George Washington Hats

{ Lemony dough enfolds a thick apricot filling in these celebration cookies. Make a batch with your nieces and give them a history lesson at the same time! The "tricorn" shape adds visual interest to cookie trays. }

Cookies:
2/3 cup butter
1 cup evaporated cane juice
1/4 cup water
1/4 cup fresh lemon juice
3 cups brown rice flour
2 teaspoons lemon peel
2 teaspoons baking powder
1 teaspoon salt
1/2 teaspoon xanthan gum

Apricot Filling:
16 ounces dried apricots
2 cups water

In a large saucepan, melt butter. Add evaporated cane juice, water, and lemon juice. Remove from heat.

In a large bowl, combine brown rice flour, lemon peel, baking powder, salt, and xanthan gum. Add to butter mixture and stir until mixed. Wrap dough in plastic wrap, shape into a disk, and refrigerate 2 or 3 hours.

Meanwhile, make filling: Snip apricots with a scissors into a medium saucepan with a tight-fitting lid. Add water. Bring to a boil, cover, reduce heat and simmer 45 minutes or until soft. Puree in blender or food processor. Turn into a bowl and cool.

Continued

Roll dough on rice-floured surface 1/8" thick. Cut with a cookie cutter into 3" rounds. Place 1 teaspoon filling in center of each round, and fold in 3 edges to make triangular shape, pinching edges to seal (filling will show a little in center of each cookie). Place on ungreased baking sheets.

Bake cookies 10 to 15 minutes, or until edges are golden and cookies are set. Cool on wire racks and store airtight.

Icebox Butter Cookies, Four Ways

{ *A roll of these rich cookies in the refrigerator or freezer is like money in the bank. · The Coconut-Macadamia version is aromatic and dressy, the Date-Nut rich and homey, the Chocolate Chip a winner all around, to aunt and nephews alike. · Though this recipe makes a large batch, I like to double it and make two variations at once.* }

> 3 1/2 cups brown rice flour
> 2 teaspoons xanthan gum
> 1/4 teaspoon salt
> 1 1/2 cups butter
> 1 cup evaporated cane juice
> 1 teaspoon vanilla extract
> 1/2 cup milk or milk substitute

In a large bowl, stir together flour, xanthan gum, and salt.

Cream butter and evaporated cane juice. Add vanilla. Add dry ingredients alternately with milk or substitute.

On a long piece of waxed or parchment paper, roll dough into a long roll 11/2" in diameter. Wrap wax paper around log and refrigerate 2 hours. Or wrap in plastic wrap and chill up to 2 weeks, or freeze up to 2 months.

Preheat oven to 375°. Slice roll into 1/4" slices and place on cookie sheets. Bake 10 to 12 minutes or until edges are just browned. Cool a few minutes on baking sheet before removing to wire racks to cool completely. Store airtight.

Variations:

Coconut-Macadamia Icebox Butter Cookies: Add to finished dough just

Continued

before forming into a roll: 2 cups lightly toasted unsweetened coconut and 1 cup chopped macadamia nuts. To toast coconut: Preheat oven to 325°. In a large rimmed baking sheet, spread coconut into a thin layer. Toast coconut, shaking pan every 2 to 3 minutes, for a total of 6 to 10 minutes, or until coconut is toasted lightly. Cool before adding to cookie dough.

Date-Nut Icebox Cookies: Add to finished dough just before forming into a roll: 1 cup chopped walnuts and 2 cups snipped whole pitted dates.

Chocolate Chip Icebox Cookies: Add to finished dough just before forming into a roll: 12 ounces semisweet chocolate chips.

Citrus Fig Bars

{ *These are fig bars, only more so. They're not the pocket-cookie kind, or the eat-three-before-supper kind; they are fig bars to be served on china. · Tender, citrus-scented pastry enfolds a lightly sweet filling. Serve them cooled for easiest handling.* }

Filling:

12 ounces dried figs
1/3 cup honey or maple syrup
1 tablespoon fresh lemon juice
2 tablespoons fresh orange juice
2 tablespoons water

Dough:

1 1/3 cups brown rice flour
1/3 cup evaporated cane juice
1 teaspoon xanthan gum
1 1/4 teaspoons baking powder
1/2 teaspoon salt
zest of lemon
7 tablespoons butter, slightly softened
1/2 cup cold water, more or less as needed

To make filling: Remove stems from figs with scissors. Grind figs in food processor or through coarse blade of a food grinder. Combine all filling ingredients in a small saucepan, bring to a boil over high heat, reduce heat, cover and cook 5 minutes or until figs are tender. Cool.

To make dough: Stir together brown rice flour, evaporated cane juice, xanthan gum, baking powder, and salt in a large bowl. Cut in butter until it is reduced to small pea-sized lumps. Stir in lemon zest. Toss with just enough water to

Continued

make a stiff but cohesive dough. Do not overwork dough. Divide dough in half. Wrap each half and chill several hours.

Preheat oven to 350°.

Place dough one half at a time on a rice-floured surface, and roll into 10" log. Roll log between 2 sheets of waxed paper to until 1/2" thick and 5" wide. Carefully spread half of filling down center third of dough. Lift long edges of dough with the help of the waxed paper, and overlap in center to seal. Repeat with remaining half of dough and filling.

Using wax paper, transfer logs to greased baking sheets, seam sides down. Press logs to flatten slightly. Bake 20 minutes or until golden. Remove from oven and cool completely on pans. With a sharp knife, cut logs into 1" bars. Store airtight.

Back-Again Brownies

{ *Yes, here they are—deeply chocolate, fudgy, and all brownie. · Oh, that brownies were as nutritious as carrots, and oh, that man were required to eat them morning, noon and night! · Measure the ingredients carefully, and don't substitute, for this recipe is a delicate balance of ingredients, and worth getting right. · Brownies really should be impromptu, but unfortunately these aren't. They need a good, long cooling time. In fact, you should have made them yesterday.* }

3/4 cup butter, softened
1 cup evaporated cane juice
1/3 cup water
1 teaspoon vanilla extract
2/3 cup unsweetened baking cocoa
1/2 teaspoon salt
1 1/2 teaspoon xanthan gum
1/2 teaspoon baking powder
1 cup brown rice flour

Preheat oven to 325°. Grease 8"x8" pan.

Cream butter and evaporated cane juice well. Add water and vanilla and beat again until homogenous and fluffy.

In a small mixing bowl, stir together cocoa, salt, xanthan gum, baking powder, and brown rice flour. Add to creamed mixture and beat until batter is fluffy and becomes a shade lighter in color.

Spread batter evenly into prepared pan. Bake 35 to 45 minutes or until almost firm in center. Brownies burn easily, so watch carefully. Cut while warm. Cool on wire rack. Brownies are best if baked at least 12 hours before serving. Makes 16 servings.

Variations:
Walnut Brownies: Add 1 cup broken walnuts to batter just before spreading in pan.

Mocha Brownies: Add 2 tablespoons instant coffee granules to batter along with dry ingredients.

Black-Bottom Banana Bars

{ *These are not only a classic after-school snack, but with chocolate glaze,* *these moist bars go places. They're sturdy enough to pack, and keep well.* }

1 cup butter, softened
1 cup evaporated cane juice
2 teaspoons vanilla extract
3 cups mashed overripe bananas
3 cups brown rice flour
2 teaspoons baking powder
1 1/2 teaspoons baking soda
1 teaspoon salt
1 teaspoon xanthan gum
1/2 cup milk or milk substitute
2 teaspoons cider vinegar
1/2 cup unsweetened baking cocoa
Posh Chocolate Glaze (see index) or frosting of choice, optional

Preheat oven to 350°. Grease 10"x15" baking pan.

Cream butter and evaporated cane juice until light and fluffy. Add vanilla and bananas and mix well.

In a separate bowl, stir together brown rice flour, baking powder, baking soda, salt, and xanthan gum. Add to creamed mixture alternately with milk and vinegar.

Divide batter in half. Stir cocoa into one portion, beating well. Spread the chocolate batter evenly in a greased 10"x15" baking pan. Spoon the light batter evenly on top.

Bake bars for 30 to 35 minutes or until nicely browned and firm to the touch in the center. Remove bars from oven and cool on a rack. Makes 24 to 30 servings.

Pumpkin Pie Bars

These are like little square pumpkin pies with a crust underneath and crumbly streusel on top. They ride happily on autumn wagon rides.

Crust:

2 3/4 cups brown rice flour

1/4 cup tapioca starch

1 tablespoon ground flaxseed

1 teaspoon xanthan gum

3/4 cup sweetener of choice

1/2 teaspoon salt

1/2 cup butter, melted

1/2 cup water

Filling:

2 1/2 cups cooked, pureed pumpkin

1 tablespoon molasses

1/2 teaspoon vanilla

1/2 cup sweetener of choice

2 teaspoons cinnamon

1/4 teaspoon salt

3 tablespoons cornstarch

1 1/2 cups milk or milk substitute, or more if needed

Topping:

1 1/2 cups reserved crumbs

1/2 cup butter, melted

1/2 cup chopped walnuts or pecans

Continued

Preheat oven to 350°. Grease 9"x13" baking pan.

For crust: In a large bowl, stir together flour, tapioca starch, flaxseed, xanthan gum, sweetener and salt. Remove 1 1/2 cups of this mixture and set aside for the topping.

To remaining dry ingredients, add melted butter and water. Stir well to make a moist, yet slightly crumbly, dough. Press into the bottom of prepared pan.

For filling: Whisk pumpkin, molasses, vanilla, cinnamon, sweetener, salt, cornstarch, and the milk or substitute until smooth. Check consistency. Filling should pour very easily—add more liquid if needed. Pour filling over crust.

For topping: Stir butter and nuts into the reserved dry mixture. Stir until crumbly and sprinkle evenly over filling.

Bake bars 30 to 40 minutes or until filling is set and topping is well browned. Cool bars before cutting. Makes 24 servings.

Lemon Toasted Coconut Bars

{ Tangy, smooth lemon filling on a shortbread crust, topped with crisp coconut. }

1 Shortbread Crust for Desserts (see index), in 9"x13" baking pan, cooled

1 1/2 cups evaporated cane juice

6 tablespoons cornstarch

pinch salt

2 cups water

1/4 cup butter

1 cup fresh lemon juice

a few drops natural yellow food coloring, optional

1 cup unsweetened coconut, toasted

In a large saucepan, stir together evaporated cane juice and cornstarch. Add salt. Stir in water until smooth. Cook over medium-high heat until mixture bubbles and thickens. Remove from heat.

Add butter and lemon juice. Stir in food coloring, if desired. Cool. Pour over shortbread crust and sprinkle with toasted coconut. Chill well. Cut into bars. Makes 20 servings.

Chocolate Shortbread

{ *Chocolaty and intense, this is a cookie grown up. · Chocolate shortbread is unmanageable warm from the oven. Cut it into slim fingers and tuck it, uncovered, on a high shelf and don't touch it for a day. After two or three days it becomes mellow and firm, and it keeps up to a week at room temperature. · The cinnamon gives an unexpected Latin flair.* }

evaporated cane juice, approximately 1 cup
1 1/2 cups butter, softened
2 cups brown rice flour
1/2 cup tapioca starch
2 teaspoons xanthan gum
1/2 teaspoon salt
1/2 teaspoon cinnamon, optional
1/4 teaspoon baking soda
5 tablespoons unsweetened baking cocoa

Preheat oven to 325°. Grease 7"x11" pan and line with waxed paper. Grease waxed paper.

Place approximately 1 cup evaporated cane juice into blender container and process 2 minutes until superfine. Measure 1 cup.

Cream butter and the 1 cup superfine evaporated cane juice until very fluffy.

In a large bowl, stir together brown rice flour, tapioca starch, xanthan gum, salt, cinnamon if desired, baking soda and cocoa. Add to creamed mixture, stirring just until well blended. Scrape down sides of bowl and mix again.

Spread dough into prepared pan. Bake 20 minutes, or until shortbread has risen, then fallen. Do not overbake. Remove from oven, allow to cool slightly, then cut into long, 31/2"x1" bars. Allow shortbread to rest 24 hours before serving. Remove from pan and remove waxed paper. Store up to 1 week airtight. Makes around 22 bars.

Toasted Coconut Shortbread

{ *These fan-shaped shortbread cookies are so natural for a ladies' tea it seems a shame not to serve them with a pot of it, even if you don't have guests. · The last time I made them, I added a cup of dried cherries to the dough. The tart cherries paired well with the toasted coconut.* }

1 cup unsweetened flaked coconut
1 3/4 cup brown rice flour
1/4 cup cornstarch
2 1/2 teaspoons xanthan gum
1/4 teaspoon salt
1 cup butter, softened
3/4 cup evaporated cane juice

Preheat oven to 325°. In a rimmed baking sheet, scatter coconut in a thin layer. Toast in oven 6 to 10 minutes, shaking pan every 2 minutes, until coconut is lightly toasted. Remove from oven and cool.

In a medium mixing bowl, stir together flour, coconut, cornstarch, xanthan gum and salt.

Cream butter and evaporated cane juice until very light and fluffy. Add dry mixture and beat just to combine.

Press dough into 9" round tart pan with removable bottom (or a 9" round springform pan). With a sharp knife, score dough into 16 wedges. To make the slices look like fans, make lines in each slice by dragging fork tines from edge to center of each slice.

Bake shortbread 40 to 50 minutes, or until lightly browned and set. Remove from oven and cool on wire rack. Cut slices along scored lines. Allow shortbread to mellow 24 hours before serving. Makes 16 servings.

Dark Chocolate-Walnut Biscotti

*{ Last winter I turned our kitchen into a biscotti bakery for a day, and
this one was a winner. Deeply flavored and drizzled with a punch
of extra-dark chocolate, they were the first of the day's successes to
disappear. They're said to be good keepers, but I can't verify it! }*

> 2 cups brown rice flour
> 1 1/4 cups evaporated cane juice
> 1/2 cup unsweetened baking cocoa
> 1 teaspoon baking soda
> 1/2 teaspoon salt
> 3/4 teaspoon xanthan gum
> 2 tablespoons ground flaxseed
> 1/4 cup butter, softened
> 2 ounces unsweetened chocolate, melted
> 3/4 cup water, or as needed
> 2 teaspoons vanilla extract
> 1 1/2 cups coarsely chopped walnuts
> 2 ounces semisweet or bittersweet chocolate, optional

Preheat oven to 350°. Grease a large baking sheet.

In a large bowl, stir together brown rice flour, evaporated cane juice, cocoa, baking soda, salt, xanthan gum, and flaxseed. Cut in butter until mixture resembles sand and no lumps remain.

Add melted chocolate, water and vanilla to flour mixture and stir well to make a stiff batter. It should hold its shape very well and be only slightly sticky. Add up to 1/4 cup more water if batter is at all dry. Fold in walnuts.

Continued

Divide dough in half. Form two 12" logs on the prepared baking sheet. With floured hands, flatten each to make a log 3" wide, 1" high and about 3" apart on the baking sheet.

Bake 35 to 45 minutes, or until logs are crusty and firm in the centers. Remove from oven and reduce heat to 325°.

Cool 20 minutes. With a large, serrated knife, cut logs into 3/4" slices. Lay biscotti cut sides down on wire cooling racks. Lay cooling racks directly on oven racks and bake an additional 20 minutes or until dried and crispy. Cool completely.

If you like, drizzle with chocolate: place racks on large baking sheet. Melt chocolate in a small saucepan over very low heat, stirring. Drizzle off the tip of a spoon in a zigzag motion across biscotti. Allow to set completely, then store airtight.

Orange-Sour Cream Biscotti

{ *What's crisp and light, the cookie of choice with a good cappuccino?* *Biscotti, of course. · Orange and sour cream are a pair, and this biscotti showcases it. · Since biscotti's second baking mutes flavors, don't skimp on the large amount of orange juice and peel in this recipe. Biscotti keeps beautifully at least a week.* }

2 1/2 cups brown rice flour
2 teaspoons baking powder
1/2 teaspoon salt
1 tablespoon ground flaxseed
3/4 teaspoon xanthan gum
1 cup evaporated cane juice
orange zest from 3 oranges
1/4 cup butter
2/3 cup fresh orange juice
1/3 cup sour cream or Sour Supreme
1/3 cup water, or more as needed
water for brushing
evaporated cane juice for sprinkling

Preheat oven to 375°. Grease a large baking sheet.

In a large bowl, stir together brown rice flour, baking powder, salt, flaxseed, xanthan gum, and evaporated cane juice. Add orange zest. Cut in butter until no lumps remain and mixture has the texture of sand.

In a small bowl, stir together orange juice, sour cream or Sour Supreme, and water. Stir into dry ingredients, mixing well, until a smooth and thick batter is formed. Check consistency: mixture should be a thick batter that's still sticky. Add more water as needed.

Continued

Divide mixture in half. Place both halves on baking sheet and form each into a 12" roll. Flatten each to 3" wide and 1" thick and about 3" apart. Brush with water and sprinkle with evaporated cane juice.

Bake 35 to 45 minutes or until rolls are browned and crusty, and middle tests done. Remove from oven and reduce heat to 325°.

Allow rolls to cool 20 minutes. Slice rolls diagonally into 3/4" slices. Lay biscotti cut sides down on wire cooling racks. Place racks directly on oven racks and bake an additional 20 minutes until they are crispy and thoroughly dried. Cool. Store airtight up to 2 weeks. Freeze up to 3 months.

Queenly Cakes

{Cakes, Sauces, Glazes & Frostings}

Mocha-Almond Birthday Present Cake

It's hard to resist the urge to

sing when you bring a cake to the table,

even if no one has a birthday to celebrate.

The simplest cake conveys a ceremony other desserts lack.

NO FLAN OR TART HAS SUCH A LOFTY STATURE,

no plate of cookies such an air of sweet ostentation.

–Celia Barbour

 chapter eight

Queenly Cakes
{Cakes, Sauces, Glazes and Frostings}

Tall and elegant, a layer cake in silky robes reigns on a footed throne. Earthy and sweet, gingerbread lies low in a cast-iron skillet, wrapping us in her comforting fragrance. As individual as they are, they're both sisters with the family name "Cake". No other baked good is as multitalented as cake; nothing else can play the part of queen or servant as successfully.

Perhaps because of this, cakes go with us through life. We dig into a one-candled cake on our first birthday so Mother can see our gooey grin. We tie on an apron and bake a cake as our first culinary accomplishment. And likely, when bridal roses bloom on a happy June day, a cake is with us, as much a friend as the smiling guests.

I have a long-held affection for cakes, especially the queenly. I'll never forget my first memory of an iced queen. When I was a tiny tot, we were invited to some of Daddy's cousins on their old homestead for Sunday dinner. I absorbed it all in wonder: the gleaming glass, ironed damask and blooming china, but mostly The Cake in the center of the table. It was a three-layered, white-iced lemon poppyseed cake and the memory of it poised in a pool of sunlight still delights my heart.

My first baking attempt (long before I could properly read a recipe) was a chocolate cake. Why try anything else? Chocolate cake, I thought, was the most wonderful thing in the world. So I perused Mom's few cookbooks and searched for a recipe. What did "tsp." mean? Why did one recipe use boiling water and another cold water? And why did every single one ask for that mysterious ingredient called "cocoa powder"? Mom didn't have any. Could I just omit it and have chocolate cake anyway?

You can't, my big sisters informed me, so I began pleading. At last our busy mom, who was happy to just get basic meals on the table, laid in a supply of cocoa, and I went to work with enthusiasm.

Chocolate cakes became a household plague as I turned them out by the dozens, each vastly different than the last. There were chocolate cakes with mountains in the middle and chocolate cakes with valleys in the middle. There were chocolate cakes long on baking soda (when I lost the teaspoon) and short on sugar (when Mom hinted that we'd had enough sweets). Then there was that particularly heavy, knobby-textured "Chocolate Potato Cake" (and the recipe *said* it was the moistest cake ever!).

Months (or maybe years) later when one cake really rose, really stayed risen, and had a moist, tender interior, I was delighted almost to tears. My family, who had heroically swallowed all the others, now deserved this unexpected treat. Jubilant, I moved on to bigger challenges, and at long last learned to make my own cake queens on footed stands.

Ask a celiac what they miss the most, and many will say "chocolate cake". I missed it intensely when the doctor forbade gluten. After enduring the craving as long as I could, I set out to see if there was a way a celiac could eat chocolate cake.

The next years were like a rerun of my preteen baking attempts. But at least this time I understood the worth of measuring spoons, knew a cup of flour was a level cup, and that substitutions must be made judiciously. After awhile, a glimmer of hope appeared: cakes are one of the easiest gluten-free baked goods to master. With the coming of xanthan gum, my last link was complete. Chocolate cake has become a staple at our house again—a welcome one. And if we want variety, we can always bake butter cake. Or carrot cake. Or apple, or shoofly, or gingerbread with orange sauce.

Though not every sister in the cake family has yet gone gluten-free, I have enough recipes to keep me happily supplied with gluten free cakes for the rest of my life. What shall we bake today? A cinnamon-scented, crumb-topped coffee cake? Or a mocha-frosted, three-layer queen? ♪

Cake Crumbs

·Liquid is the Number One, Most Important Ingredient in cakes. Liquid will make all the difference between a moist, light cake and a crumbly, dry one. Every time you make the same recipe, it will take a slightly different amount of liquid. I give variable liquid amounts in my recipes, plus visual signs for you to tell when you have the batter right. Watch the batter carefully. How does it pour? How much resistance do you feel when you stir it? Does a spoon stand or fall in it? A few cakes (South Seas Sun Cake, Fudgy Date Cake) require a thicker batter, but most gluten-free cake batters are best thin. Err on the side of too much liquid.

·You'll notice cakes require less xanthan gum than cookies or pie crusts. This is because cakes have a much higher ratio of liquid to flour.

·Carrot, banana, zucchini, or almost any pureed fruit or vegetable do wonderful things for gluten free cakes. Not only do fruit- or vegetable-enriched cakes bake up moist, they stay moist as well. ♪

Yours Truly Chocolate Cake

{ Like a friend who will never leave you, this recipe will be there for you again and again. It is the Basic, the Stand-by, the Fool-proof Cake of cakes. · This recipe has been 2-layer special-occasion cakes, dressed-up desserts, and even a slinky birthday worm (see Crawly Caterpillar Cake). · Eat this cake in wedges completely unadorned, or pretty it up with frosting, sauce or icing, as you please. }

- **2 1/2 cups brown rice flour**
- **1/2 cup tapioca starch, cornstarch, or potato starch**
- **1/2 cup unsweetened baking cocoa**
- **1/2 teaspoon xanthan gum**
- **2 teaspoons baking soda**
- **1/2 teaspoon salt**
- **1 cup sweetener of choice**
- **3/4 cup light olive or vegetable oil**
- **2 tablespoons apple cider vinegar**
- **1 tablespoon vanilla extract**
- **2 1/2 to 3 cups cold water, or more as needed**

Preheat oven to 350°. Grease 9"x13" baking pan.

In a large bowl, whisk together brown rice flour, starch, cocoa, xanthan gum, baking soda, salt, and sweetener. Make a well and pour in oil, vinegar, vanilla and 2 1/2 cups water. Whisk just to combine. Check consistency: batter should be very soft, running in a thin stream from spoon when lifted. Add up to 1/2 cup more water if needed. Usually a total of 2 3/4 cups is close.

Pour batter into prepared pan. Bake 30 to 40 minutes or until cake is springy in center. Cool on wire rack. Serve as is or with desired icing or sauce, warm or cooled. Makes 24 servings.

Rich Butter Cake

{ *This is my answer for a gluten-free yellow cake. It's not as light as its gluten competitor, but the flavor is buttery and sweet. I've tweaked and twisted it into all kinds of variations. One of my favorites is Boston Cream Pie. · Serve this cake soon after baking for top satisfaction.* }

2/3 cup butter, softened
2/3 cup evaporated cane juice
1 tablespoon liquid lecithin, optional
2 teaspoons vanilla extract
1 3/4 cup milk, milk substitute or water, or more as needed
2 1/2 cups brown rice flour
1/2 cup tapioca starch or cornstarch
1 teaspoon xanthan gum
1/2 teaspoon salt
4 teaspoons baking powder

Preheat oven to 350°. Grease 9"x13" baking pan.

Cream butter and evaporated cane juice until very light and fluffy, up to 5 minutes. Add lecithin (if using) and vanilla.

In a medium mixing bowl, combine brown rice flour, tapioca starch or cornstarch, xanthan gum, salt, and baking powder. Add to creamed mixture alternately with milk or substitute. Check consistency—mixture should be a light batter that just holds its shape when mounded with a spoon. Add up to 3/4 cup more liquid if needed to make this consistency. Beat batter on high speed for 2 minutes.

Pour batter into prepared pan. Bake 20 to 30 minutes, or until cake is nicely browned and center is springy. Remove from oven and cool on wire rack. Serve warm or just cooled and within 24 hours. Makes 24 servings.

Apple Cake With Cinnamon-Nut Glaze

{ *We used to visit friends with a family full of girls and a Wolf River apple tree in their back yard. The tart, red-blushed apples were so huge that half an apple yielded enough to make this cake. They often made it for us when we'd drive over for a Sunday evening hymn sing.* }

1 cup light olive or vegetable oil
1 cup evaporated cane juice
1 teaspoon vanilla extract
2 1/2 cups brown rice flour
2 teaspoons xanthan gum
1 teaspoon baking powder
2 teaspoons ground cinnamon
1/2 teaspoon salt
**1 1/2 cups buttermilk, or milk substitute with
2 tablespoons cider vinegar**
1 teaspoon baking soda
2 cups cored and diced apples
water, if needed, to correct consistency
Cinnamon-Nut Glaze (see index)

Preheat oven to 350°. Grease a 9"x13" baking pan.

In a large mixing bowl, whisk together oil and evaporated cane juice. Add vanilla.

In a liquid measuring cup, stir together buttermilk (or substitute and vinegar) with the baking soda.

In a separate bowl, stir together brown rice flour, xanthan gum, baking powder, cinnamon, and salt. Add to oil/evaporated cane juice mixture alternately with buttermilk or substitute. Whisk well. Check consistency:

Continued

batter should be a medium-thin cake batter. Add small amounts of water, if needed. Fold in apples.

Transfer batter to prepared pan. Bake cake 35 to 45 minutes, or until center springs back when lightly touched. Cool slightly before icing.

Spread icing thinly on warm cake. Serve cake warm. Makes 20 servings.

Crumb-Topped Coffee Cake

{ *You can do a lot with this basic coffee cake. I like to sprinkle berries with the middle layer of streusel, then serve the cake with a sauce. Try blueberry coffee cake with Orange Sauce or raspberry with Classic Vanilla Pudding.* }

Cake:

 2 1/2 cups brown rice flour
 1/2 cup tapioca starch or cornstarch
 1 teaspoon xanthan gum
 1/2 teaspoon salt
 4 teaspoons baking powder
 1/2 cup butter, softened
 3/4 cup evaporated cane juice
 1 1/2 cups milk or milk substitute, or more if needed

Topping:

 1/2 cup brown rice flour
 1/3 cup evaporated cane juice
 1 1/2 teaspoons ground cinnamon
 1/2 cup chopped pecans or walnuts, optional
 3 tablespoons butter, melted

Preheat oven to 350°. Grease 9"x13" baking pan.

In a large bowl, combine brown rice flour, tapioca starch or cornstarch, xanthan gum, salt, and baking powder.

In a mixer, cream butter and evaporated cane juice. Add dry ingredients alternately with milk or substitute and beat well. Check consistency—batter should be just stiff enough to mound when dropped off a spoon. Add more liquid if needed. Beat batter 2 minutes.

Continued

Make topping: In a small bowl, combine brown rice flour, evaporated cane juice, cinnamon, nuts, and butter. Stir until crumbly.

Spread half of cake batter in prepared pan. Sprinkle with half of topping mixture. Carefully spread remaining batter over crumbs. Sprinkle with remaining topping.

Bake 25 to 30 minutes or until center is firm and edges are nicely browned. Serve warm. Makes 24 servings.

Pennsylvania Shoofly Cake

{ *Here the classic shoofly pie has a new vocation, and performs it beautifully. This cake is moist and soft and will keep a day or so airtight.* }

3 1/2 cups brown rice flour
1/2 teaspoon salt
1 1/2 teaspoons xanthan gum
1/2 teaspoon cinnamon
3/4 cup evaporated cane juice
1 cup butter, slightly softened
2 cups water
1 cup light baking molasses
1 tablespoon baking soda

Preheat oven to 350°. Grease 9"x13" baking pan.

Stir together flour, salt, xanthan gum, cinnamon, and evaporated cane juice in a large bowl. With a pastry blender or your fingers, cut in butter until just small lumps remain. Reserve 13/4 cups of this mixture for topping.

In a large saucepan, bring water to a boil. Add molasses. Add baking soda, stirring. When foaming subsides, pour over remaining dry ingredients in bowl. Stir just until combined and spread into a greased 9"x13" baking pan. Sprinkle reserved crumbs on top.

Bake cake for 30 to 45 minutes or until cake is firm in center. Remove to wire rack to cool. Serve warm or cooled. Makes 24 servings.

Cinnamon-Nut Zucchini Cake

{ *We discovered this easy-to-stir-together cake last fall during a bumper crop of zucchini. We liked it so well, it became a fixture. You can skip the glaze, but I think it's a wonderful counterpart to the moist, lightly spiced cake.* }

2 cups brown rice flour
1 cup evaporated cane juice
2 tablespoons ground flaxseed
2 teaspoons ground cinnamon
1 1/2 teaspoon baking powder
1 teaspoon baking soda
3/4 teaspoon salt
1/2 teaspoon xanthan gum
2 cups finely grated zucchini
2/3 cup light olive or vegetable oil
1 teaspoon vanilla extract
1 tablespoon cider vinegar
1 1/4 cups water, or more as needed
Cinnamon-Nut Glaze (see index)

Preheat oven to 350°. Grease 9"x13" baking pan.

In a large bowl, stir together the brown rice flour, evaporated cane juice, flaxseed, cinnamon, baking powder, baking soda, salt, and xanthan gum.

In another bowl, stir together zucchini, oil, vanilla, vinegar, and water. Add to dry ingredients, beating until combined.

Test consistency—batter should be soft, with a medium consistency. Add up to 1/4 cup more water if needed. Pour into prepared pan and bake 35 to 40 minutes, or until cake is springy in the center and tests done.

Ice cake while warm with Cinnamon-Nut Glaze. Serve warm or cooled. Cake keeps well up to 2 days, airtight. Makes 20 servings.

Date & Orange Cake

{ *This dense, full-flavored cake is rich with dates, nuts, and a piquant orange glaze. · Grandma Hobbs is famous for her wonderful Penny Candy Cake, and she'll make it for my sisters with minimal begging. This cake has some of the same flavor notes as hers, and I like to pretend it is. Serve it in hefty wedges with mugs of tea or coffee.* }

1/2 cup butter, softened
2/3 cup evaporated cane juice
1/2 cup unsweetened applesauce
1/2 cup fresh orange juice
1 tablespoon orange peel
2 1/2 cups brown rice flour
1 teaspoon baking powder
1 teaspoon baking soda
1/2 teaspoon salt
3/4 teaspoon xanthan gum
1 cup water, or more as needed
1 teaspoon cider vinegar
1 cup whole pitted dates
1 cup chopped walnuts or pecans
Orange Glaze (see index)

Preheat oven to 350°. Grease 9" springform pan.

Cream butter and evaporated cane juice very well. Add applesauce, orange juice and peel.

In a large bowl, stir together brown rice flour, baking powder, baking soda, salt, and xanthan gum. Add to creamed mixture alternately with water and vinegar. Beat batter at high speed 2 minutes. Check consistency—batter

Continued

should hold its shape when dropped from a spoon, but still be very soft. Add more water if needed to reach this consistency.

Snip dates into small pieces with scissors. Fold into batter with the nuts. Spread batter into prepared pan. Bake 55 to 65 minutes or until crusty and browned, and toothpick inserted in center comes out clean.

With a skewer or ice pick, poke holes in 1/2" intervals in hot cake. Pour Orange Glaze slowly over warm cake. Cool on wire rack and remove sides of pan. Makes 10 to 12 servings.

South Seas Sun Cake

{ *Pineapple, carrot and coconut sing in harmony here—all blanketed by a fluffy frosting. · The batter of this cake needs to be thicker than most. A spoon should almost stand upright in it. · Though nicest just cooled, this cake keeps well.* }

2 cups brown rice flour
3/4 cup evaporated cane juice
1/2 teaspoon xanthan gum
1 1/2 teaspoons baking soda
1 teaspoon salt
2 cups grated carrot
1 cup unsweetened flaked coconut
1 cup chopped walnuts
3/4 cup olive or vegetable oil
1 teaspoon vanilla
1 (20 ounce) can crushed pineapple, undrained
2 tablespoons lemon juice
1/4 cup water, or more as needed
1 recipe Pineapple-Nut Frosting (see index)

Preheat oven to 350°. Grease 9"x13" pan.

Cake: In a large bowl, whisk together flour, evaporated cane juice, xanthan gum, baking soda, and salt. Stir in carrot, coconut, and walnuts.

Add oil, vanilla, pineapple with its juice, lemon juice, and water. Stir just to combine. Batter should be soft, but able to hold its shape well when dropped with a spoon. Add up to 2 tablespoons more water if needed to reach this consistency.

Pour batter into prepared pan, and smooth with a spatula. Bake 35 to 45 minutes, or until cake feels springy in the center. Remove to wire rack to cool completely.

Ice cake generously with Pineapple-Nut Frosting. Store leftovers, airtight, in refrigerator. Makes 24 servings.

Old-Fashioned Gingerbread With Orange Sauce

{ Citrus and ginger are always happy companions. Grandma used to make gingerbread and Mom used to make it, and now I'm happy to have it again, gluten-free. }

1/2 cup butter, softened
1/4 cup sweetener of choice
1/4 cup water
1 cup baking molasses
2 1/3 cups brown rice flour
1/2 teaspoon xanthan gum
1/2 teaspoon baking soda
1 teaspoon baking powder
1 teaspoon ground ginger
1 teaspoon ground cinnamon
1 cup hot water
Orange Sauce (see index), optional

Preheat oven to 350°. Grease 9" or 10" cast-iron skillet or a 9"x13" baking pan.

Cream butter and sweetener. Add water and molasses, and beat until light. Add brown rice flour, xanthan gum, baking soda, baking powder, ginger, and cinnamon and beat well. Add hot water and stir just until incorporated. Batter will be thin.

Pour into prepared pan. Bake 30 to 40 minutes, or until cake is springy in center. Serve in small wedges or squares with Orange Sauce.
Makes 10 to 12 servings.

Fudgy Date Cake

{ Deep-flavored and seriously rich, this is dessert in a Sunday suit. Served in squares with a drizzle of Posh Chocolate Glaze, it deserves candles and roses. · This cake batter needs to be thicker than most. Whenever I add more water than specified, I wish I hadn't. Surprisingly, it also needs a lot of xanthan gum. · Because of the moist dates, this cake will keep happily, airtight, for several days. }

1 1/2 cups boiling water
2 cups chopped dates from whole pitted dates
1/2 cup butter, softened
1/2 cup light olive or vegetable oil
3/4 cup evaporated cane juice
2 teaspoons vanilla extract
2 3/4 cups brown rice flour
2 teaspoons xanthan gum
3/4 teaspoon salt
1 1/2 teaspoons baking soda
3 tablespoons unsweetened baking cocoa
1 1/2 cups chocolate or carob chips, sweetened or unsweetened
3/4 cup chopped pecans or walnuts
1 additional tablespoon evaporated cane juice, for sprinkling

In a small bowl, pour boiling water over dates and allow to stand until just warm.

Preheat oven to 350°. Grease 10"x15" baking pan.

Cream butter, oil, and evaporated cane juice until light and fluffy. Add vanilla.

In a large bowl, stir together flour, xanthan gum, salt, baking soda, and cocoa. Add to creamed mixture alternately with cooled date mixture, stirring just to combine.

Continued

Spread batter into prepared pan. Sprinkle with chocolate or carob chips and pecans or walnuts. Sprinkle with evaporated cane juice. Bake 25 to 30 minutes or until firm to the touch. Serve warm or cooled.
Makes 24 to 35 servings.

Chocolate & Cream Cake

{ *Combining three favorite recipes in one, this is special-occasion cake. Bake the cake the same day you serve it, but the frosting and glaze can be made a day or two ahead of time.* }

1 recipe Chocolate Cake batter (see index)
1 recipe Fluffy Filling and Frosting (see index)
1 recipe Posh Chocolate Glaze (see index)

Preheat oven to 350°. Bake Chocolate Cake batter in a greased 9"x13" baking pan. Cool cake completely. Assemble and serve cake within a few hours.

To assemble cake: Spread filling over cake to edges. Warm or chill chocolate glaze as needed to obtain a "glazing" consistency. Drizzle glaze over filling. Chill until glaze is set. Serve immediately. Chill any leftovers.
Makes 24 servings.

Upside-Down Cornmeal Berry Cake

{ *Did you go berrying—not a big, all-day hunt, but a short, eat-as-many-as-you-save foray? Here's a recipe for you. · This upside-down cake doesn't use as many berries as a pie, and it showcases them where everybody can see their goodness: on the top.* }

> 2 cups fresh blackberries, blueberries, and/or raspberries
> 1/2 cup butter, softened
> 3/4 cup evaporated cane juice
> 2 cups brown rice flour
> 1/2 cup yellow cornmeal
> 1 1/2 teaspoons baking powder
> 1/2 teaspoon baking soda
> 1/2 teaspoon salt
> 1 teaspoon xanthan gum
> 2 cups milk or milk substitute, or more as needed
> 2 tablespoons apple cider vinegar
> Orange Glaze (see index), optional

Preheat oven to 350°. Grease 9" round baking pan and line with waxed paper. Grease paper. Scatter berries into bottom of pan.

Cream butter and evaporated cane juice. In a large bowl, combine brown rice flour, cornmeal, baking powder, baking soda, salt, and xanthan gum. Add to creamed mixture alternately with milk or substitute and vinegar, blending just to combine. Add more milk or substitute, if needed, to make a soft batter. Pour batter carefully over berries.

Bake cake 40 to 50 minutes until center springs back when touched. Cool 5 minutes, then invert on plate. Drizzle with Orange Glaze, if desired. Serve slightly warm. Makes 10 servings.

Crawly Caterpillar Cake

{ Fun? A little creepy? A snap to make? Yes, yes and yes. This slinky critter has attended more birthday parties than I can count, and just recently it went gluten-free for my allergic nephew. · Candy is used for face, feet and "ruff", but if sugar is a no-no, try whole dates for the feet, dried unsweetened coconut ribbons for the ruff, and the eyes... hmm, let's see... how about two Dark Chocolate truffles? Natural food coloring is available at many health food stores. · Light the curving line of candles and listen to the squeals! }

2 recipes Chocolate Cake batter (see index)
2 recipes Fluffy Filling and Frosting (see index)
1/2 teaspoon mint extract or 10 drops peppermint essential oil
green food coloring, as needed
flaked coconut, sweetened or unsweetened, as needed
about 4 large marshmallows
1 large gum ball
multicolor party cake sprinkles, as needed
gummi orange or lemon slices, as needed

Preheat oven to 350°. Grease a large Bundt pan and dust it with rice flour. Grease an oven-proof 11/2 cup capacity custard cup, and dust it with rice flour.

Pour cake batter into Bundt pan and custard cup, filling both 2/3 full. You might have batter left which you can bake for another use.

Bake cakes until they pull from sides of pan and center springs back when lightly touched: about 20 minutes for the smaller cake, 45 to 55 minutes for the larger cake. Cool cakes 15 minutes on a wire rack, then remove pans and cool completely.

Prepare frosting: Reserve 1 cup frosting and add mint extract or peppermint oil to remaining frosting. Tint mint frosting a bright green. *Continued*

Caterpillar body: With cake inverted side up, slice large Bundt cake vertically in exact thirds to make semicircles. Arrange cake into caterpillar shape on serving tray as follows: Place semicircles with the first curving to left, the next to the right, and the last to the left again, with cut ends connecting. Ice body with mint frosting. Swirl frosting with a spoon into ridges crosswise to make the caterpillar body look "slinky".

Caterpillar head: Frost small cake with the untinted frosting on all sides. Cover generously with flaked coconut. Position head on one end of the caterpillar body, tipping face slightly upward.

Caterpillar eyes: Place gum ball on cutting board. With a very sharp knife, carefully slice gum ball exactly in half. Position eyes, rounded sides out, on head. Use toothpicks to secure if necessary.

Caterpillar "ruff": With scissors, snip long edges of marshmallows into triangular "petal" shapes. Tuck a row of these marshmallows "petals" between head and body to form a ruff.

Caterpillar feet: Position gummi orange or lemon slices, rounded sides up, about 4" apart along both sides of caterpillar body.

To finish: Sprinkle a row of party sprinkles along top of caterpillar. Parade a row of birthday candles down the caterpillar's back.

Serve within several hours of preparing.
Refrigerate leftovers. Makes 18 to 20 servings.

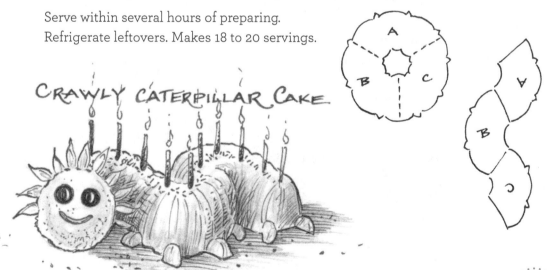

CRAWLY CATERPILLAR CAKE

Mocha-Almond Birthday Present Cake

{ *This could be named "A Birthday Present for Your Best-est Friend".*
Wrapped in a ribbon, topped with roses, it's a gift in itself. · This outsized
cake can serve a party of 18. It's best to make the cake less than 12 hours
before serving, but part of the filling can be done 2 days ahead of time.
· I think mocha is one of the most inspired flavors invented, but some
of my sisters consider all coffee inedible, no matter how it's dressed. If
your best-est friend happens to be of this mind, omit coffee in cake and
frosting and call it "Fudge-Almond Birthday Present Cake". }

Cake:
- 3 3/4 cups brown rice flour
- 3/4 cup cornstarch
- 1 1/2 cup evaporated cane juice
- 3/4 cup unsweetened baking cocoa
- 1 tablespoon baking soda
- 1 1/2 teaspoon salt
- 1 teaspoon xanthan gum
- 4 1/2 cups water, or as needed
- 1 cup oil
- 1/2 cup unsweetened applesauce
- 4 teaspoons vanilla
- 2 tablespoons cider vinegar
- 3 tablespoons instant coffee granules

Almond Filling:
- 2/3 cup evaporated cane juice
- 1/2 cup water
- 3/4 cup butter, very soft
- 1/2 teaspoon vanilla extract

Continued

pinch salt
1 1/4 cups ground almonds

Mocha Fudge Frosting:
1 1/2 cups cream cheese or Tofutti Better Than Cream Cheese
1 tablespoon water
2 tablespoons instant coffee granules
1 cup evaporated cane juice
1/2 teaspoon vanilla extract
8 ounces unsweetened chocolate, finely chopped

For decoration, optional:
2 (12") lengths of ribbon at least 1" wide
roses, pansies, or other fresh flowers

For cake: Preheat oven to 350°. Grease three 8"x8" square baking pans. Sprinkle a little rice flour in each pan, then shake to coat bottom and sides.

In a very large mixing bowl, combine brown rice flour, cornstarch, evaporated cane juice, cocoa, baking soda, salt, and xanthan gum. Make a well and add water, oil, applesauce, vanilla, vinegar, and instant coffee. Stir until smooth. Check consistency. You should be able to pour batter from the bowl in a medium-thin stream. Add up to 1 cup more water if needed.

Pour batter into prepared pans. Bake 35 to 40 minutes until cake tests done in centers and pulls away from edges of pan. Cool on wire racks 15 minutes, then invert and cool completely on racks. Assemble and serve cake within 12 hours for very best consistency.

To make filling: Stir together water and evaporated cane juice in a small saucepan. Bring to a boil over high heat and boil rapidly 3 minutes. Remove from heat and cool. Cover and store up to 24 hours if needed.

Continued

To finish filling, combine cooled syrup with butter, vanilla, and salt and beat until very fluffy. Stir in ground almonds.

To assemble and fill cake: Transfer one cake layer to serving plate, and spread half the filling on top to within 1/2" of cake edges. Top with second layer. Spread remaining filling, then add third layer.

To make frosting: Have cake ready for frosting. In a medium saucepan, stir together cream cheese or Better Than Cream Cheese, water, coffee, evaporated cane juice, and vanilla. Bring to a boil over medium heat, stirring constantly. Remove from heat. Add chocolate. Stir until chocolate is melted. As soon as frosting is thick enough to spread, generously frost top and sides of cake. If frosting thickens too much to spread, add hot water, a few drops at a time, to thin slightly. If you prefer a smooth surface, dip knife in hot water as you spread.

Allow icing to harden. To decorate, lay the two lengths of ribbon crossed over center top of cake. Bring one end of ribbon down each side of cake, and tuck excess under cake with a butter knife. Just before serving, place short-stemmed bouquet of flowers in center top of cake. If desired, tuck two ribbon pieces under bouquet like the tag ends of a bow.
Makes (18) 1" slice servings.

Orange Sauce

A drizzle of this sauce will lift cakes to new heights. A dense, spicy cake or a fruited coffee cake will be especially happy recipients.

2 cups fresh orange juice
2 teaspoons fresh lemon juice
1/4 to 1/2 cup sweetener of choice
2 1/2 tablespoons perma-flo or cornstarch
1 tablespoon cold butter

Whisk together orange juice, lemon juice, sweetener and perma-flo or cornstarch in a medium saucepan. Heat over medium-high heat, whisking constantly, until mixture boils. Boil 30 seconds. Remove from heat and whisk in cold butter. Serve over cake slices.

Posh Chocolate Glaze

{ Keep a jar of this glaze in the refrigerator and make it your new best trick. Spread over cake, drizzle over shortbread fingers or brownie squares, and dessert is served. · It will thicken once chilled. Just heat a spoonful in a metal measuring cup until it reaches drizzling consistency. Too thin? Pop it in the freezer for a few minutes. }

6 ounces bittersweet or semisweet chocolate
1 tablespoon butter
1/2 teaspoon vanilla extract
pinch of salt
1/4 cup cream, milk, milk substitute or Sour Supreme

Place chocolate, butter, vanilla, and salt in blender or food processor.

In a small saucepan, heat cream or substitute over medium heat until simmering, stirring often to prevent scorching.

Pour hot liquid over mixture in blender or food processor and process until melted. Check consistency: it should be the texture of a medium-thick glaze. If it's too thick, add a bit more of the liquid. If it's too thin, chill 15 minutes, then blend again.

Drizzle, pour, or spread over cake, cookies or desserts.

Cinnamon-Nut Glaze

{ This thinly-spread, rich glaze is shiny and sweet. It's perfect for apple cakes. · To date it has cooperated beautifully with any sweetener I've tried. }

1/2 cup butter
1/2 cup chopped walnuts or pecans
1 teaspoon ground cinnamon
1/2 cup sweetener of choice
1 tablespoon water

Melt butter in a small saucepan. Add nuts and simmer 2 to 3 minutes, or until nuts are toasted, but not burned. Add cinnamon, sweetener, and water. Stir until smooth, bring to a boil, and boil 1 minute.

Remove from heat and spread or drizzle over warm cake. Makes enough to glaze one 9"x13" cake.

Orange Glaze

{ *Here's a simple glaze that's citrusy, perky and sweet.* }

1/3 cup evaporated cane juice
1/4 cup orange juice concentrate, undiluted
1 tablespoon butter
1 teaspoon orange peel

Stir all ingredients together in a small saucepan. Bring to a boil over high heat, reduce heat and cook 3 minutes, stirring often. Remove from heat and allow to cool 10 minutes. Drizzle, brush or spread thinly on cooled cake, cookies or bars.

Broiled Icing For Cakes

{ *Broiled icing is an old cake trick. Grandma Kennell often spread it on birthday cakes. It's a cousin to German chocolate cake icing. The difference? Broiled icing is (can you guess?) broiled, and the sugar- and butter-coated coconut toasts to a dreamy crunch. · Broiled icing can be used on almost any cake, but it's a natural on chocolate cake.* }

> 1/4 cup milk or milk substitute
> 1/2 cup evaporated cane juice
> 1/4 cup butter
> pinch of salt
> 2 cups unsweetened coconut
> 1/2 teaspoon vanilla
> 1/2 cup chopped pecans, optional

In a medium saucepan, over high heat, bring the milk or milk substitute, evaporated cane juice, salt, and butter to a boil, stirring constantly. Reduce heat and cook 3 minutes.

Remove from heat. Add coconut, vanilla, and pecans, if desired. Stir well, and spread evenly on cake. Broil, watching carefully, for 5 minutes. Rotate pan if necessary to brown evenly. Cool before serving. Makes enough to cover one 9"x13" cake.

Silky Chocolate Frosting

{ This smooth frosting cooks up quickly, and goes on the cake fast. It's especially tasty on chocolate cake. }

1 cup water
1/3 cup sweetener of choice
3 tablespoons cornstarch
1/4 cup unsweetened baking cocoa
1 teaspoon vanilla extract
1/4 cup butter, softened

In a small saucepan, combine water, sweetener, cornstarch, and cocoa. Whisk until smooth. Bring to a boil over high heat, whisking constantly, until thickened and bubbly.

Remove mixture from heat. Add vanilla and butter, beating until butter is fully incorporated. Spread immediately over cooled cake. Makes enough to cover one 9"x13" cake.

Fluffy Filling & Frosting

{ *This all-purpose filling and frosting is like pseudo whipped cream, and almost as useful. It's rich, holds its shape, and adapts from piping to combining with other elements to make dressy desserts. · Since it's emulsified, this recipe can be tricky on cold days. Be sure your butter is as soft as possible, and that the cooked mixture is cooled but not chilled. If it doesn't come together in a thick, creamy mixture after 5 minutes of beating, try this: melt two additional tablespoons butter and add it, hot, to the beating mixture. This rescues erring frosting every time.* }

> **1 cup milk or milk substitute**
> **3 tablespoons cornstarch**
> **pinch salt**
> **1 cup butter, at room temperature**
> **1/2 cup sweetener of choice**
> **2 teaspoons vanilla extract**

In a small saucepan, combine milk or milk substitute and cornstarch, whisking well to combine. Bring to a boil over medium-high heat, whisking constantly, until mixture is thickened and bubbly. Remove from heat and cool completely. Do not chill.

In a mixer bowl, combine cooled mixture, salt, butter, sweetener, and vanilla. Beat on high speed 5 minutes. Check consistency: frosting should be completely creamy and very fluffy. Beat longer if necessary. Makes enough to cover one 9"x13" cake. Refrigerate leftovers.

Pineapple-Nut Frosting

{ I missed the usual cloak of cream cheese frosting on carrot or pineapple cakes. One day I was tinkering and came up with this new take—not exactly the same, but an acceptable frosting in itself. It can clothe not only carrot, but any other cake as well. }

1 (12 ounce) can crushed pineapple (in its own juice)
1/3 cup sweetener of choice
1 tablespoon lemon juice
4 teaspoons cornstarch
1/2 cup sour cream or Sour Supreme
1/2 cup chopped walnuts or pecans

Drain pineapple well, reserving juice. Combine juice, sweetener, lemon juice, and cornstarch in a small saucepan. Whisk until smooth. Bring to a boil over high heat, whisking constantly, until thickened and bubbly. Remove from heat. Cool completely.

Fold drained pineapple, sour cream or Sour Supreme and nuts into cooled mixture. Spread generously onto cooled cake. Makes enough to cover one 9"x13" cake. Store leftover cake chilled.

A Spoonful of Fellowship
{Puddings, Cobblers and Other Spoon Desserts}

Tiramisu with Raspberries

Our favorite foods connect us

WITH OTHER TIMES AND SPECIAL PEOPLE...

whose presence made them so pleasurable:

the grandmother whose Sunday supper gathered the clan,

the father who carefully loaded a spoon and blew on it gently,

until it was just cool enough to eat.

–Unknown

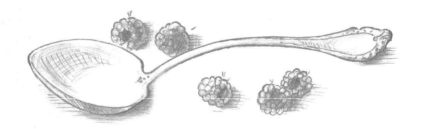

chapter nine

A Spoonful of Fellowship
{Puddings, Cobblers and Other Spoon Desserts}

Recently I met the term "spoon desserts", and liked it. It brings harmony to an otherwise miscellaneous bunch, agreed only on what they are not: cakes, cookies, or pies. They're as dressy as tiramisu for a women's tea and as simple as tapioca for a farmer's supper. They're light, frosty sherbet and warming Indian Pudding. They're layered puddings in trifle bowls and simple boiled custards adorned or unadorned. It's a collection of desserts as hodgepodge as a fellowship meal, united because you eat them with a spoon.

Likely you'll see spoon desserts at any church fellowship meal across the nation. Fellowship meals, otherwise known as potlucks, basket dinners, church suppers, and carry-ins, are an old tradition. This spreading of cloths and laying out of good things began with the earliest settlers, who traveled far to hear the occasional circuit-preacher. A hefty meal under trees plus several hours of "catching up" between far-flung neighbors sustained them on the long drive home in time to milk the cow.

America has changed in many ways, but basket dinners are still with us. Nowhere are they more alive and flourishing than in our Mennonite communities. They're still a custom when a visiting minister holds a series of meetings, but they don't stop there. We bring full baskets and lay out potlucks after baptisms, communion services, or Sundays after weddings.

I love these dinners. Maybe it sounds strange for a gluten-intolerant to say so. For most celiacs, a potluck is a minefield—you either choose carefully between least-suspicious dishes, or forgo them and eat your own contribution. Maybe, as a foodie, just seeing the slow cookers, nine-by-thirteens, and Tupperwares full of beautiful things is as satisfying as eating for me. But mostly, I think, it's the Little White Tags.

Our ladies are gracious about making and marking gluten-free edibles. Sometimes these tags perch like butterflies all down the table. My nephews keep a sharp lookout for them.

"Look, it's gluten-free!" they chortle, and proceed to heap their plates.

"Save a little for the rest of us!" their mom might chide… but for me, watching their blissful smiles is a feast itself.

These little labels spell love. They also convince me that labeling everything you serve to allergic guests is a very good thing. Non-cooks, who can only guess, and tiny tots, who must ask the closest adult, "Does this have wheat in it?" get their questions answered at the serving line.

Food is so sharing. It's no wonder Jesus asked us to feed the hungry, to bless with bread. This caring can go many ways—a meal to the bereaved in "the valley of the shadow", a basket of fruit for those tired of hospital fare, and maybe, too, handing a celiac child a gluten-free cookie.

"Food is fellowship!" my Romanian friend, once hungrier than most of us ever were, agrees. She's as much a foodie as I am. "We're coming over—" I told her over the phone when she was sick. "Now don't bother—no food, nothing. We just ate lunch. We're absolutely fine. We'll just sing… pray… then come home for supper."

"Just a *little* fruit?" she begged. We went to find the table spread with fruit, yes, and many other things. She'd asked a friend to bring food over for us! But I couldn't scold her as I viewed the beautiful array. I understand foodies too well.

Yes, I love fellowship meals. It's a delight to sit, plate full, and eat among friends. The weekday carpenters and farmers, housewives and schoolteachers feast in one harmonious bunch, focusing on things that unite, not vocations, traits or personalities as opposite as the Poles. Our souls fed, and bodies warmed by good comfort food, we compare tastes, beg recipes, share God's goodness of the past week. Really, fellowship meals are aptly named. And among the pies, cakes and cookies on the table, "spoon desserts" are there, holding their own, often the first to disappear.

How can a pudding, a unity of a few simple ingredients, satisfy and comfort so completely? Why does a warm cobbler on a frigid night warm us to the toes? How can the homely baked apple, roasted to an earthly brown, look so elegant on a china plate? Questions that will remain mysteries, perhaps, but we can enjoy these mysteries by the bite, each one lingering on the tongue as only a "spoon dessert" can. ♪

Spoon Secrets

·A layered, creamy sweet is a worry-free way to serve a dessert at a dinner party. Cut in squares, portion on plates, hand them all around and the dessert is served.

·A creamy dessert precludes the need to serve ice cream. This is especially nice if there are any sensitive to dairy at the table.

·With shortbread or other cookies, simple fruit tapiocas and puddings make elegant "ladies' luncheon" desserts. Serve them frosty cold in chilled sherbet glasses. ♪

Classic Vanilla Pudding

{ *Hot from the pan or chilled for an hour, pudding is comfort food. · Learning to make pudding dairy- and egg-free was a drawn-out lesson. I tried rice milk, but no sooner had the pudding thickened than it would thin again. Thoroughly frustrated, I finally read that protein has a part to play in the consistency of puddings. Rice milk is considerably lower in protein than milk... but would soy milk work? It did. It thickened as well as milk. But I don't use soy milk regularly, and I couldn't get around the bean-y flavor, perhaps exaggerated by heating. So I tried almond milk, and it thickened with a lovely, creamy flavor. Pudding is back. · Lecithin replaces egg in this recipe. If you prefer, omit lecithin, use only two tablespoons cornstarch, and add one beaten egg with the shaken ingredients.* }

1 cup milk, soy milk or almond milk (do not use rice milk), divided
2 1/2 tablespoons cornstarch
pinch salt
1/4 teaspoon liquid lecithin
2 tablespoons sweetener of choice, or more to taste
1 tablespoon cold butter, optional
1 teaspoon vanilla extract

In a small saucepan, heat 3/4 cup milk to the simmering point.

In a small bowl or shaker, combine remaining 1/4 cup milk, cornstarch, salt, and lecithin. Pour in a thin stream into simmering milk, whisking constantly, until thickened. Boil 30 seconds. Remove from heat.

Add sweetener, butter (if using), and vanilla to pudding. Stir to incorporate. Serve warm or chilled. Makes 2 servings.

Classic Chocolate Pudding

{ How did we survive without this classic? Well, never mind, it's back again. · For over-the-top richness, I sometimes stir semisweet chocolate into the warm pudding. }

1 cup milk, soy milk or almond milk (do not use rice milk), divided
2 tablespoons cornstarch
1 1/2 tablespoons unsweetened baking cocoa
pinch salt
1/4 teaspoon liquid lecithin, optional
3 tablespoons sweetener of choice
1 tablespoon cold butter, optional
1/2 teaspoon vanilla extract

In a small saucepan, place 3/4 cup of the milk, soy milk or almond milk. Heat over medium heat until milk just begins to simmer.

Meanwhile, combine remaining 1/4 cup of the milk or substitute, cornstarch, cocoa, salt, and lecithin, if using. Mix very well until mixture is completely smooth. Stir into hot milk in a thin stream, whisking constantly, until pudding is thickened and bubbly. Remove from heat and add sweetener, butter, and vanilla. Stir until butter is fully incorporated. Serve pudding warm, or cover and refrigerate until deeply chilled. Makes 2 servings.

Indian Pudding

Back in my school days, I wondered what hasty pudding was—the kettle of something pioneer mothers always seemed to be cooking. I was glad to grow up and find out what it is, and better yet, that it can be made without eggs and milk quite successfully. This version of hasty pudding is spiced and sweetened with earthy molasses. It's simple and satisfying.

3 cups milk, soy milk or almond milk
1/3 cup yellow cornmeal
1/2 cup baking molasses
1/2 teaspoon salt
1 teaspoon ground cinnamon
1 teaspoon ground ginger
2 tablespoons butter

Preheat oven to 300°. Grease 1 quart casserole or 9"x13" baking pan.

Place milk in a heavy-bottomed saucepan. Whisk in cornmeal, molasses, salt, cinnamon, and ginger. Heat over medium heat, whisking occasionally, until mixture boils. Add butter and whisk until melted.

Turn pudding into prepared casserole or pan. Bake pudding 1 hour or until set and browned. Serve warm or chilled. Makes 6 to 7 servings.

Layered Date Pudding

{ *This is a version of English baked puddings, piled in a bowl in trifle-like layers oozing with caramel-y sauce. It's a classic Mennonite dessert, often served to Sunday dinner guests.* }

8 ounces pitted whole dates
1 cup boiling water
1 teaspoon baking soda
2 tablespoons butter
3/4 cup evaporated cane juice
1/2 teaspoon salt
1 teaspoon xanthan gum
1 1/2 cups brown rice flour
1/2 cup chopped walnuts, optional

Sauce:
2/3 cup evaporated cane juice
2/3 cup water
1 tablespoon cornstarch
1 teaspoon vanilla
1 tablespoon butter
pinch of salt
whipped cream or non-dairy whipped topping, optional

Preheat oven to 350°. Grease 9"x9" baking pan.

Snip dates with scissors into a large bowl. Add boiling water and baking soda. Add butter. Cool mixture to lukewarm, then add evaporated cane juice, xanthan gum, salt, and flour. Beat well. Fold in walnuts, if using. Spread mixture into prepared pan.

Bake 30 to 45 minutes, or until browned and crusty. Cool. Cut into small cubes.

Continued

For sauce, stir together evaporated cane juice, water, cornstarch, and salt in a small saucepan. Bring to a boil, stirring, and boil 2 minutes. Add vanilla and butter. Cool.

In a 2 quart serving bowl, layer half the cake cubes, half the sauce, and a layer of cream or topping, if using. Repeat with cake and sauce, ending with a generous dollop of cream, if using. Chill before serving. Makes 8 to 10 servings.

Aloha Pudding

{ *Pick yourself a red posy and sit down to watch the sunset with a bowl of this coconut-y dessert. Its shining gift is the crunch of toasted coconut and almonds against velvety pudding.* }

1 cup unsweetened flaked coconut
1/4 cup evaporated cane juice
1 cup brown rice flour
1 teaspoon xanthan gum
1/2 cup sliced almonds
1/2 cup butter, melted
3 recipes Classic Vanilla Pudding (see index), chilled
1/2 teaspoon coconut extract

Stir together coconut, evaporated cane juice, brown rice flour, xanthan gum, almonds and butter in a large bowl until crumbly. Spread in a 10"x15" baking pan and bake at 350° for 25 minutes, stirring every 5 minutes to toast evenly. Allow to cool. Crumbs may be stored airtight up to 2 days, or frozen several months.

Stir coconut extract into the chilled pudding until thoroughly combined.

In a 1 quart glass serving bowl, layer one-third of the crumbs, half the pudding, one-third of the crumbs and the rest of the pudding. End with the remaining crumbs. Chill well before serving. Makes 8 servings.

Apple Tapioca

{ Simple, yet full-flavored, apple tapioca is at home in earthen bowls or footed crystal. }

6 cups sliced, cored and peeled apples
1/3 cup minute tapioca
1/3 cup sweetener, more or less to taste
1/4 teaspoon salt
1 tablespoon fresh lemon juice
1 cup water
2 tablespoons butter

Stir together apples, tapioca, sweetener, salt, lemon juice, and water in large saucepan with tight-fitting lid. Bring to a boil over medium-high heat, stirring. Reduce heat, cover and simmer slowly 15 to 20 minutes. Remove from heat and drop in butter. Allow to cool slightly before stirring. Serve warm or chilled. Makes 8 servings.

Rhubarb-Blueberry Tapioca

*{ Tart rhubarb plays up mild blueberries in this quick dessert. Its homey-
ness makes it a good everyday (and maybe every-single-day) dessert. }*

4 cups sliced rhubarb, fresh or frozen
2 cups blueberries, fresh or frozen
1/2 to 3/4 cup sweetener of choice
2 tablespoons minute tapioca

In a medium saucepan with tight-fitting lid, place rhubarb and blueberries. Do not add water. Cover tightly and place over medium-low heat.

Bring mixture to a boil, increasing heat as juice is extracted from fruit. Add sweetener, and simmer mixture until rhubarb is soft, about 5 minutes.

Add tapioca. Cover and continue to cook over low heat until tapioca is clear, about 5 more minutes. Remove from heat and chill before serving. Makes 8 to 10 servings.

Strawberry Danish Dessert

{ This is "home food"—a revision of Mom's classic dessert she stirred up for company and basket dinners. · "I like the strawberries," said a little visiting friend. "I like the pink sauce," I said and together we quite literally slurped the bowl clean. · If you use partially frozen strawberries, it's a very quick dessert. }

1 tablespoon unflavored gelatin
3 1/2 cups water, divided
6 oz. red 100% raspberry-white grape juice concentrate
1/3 cup sweetener of choice, or stevia to taste
1/2 cup perma-flo or cornstarch
1 quart sliced strawberries, fresh or frozen, slightly thawed if frozen

In a small bowl, sprinkle gelatin over 1/2 cup of the water. Allow to rest 5 minutes.

In a large saucepan, stir together 2 1/2 cups of the water, juice concentrate, and sweetener. Bring to a boil. Combine remaining 1/2 cup water with perma-flo or cornstarch until smooth. Stir into boiling mixture, and bring back to a boil, whisking until smooth and bubbly. Remove from heat.

Add gelatin mixture and stir to dissolve. Add strawberries, and pour into serving bowl. Chill until set. Makes 10 servings.

Tiramisu With Raspberries

{ *Coffee, chocolate, cream. All topped with crimson raspberries.* }

1 recipe Rich Butter Cake (see index), baked and cooled
3 recipes Classic Vanilla Pudding (see index), chilled
1 cup Sour Supreme
2/3 cup strong brewed coffee, cooled
2 ounces unsweetened or bittersweet chocolate, grated
2 cups fresh raspberries
whipped cream or non-dairy whipped topping, optional

Cut cake in half. Reserve one half for another use. Crumble remaining cake.

Fold Sour Supreme into pudding.

In a trifle bowl or other deep glass bowl, layer half of cake; drizzle with half the coffee. Layer half the pudding mixture over cake, and sprinkle with half the grated chocolate. Repeat cake, coffee, pudding, and chocolate layers. Top with a large dollop of whipped cream or topping, if desired. Sprinkle with raspberries. Chill at least 2 hours before serving. Makes approximately 10 servings.

Baked Caramel Apple Pudding

{ *Here's homey goodness for a late-autumn night. Served with cream, milk, or milk substitute, it can be supper by itself.* }

1/2 cup butter
2 cups brown rice flour
2/3 cup evaporated cane juice
1 teaspoon xanthan gum
1/2 teaspoon salt
1 1/2 teaspoon baking powder
1 teaspoon baking soda
1 cup milk or milk substitute
2 tablespoons apple cider vinegar
4 cups apples, cored and chopped, unpeeled

Topping:
1/2 cup chopped walnuts or pecans
3/4 cup evaporated cane juice, divided
1 3/4 cup water
2 tablespoons butter

Preheat oven to 350°. Place butter in a 9"x13" baking pan and place in oven to melt.

In a large bowl, stir together brown rice flour, evaporated cane juice, xanthan gum, salt, baking powder, and baking soda. Add melted butter, milk or substitute, and vinegar, stirring well. Add apples. Spread in the baking pan.

Topping: Sprinkle walnuts or pecans and 1/4 cup evaporated cane juice over batter in pan. In a small saucepan, stir together the remaining 1/2 cup evaporated cane juice, water, and butter. Heat over high heat until mixture boils. Remove from heat and pour over batter. Do not stir.

Continued

Bake 35 to 45 minutes until browned and bubbly, and cake springs back in center when touched. Serve warm. Makes 10 to 12 servings.

Boston Cream Pie

{ *This was Mom's favorite girlhood dessert, so I recreated it for her birthday, gluten-free. · Mom's birthday is in March, before wildflowers are blooming, but I think I'll make this creamy dessert again in late spring. The ganache-like chocolate top would be a perfect field for displaying a circlet of purple violets.* }

1 recipe Rich Butter Cake batter (see index)
2 recipes Classic Vanilla Pudding (see index), chilled
1 recipe Posh Chocolate Glaze (see index)

Preheat oven to 350°. Pour cake batter into greased 10" round baking pan. Bake cake 45 to 50 minutes or until cake is springy in center and nicely browned. Cool cake 10 minutes, then remove pan. Assemble and serve dessert within several hours.

To assemble: Place cake on cake plate or cake stand. Split cake horizontally into 2 layers with a long serrated knife.

Spread chilled pudding on first layer. Replace top layer.

Warm or chill glaze to obtain a thick glazing consistency. Pour chocolate glaze over cake until top of cake is covered and glaze begins to drip down sides. Allow to set a few minutes. Serve. Makes 12 servings.

Brownie Pie

{ My oldest sister used to have a children's cookbook, and we pored over the recipes. Brownie Pie was one of them. I couldn't believe how wonderful it tasted. I liked best the rich syrup the "pie" created as it baked. · Warm, served with milk or milk substitute, it's both an everyday and company dessert. }

1/4 cup butter
1 1/2 cups brown rice flour
1 cup evaporated cane juice, divided
1 tablespoon baking powder
1/2 teaspoon salt
1/2 teaspoon xanthan gum
2/3 cup unsweetened baking cocoa, divided
1 teaspoon vanilla extract
1 1/4 cups water, for batter, or as needed
2 1/2 cups water, for pouring over all

Preheat oven to 325°. Place butter in 9"x13" baking pan, place in oven, and allow butter to melt, about 5 minutes.

Meanwhile, in a medium mixing bowl, stir together brown rice flour, 1/2 cup of the evaporated cane juice, baking powder, salt, xanthan gum, and 1/3 cup of the cocoa. Add the melted butter, vanilla, and about 1 1/4 cups water. Stir just to combine. Check consistency. Batter should be thick but easy to stir. Add more water if necessary, but do not overmix.

In a small bowl, stir together remaining 1/2 cup evaporated cane juice and 1/3 cup cocoa.

Spread batter into butter-lined pan. Sprinkle cocoa/evaporated cane juice mixture on batter. Pour the 2 1/2 cups water over all. Do not stir.

Bake dessert 35 to 45 minutes until cake tests done, and syrup is bubbly. Serve warm with milk, milk substitute, or ice cream. Makes about 8 servings.

Winter Peach Cobbler

{ When blizzards howl and the mercury drops, this cobbler will warm you. · You can use any canned fruit in this recipe, but I give the peach version because it's especially satisfying. }

> **1/4 cup butter**
> **1 cup brown rice flour**
> **1 tablespoon baking powder**
> **1/2 teaspoon xanthan gum**
> **1/3 cup sweetener of choice**
> **1/4 teaspoon salt**
> **1/2 cup milk, milk substitute or water, or more as needed**
> **1 quart canned peaches, with juice**
> **evaporated cane juice for sprinkling**

Preheat oven to 350°.

Place butter in 9"x13" baking pan. Place in oven to melt, about 5 minutes.

In medium mixing bowl, stir together brown rice flour, baking powder, xanthan gum, sweetener, and salt. Remove butter from oven and pour half over dry ingredients. Reserve remaining butter in pan. Add milk or substitute to dry ingredients and mix until combined. Consistency should be fairly stiff but soft enough to spoon easily into pan. Add more liquid to batter as needed, up to 1/4 cup more.

Turn batter into butter-lined pan. Sprinkle with evaporated cane juice. Pour the peaches with juice over all. Do not stir. Bake 35 to 45 minutes or until browned, bubbly and cobbler tests done in center. Serve warm with milk or milk substitute. Makes 6 to 8 servings.

Black & Blue Berry Cobbler

{ On an August afternoon, the scent of cobbler in the oven is pure richness. · I like the flavor of this berry combination. You can substitute any berry or berries at whim. Simply adjust lemon and sweetener to suit the tartness or sweetness of the fruit. }

1 pint blackberries, fresh or frozen
1 pint blueberries, fresh or frozen
3/4 cup water, divided
1/2 cup sweetener of choice
2 teaspoons lemon juice
1/4 cup perma-flo or cornstarch
1 recipe Rich Butter Cake batter (see index)
evaporated cane juice for sprinkling

Preheat oven to 350°.

In a large saucepan, place blackberries, blueberries, 1/2 cup of the water, sweetener, and lemon juice. Bring to a boil over medium-high heat.

In a small bowl or shaker, stir perma-flo or cornstarch with remaining 1/4 cup water until no lumps remain. Pour into boiling berries in a slow stream while stirring rapidly. Cook until thick and bubbly. Pour into 9"x13" pan.

Pour Rich Butter Cake batter over berries. Sprinkle with evaporated cane juice. Bake 40 to 50 minutes or until browned and bubbly.

Strawberries & Cream Dessert

{ First a crust, then a creamy layer, then glazed fresh strawberries—this is celebration dessert. Serve it deeply chilled in very small squares. }

1 recipe Shortbread Crust for Desserts (see index), baked in 9"x13" baking pan and cooled

1 recipe Fluffy Filling and Frosting (see index)

1/4 cup water

1 tablespoon unflavored gelatin

6 cups sliced fresh strawberries

1 recipe Strawberry Glaze (see index)

Chill crust. For filling, sprinkle gelatin over water in a small saucepan. Allow to soak 5 minutes. Heat gently to dissolve, then cool completely. Beat into Fluffy Filling.

Spread filling over crust. Slice strawberries over filling. Drizzle Strawberry Glaze generously over berries. Cover dessert with plastic wrap and chill until serving, up to 6 hours. Makes 20 servings.

Blueberry & Lemon Dessert

{ *This is* almost *cheesecake. It's rich—serve in teeny squares, well chilled.* }

Crust:

1 recipe Shortbread Crust for Desserts (see index), baked in 8"x11" glass baking pan and cooled

Filling:

1 recipe Fluffy Filling and Frosting (see index)
1 tablespoon unflavored gelatin
1/4 cup water
1 teaspoon vanilla extract
2 teaspoons lemon extract

Topping:

1 recipe filling from Fresh Blueberry Pie recipe (see index)

Chill shortbread crust. Prepare Fluffy Filling and Frosting as directed. Prepare Fresh Blueberry Pie filling. Chill filling until needed.

In a saucepan, combine water and gelatin. Allow to soak 5 minutes, then heat gently until dissolved. Cool. Beat into Fluffy Filling and Frosting. Add vanilla and lemon extract. Spread carefully over chilled crust. Top with pie filling.

Chill 2 to 4 hours, or until chilled deeply. Makes 24 servings.

Stained-Glass Window Dessert

{ *We reinvented this chilled dessert for a summer picnic under a maple tree. The jewel-tone gelatins look like panes of colored glass.* }

4 cups water, divided
6 tablespoons unflavored plain gelatin, divided
6 ounces 100% red juice concentrate
12 ounces 100% light juice concentrate
2 cups pineapple juice
1 cup sweetener of choice
1/2 cup cornstarch
2 tablespoons lemon juice
2 cups crushed pineapple, well-drained
1 1/2 cups sour cream or Sour Supreme
1 recipe Shortbread Crust for Desserts (see index), baked in 9"x13" pan and cooled

Make gelatin cubes: In two small saucepans, combine 1 cup water and 1 1/2 tablespoons gelatin in each. Allow to rest 5 minutes. Heat each gently, stirring, just to dissolve. To one pan add the 6 ounces red juice concentrate, to the other pan add 6 ounces (or half, about 3/4 cup) of the light juice concentrate. Pour each into greased 9" square pan to make two pans of gelatin. Chill until well set, about 2 hours.

Make filling: In a medium saucepan, place remaining 2 cups water and remaining 3 tablespoons gelatin. Add sweetener, lemon juice, pineapple juice, remaining 6 ounces of light juice concentrate, and cornstarch. Bring to a boil, whisking well until thick and bubbly. Cool. Add sour cream or substitute. Fold in pineapple.

Cut gelatin into 3/4" cubes. Fold lightly into filling. Spread over crust and chill several hours before serving. Makes 24 servings.

Fruit-and-Nut-Stuffed Baked Apples

{ *Here's a hearty baked apple crammed with good things. For special occasions, top each apple with whipped cream.* }

6 firm, sweet apples
1 cup walnuts
1/2 cup raisins
1/4 cup unsweetened flaked coconut
2 tablespoons pure maple syrup
1 teaspoon grated lemon zest
1/4 teaspoon ground cinnamon
1/4 teaspoon ground nutmeg, optional
1 tablespoon butter
1/2 teaspoon vanilla extract
1 1/2 cups apple cider

Preheat oven to 375°.

Core apples and peel upper third of each. Cut shallow craters around holes so apples hold more filling.

In a food processor or blender, place walnuts, raisins, and coconut. Process to a medium-fine consistency. Place mixture in a small bowl, then add syrup, zest and spices. Blend to combine.

Place apples in greased 8"x12" baking pan. Stuff apples tightly with nut mixture. Pour cider, butter and vanilla into pan around apples.

Bake, basting apples occasionally with pan liquids, for 45 minutes to 1 hour until apples are tender. Serve warm with pan juices and milk or milk substitute. Makes 6 servings.

Individual Berry Shortcakes

{ Is the queen dropping in for tea? Don't panic. Serve her warm shortcakes, buttered, and oozing with cream and berries. }

1 cup brown rice flour
1/3 cup cornstarch, tapioca starch or arrowroot starch
1/4 teaspoon salt
1/2 teaspoon xanthan gum
2 teaspoons baking powder
1/4 cup butter, slightly softened
1/3 cup milk, milk substitute or water, or more as needed
2 tablespoons honey
evaporated cane juice, for sprinkling
berries
Classic Vanilla Pudding (see index), chilled, or whipped cream

Preheat oven to 400°.

In a medium mixing bowl, combine brown rice flour, cornstarch, tapioca starch, or arrowroot starch, salt, xanthan gum, and baking powder. With pastry blender or fingers, cut butter into flour mixture until only pea-sized lumps of butter remain.

In a small bowl, stir together milk or substitute and honey. Drizzle over flour/butter mixture and stir with a few strokes until barely combined. Consistency should be fairly stiff but still very sticky. Add a little more liquid if needed.

Drop batter into mounds on baking sheet to make 6 to 8 individual shortcakes. Sprinkle with evaporated cane juice and bake 10 to 15 minutes or until browned and crusty. Cool. Serve while warm, split and filled with fresh berries and chilled vanilla pudding or whipped cream. Makes 6 to 8 servings.

Frosty Fruit Sherbet

{ This recipe is packed with memories. We sisters invented it one summer, and whipped it up for every possible occasion, from orchard tea parties to youth hymn sings on hot July nights. We made it sugar-free from the beginning, because Brother-in-law No. 1 (who was regularly appearing) is hypoglycemic, and we wanted him to enjoy bowls of this frosty dessert with the rest of us. · We used fructose, but most sweeteners perform well here. }

1 tablespoon unflavored gelatin
1 cup water
2 tablespoons lemon juice, or to taste
1/2 cup sweetener of choice, or to taste
3 cups milk or milk substitute
1 (12 ounce) can 100% juice concentrate of choice, undiluted
whole berries or fruit sauce for garnish, optional

In a saucepan, sprinkle gelatin over water. Allow to rest 5 minutes, then heat gently to dissolve. Add remaining ingredients, stirring well. Adjust lemon/sweetener ratio to suit your taste. Pour into a 9"x13" pan and place in freezer.

When sherbet is frozen several inches around edges, stir well. Return to freezer and freeze completely. If you like, beat mixture with a mixer to give it a creamier texture, and refreeze if necessary. Serve in sherbet glasses, garnished with berries or a fruit sauce if desired. Makes 10 to 12 servings.

Shortbread Crust for Desserts

{ This crust can be the springboard for many desserts. Try it in place of graham cracker, wafer or cookie crusts in your old favorites. · Any kind of nut works well here. Mix and match them with the filling, like almonds with cherry, macadamias with cheesecake, pecans with pumpkin. }

2 cups brown rice flour
1/2 cup ground pecans or almonds
1/4 cup evaporated cane juice
1/2 teaspoon xanthan gum
1 cup butter, melted
2 to 4 tablespoons water, as needed

Preheat oven to 350°.

In a large bowl, stir together brown rice flour, nuts, evaporated cane juice, and xanthan gum. Add butter, tossing to make a sandy texture.

Stir water into mixture just until dough holds together. Pat into one 9"x13" baking pan or two 8"x8" pans. Bake 15 minutes, or until crust(s) are slightly browned around edges and firm to the touch. Cool completely.

Strawberry Glaze

{ *This transparent red glaze is great on strawberry pie and beyond. It can be used in any dessert that needs something sweet and bright. Try it drizzled lightly on whole raspberries.* }

1 tablespoon unflavored gelatin
1 cup water, divided
1/2 cup red 100% juice concentrate, undiluted
2 tablespoons perma-flo or cornstarch
1/3 cup sweetener of choice

In a small bowl, sprinkle gelatin over 1/4 cup of the water. Allow to soak 5 minutes.

In a small saucepan, combine remaining water, juice concentrate, perma-flo or cornstarch and sweetener. Bring to a boil over medium-high heat, whisking constantly. Cook 1 minute.

Remove from heat and add soaked gelatin, whisking to dissolve. Chill glaze until syrupy before using. Refrigerate up to 1 week, heating gently to glaze consistency before using.

A Celiac's Pantry

The can-haves, the can't-haves, and the try-mes
to help you stock your shelves.

Agave Nectar   (ah-GAH-vee; ah-GAH-vay): see SWEETENERS

Amaranth Flour   (AM-ah-ranth): A gluten-free flour milled from the seeds of the amaranth plant. Amaranth was once considered a common weed (and looks it!), but is now recognized as the highest source of protein among plants. Use amaranth flour while fresh, and store cold; stale amaranth flour has a bitter aftertaste. Amaranth flour is a very moist flour; use with other flours for best texture. Just a tablespoon or two in a recipe will boost nutrition considerably.

Arrowroot Powder, Arrowroot Flour: An easily-digested gluten-free starch often used with other flours to lighten baked goods. It's also a thickener, and has about twice the thickening power of flour. Use conservatively or you'll have stringy-textured gravy.

Baking Powder: The little tin can of white leavening in almost every kitchen. Alas, in gluten-free baking, we must be suspicious even of old standbys! Baking powder is a blend of baking soda, an acid, and a binder and moisture absorber, which sometimes contains gluten. Find gluten-free baking powder in large grocery stores.

Barley, Barley Grits, Pearl Barley, Barley Flour: Though lower in gluten than wheat flour, all barley and barley products contain gluten.

Beans: Protein-rich legumes which have nourished mankind thousands of years. Even today, it's the primary source of protein in third world countries;

and in America, beans star in many regional dishes. You'll find homey Boston baked beans in the Northeast, *frijoles refritos* in the Southwest, pork and beans on the prairie, beans and cornbread in the deep South.

Beans are available to the cook several ways (listed from tastiest down): fresh, dried and canned. Fresh aren't readily available; we're privileged to grow our own, and let me tell you, the flavor is incredible. The work is also incredible—picking, shelling, canning. But winter comes, and we open jars of our fresh-canned beans; we peruse seed catalogs and exclaim over spotted Jacob's Cattle and black and white Calypso and golden Tiger's Eye, and we order seed for next year. Fresh-canned beans in gleaming Mason jars, ready at a cook's whim, is like gold in the house.

That said, fresh beans aren't practical for everyone (like if you live in an apartment or lack an iron back), but there's second best—and dried beans aren't to be disdained. Home cooked to a mashable texture with plenty of garlic, if they aren't king's food, they're close to queen's. Get to know beans, and you'll find beans have different personalities to fit different dishes. Here are my personal favorites: earthy *black beans* for refried beans; mealy *pinto beans* for chili (and anything beef and beany); firm-textured *pea beans* for baked beans; big *garbanzo beans* (cooked until very soft) for dips and hummus; and occasionally scarlet *kidney beans* for salads.

Are you buying canned beans? Some kinds are better than others. When you want firmer beans, for salads, in baked beans, and even with beef, they perform. Don't try to hand-mash them for refried beans or hummus—you may need a blender.

Bean Flours: Flours milled for legumes, usually *garbanzo, fava,* and sometimes *cranberry* beans. These nutritious flours are high in protein and produce soft, springy baked goods. When milling your own make the grind as fine as possible. Bean flours tend to taste beany; they're best combined with other flours; ¼ to ⅓ of the total flour measurement is the max. I especially like garbanzo bean flour in yeast breads. *Soy flour* is not for timid tummies.

Brown Rice Flour: Flour milled from unpolished rice. Brown rice flour is my cornerstone flour. It is pleasant-tasting, has a better texture than white rice flour, and works seamlessly into both savories and sweets. But I've learned not all brown rice flour is created equal. Home mills rarely grind it fine enough, and since the grind of rice flour drastically affects baked goods, I buy it. Again, not all flour is the same. Look for brown rice flour that is very finely ground. Here's a simple test: rub a pinch of flour between your fingers (you can do this carefully right through the bag). It should feel light and powdery, with almost no "grit". Brown rice flour can be expensive; to cut costs, we order 50-pound quantities from my sister's bulk food store. Their supplier is Dutch Valley Foods, which presently carries two grades: organic and regular. The organic tends to be gritty; the regular very fine. Because brown rice flour contains the bran, it's perishable. Keep it in the freezer.

Bran: The outer layer of grain kernels. Whole wheat and oats are a good source of bran, and removing them from your diet removes a lot of fiber. The traditional celiac diet of white rice flour and starches is very bran-deficient. Not good, because bran is high in calcium, phosphorus, B vitamins, and is known to prevent colon cancer. Now the good news; tablespoon for tablespoon, *rice bran* has four times more soluble fiber than oat bran. Increase your bran intake considerably by using brown rice flour instead of white. Boost it further by adding a few tablespoons of rice bran to each recipe. Rice bran is delicate, lightly sweet, and very tasty. Bob's Red Mill is good; check the freshness date before you buy, then store it in the freezer. Rice bran gets rancid quickly. I'd like to try *corn bran*, which is said to be high in insoluble fiber.

Brewer's Yeast: A non-leavening yeast often used as a flavoring or supplement. Many kinds of brewer's yeast contain gluten.

Brown Sugar: see SWEETENERS.

Buckwheat Flour: A flour milled from the seeds of the buckwheat plant. "Buckwheat" is a misnomer. It's neither wheat nor a grain; it's really a plant in the rhubarb family, and it's gluten-free. Dark buckwheat flour is made from roasted buckwheat groats; it has the distinctive flavor of old-fashioned buckwheat pancakes. You can't use much in baked goods before you can detect it. Light buckwheat flour is ground from unroasted groats; it's mild and nutty, and bakes beautifully. I recently spotted whole-grain buckwheat flour; I'd like to try it. Use buckwheat flour for up to 50% of total flour in baked goods (try half and half with brown rice flour). If you use more, the texture will become too moist.

Bulgur   (BULH-guhr): Steamed, dried, and crushed wheat; not gluten-free.

Butter: Every cook's best ingredient. Despite the marks against it (saturated fat; dairy), there's nothing like sweet, creamy butter in cookies and cakes, or spread on warm biscuits and scones. Here's a loophole: butter is low in lactose, some dairy-sensitive people can handle it better than other dairy products. Thankfully, most of my family is okay with it, and that's why you'll find real butter in these recipes. That said, there are lactose-intolerant people who can't have anything dairy, butter or otherwise, and so substitution is a must. I tried dairy-free substitutes in some key recipes in this cookbook (Rich Butter Cake, Basic Butter Pie Dough) and found *EarthBalance* works reasonably well (find EarthBalance Buttery Spread in bigger grocery stores). It seems to have the same ratio of fat to liquid as butter (80% fat to 20% liquid). Because of this, and the buttery flavor, I think it would perform well in most recipes. I've just discovered EarthBalance now offers a soy-free version. Don't substitute oil, palm oil, coconut oil, or lard for butter without adjustments in the fat/liquid ratio. All these oils are 100% fat (butter is 80%), and this can alter results. One more product to consider: *ghee*, traditional in Indian cooking. Ghee is butter with all liquids removed. Because of this, it's almost completely lactose-free. Again, since it's 100% fat, use less when substituting for butter. To make a form of ghee, melt butter, allow liquids to settle, then dip off the pure butterfat which rises to the top.

Buttermilk: A cultured, acidic dairy product, a favorite baking ingredient. If you can't handle lactose, try homemade buttermilk replacement when baking: 2 tablespoons cider vinegar plus milk substitute to equal 1 cup. Allow to stand five minutes before using—some milk substitutes, such as soy, thicken nicely; others don't, but are still usable). If you can handle yogurt, try it for a good buttermilk stand-in.

Cane Syrup: see SWEETENERS.

Caramel Color: An additive once suspected of gluten, now considered gluten-free.

Carob Powder: A powder ground from the dried pulp of the tropical carob tree. It has a sweet, roasted flavor, and is often substituted for chocolate. Carob is pleasant-tasting, but not exactly like chocolate. For those allergic to chocolate, however, carob is an easy-to-digest alternative.

Casein: Milk protein; sometimes found in cheese substitutes. Some people allergic to milk can't tolerate casein. Read labels carefully, even if something says "lactose-free".

Cassava Flour   (kuh-SAH-vuh): see TAPIOCA STARCH

Chickpea Flour: Another name for garbanzo bean flour; see BEAN FLOURS.

Chili Powder: A blend of spices including ground chiles, garlic powder, oregano, cumin, and occasionally monosodium glutamate (see MONOSODIUM GLUTAMATE OR MSG). If MSG bothers you, be a savvy label reader. MSG can lurk under "natural flavoring" in some brands of chili powder. Spice Islands makes a wonderful MSG-free chili powder. You can also make delicious chili powder by grinding dried and toasted chiles (try

New Mexico and ancho chiles). If you like a little more heat, add a judicious amount of jalepeno to the chili.

Chile Paste: A paste made of fava beans, chiles, wheat flour and garlic; a popular seasoning in Chinese restaurant cooking; not gluten-free.

Chocolate: Dried, roasted, fermented and ground beans of the tropical cacao tree. Chocolate has borne a lot of imitations, a bad name, and "healthier alternatives", and has emerged a "miracle food". Please let me tell you why: research shows minimally processed chocolate may contain the highest flavanol content of any edible on earth. Flavanol? It's an antioxidant good for many things. It's thought to be heart-healthy and help fight diabetes and high blood pressure. What's more, chocolate is a nourishing food, high in protein, iron, and copper. Where was chocolate hiding these good things all this time? Right in the midst of every melt-on-the-tongue mouthful.

Chocolate comes very sweet to very bitter, with many gradations between. Find a few choices in the baking section of grocery stores (staples like unsweetened baking chocolate and cocoa powder), but for a dazzling selection, look in the candy aisle. Milk chocolate, America's favorite, is mild and sweet, and often contains more milk than chocolate. Don't touch if sugar or dairy bother you. *Semisweet Chocolate* is darker, containing from 15% to 35% cacao. Most chocolate chips are semisweet. Dark Chocolate varies greatly in intensity, from 35% to 90% cacao. The higher the cacao content, the less sugar, dairy or soy additives chocolate contains. Dark chocolate's varying intensities is an enthusiast's testing grounds. Tasting chocolate is a great thing to do among friends. ("Can you handle 60%? Here, try a little 65%!")

As chocolate makers specialize, interesting chocolate/herb/spice/citrus/ coffee combinations are born. Coffee and chocolate are always winners. Orange and chocolate share a special affinity. Hazelnuts and chocolate are happy counterparts. I just tried a dark chocolate/sea salt combination. The harmony of smooth, bittersweet chocolate against little bursts of crunchy salt was incredible.

You can bake with one chocolate or a combination. More than one kind of chocolate in one recipe is *not* too much of a good thing. Unsweetened chocolate (which most chocolate aficionados can't eat out of hand) does wonderful things to a recipe. One square of this unadulterated cacao adds depth other chocolates can't give. It's less processed than other kinds of chocolate, and contains more flavanols.

Let's not forget baking cocoa, the humble ingredient that makes such chocolaty good things. There are two kinds you can buy: natural and Dutch-process. Dutch-process has been treated with alkali to reduce chocolate's acidity, and it is very rich, and full bodied. I use Dutched cocoa in my recipes.

Cider Vinegar: see VINEGAR

Citric Acid: A food additive once suspected of gluten; now considered gluten-free.

Citrus: Both the zest and juice of citrus fruits are used the world over in cooking and baking. In allergy-free baking, we find that removing some elements (egg, dairy) make the recipe more dependent for flavor on other elements. This is especially true of citrus. Whenever possible, buy fresh lemons, oranges or limes, and juice or zest them. Fresh lemon juice in recipes is almost incomparable to bottled. Both have the same acidity, but the bottled lacks the floral complexity of the fresh.

Don't bother with purchased dried zest. What is meant to be bursts of concentrated citrus demoralizes into flavorless UFOs. A citrus zester is a must-have; it removes the colored rind and leaves the bitter white skin behind.

Cheese: The protein and calcium-packed queen of the dairy world, often missed most by the dairy-sensitive. If you're only mildly intolerant to lactose, try aged or hard cheeses (such as aged Swiss, Parmesan, aged Cheddar). They contain less lactose than fresh, soft cheeses. For the rest, try cheese substitutes made from soy, almond or rice. They're not the same for out of hand eating, but are fine in toasted cheese sandwiches or casseroles.

Coconut: The fruit of the tropical coconut palm, high in fat, fiber, and minerals. If you have coconut trees in your backyard, then you know more about coconuts than most of us. End here! But for those of us thousands of miles from the equator, eating coconut isn't as simple. We can choose fresh coconuts (the best—and pricey!), sweetened shredded coconut (the easiest to find anywhere), or unsweetened shredded coconut (found in health food stores). Sweetened shredded coconut is a class apart; the texture isn't like fresh or dried. It's America's favorite coconut, and it comes out of the bag in moist, sugary curls—admittedly yummy for out-of-hand eating. Obviously, it doesn't fit in a low-sugar diet, so I buy unsweetened coconut. Unsweetened coconut isn't the snitching kind—you have to bake with it to make it palatable (the exception is coconut ribbons—wide shreds of unsweetened coconut that go nicely in trail mixes). Dried unsweetened coconut falls short of fresh coconut, but I've learned a few tricks. It's okay baked as is, but it really shines when toasted. Toasted coconut in shortbread is nothing less than harmonious. It tastes and looks lovely on fluffy desserts. And (a trick I learned one July in Costa Rica) enormous amounts of coconut in granola (about half and half with rolled grain) is a very good thing.

Coconut Oil: see FATS AND OILS

Coffee: The roasted beans of the tropical coffee plant. Coffee, America's get-folks-off-to-work morning beverage, has recently sprouted in a new direction with class. Those who didn't like it black are now devotees of lattes, macchiatos, and cappuccinos. In these Italian specialities, coffee's edge is muted by frothy milk and sweet syrups into full-flavored drinks.

Drinking coffee together is bonding—mankind has known that for a long time. Some of my happiest moments with friends have been spent knee to knee over steaming mochas. So if sugar and dairy have been ruled out of your life, it can leave you in the cold. Upper-end coffeehouses make dairy-free, sugar-free coffees—for a price. I enjoyed a peppermint mocha one snowy day which has lingered in my mind as the ideal of coffee. But these amazing cappuccinos and mochas put me in a quandary—every time I drive past a coffeehouse, the temptation is huge. I'd yield every time, if it weren't for the exorbitant prices. These prices have driven me to my own resources. How can I recreate a mocha, a latte?

Someday I want to own an espresso machine, and invite all my friends for cappuccinos. Meanwhile, I imitate (rather feebly) with my own substitutions. Non-dairy creamer is an option—until you look at the ingredients (which makes you wonder if you're reading Spanish by mistake!). So I went on a hunt and found Silk brand creamer made from soy. There are several flavors available, with ingredients that read like *Back to Eden* in comparison. I happily bought French Vanilla ("*I'm doing this for my cookbook!*" I justify) and brought it home and tasted it. The flavor was comparable, with slight beany overtones. It was less creamy, so I doubled the serving amount (I drink cappuccinos, not black coffee). I could definitely live with it. I've found, by the way, that agave nectar is a fine coffee sweetener.

Have you heard of coffee's "new" phytonutrient? It's called chlorogenic acid and may help the body process glucose, which makes it good for diabetics, hypoglycemics, and dieters. Both caffeine and decaf coffee contain the same amounts of chlorogenic acid. So have a cappuccino for your health!

Cornmeal: Coarsely ground corn, gluten-free. Cornmeal broadens the horizon of the gluten-free diet immensely. Because of it we still have cornbread, cornmeal mush, corn "dodgers" (my sister's name for cornmeal pancakes) and a host of other homey things. Cornmeal comes in different textures, grinds, and even colors. You'll find white cornmeal in the South, yellow in the Midwest and North, and sometimes blue in the Southwest.

Southerners and Northerners can get opinionated over color. With a nod to my Midwestern roots, I prefer yellow. I like the fuller flavor and the sunnier color (besides, yellow has a teensy bit more vitamin A!). I hesitate to put blue cornmeal in cornbread, but blue corn chips are pretty on chili or guacamole buffets.

How cornmeal is ground is something to consider. Commercial cornmeal, ground in steel mills, has nearly all the nutrient-rich germ removed. Old-fashioned water-ground or stone-ground (available in some grocery and health food stores) retains some of the germ. Since fiber is important in the gluten-free diet, this is a big detail. Store stone-ground cornmeal in the refrigerator because the oil in the germ is very perishable. Another option: grind your own. Home-ground cornmeal retains everything in the corn kernel.

The texture of the cornmeal is a matter of taste and recipe. In my recipes I use finely ground cornmeal; a coarser grind will change batter consistency. If you think your cornmeal may be too coarse, allow the finished batter to rest 10 minutes before checking consistency and baking.

Cornstarch: Starch ground from the endosperm of corn; gluten-free. Cornstarch is a standard thickener; it makes translucent sauces and puddings with a lovely texture. In gravy, it lacks the full flavor of flour; it's best half and half with rice flour (rice flour gives body, cornstarch silkiness). Cornstarch also does beautiful things for gluten-free cakes. I use it interchangeably with tapioca starch or arrowroot starch to lighten cakes. Rice flour and cornstarch together perform much like cake flour.

Corn Syrup: see SWEETENERS

Corn Tortillas: Made from corn masa, most corn tortillas are gluten-free. (Read labels! Some aren't.) Once considered Mexican cuisine, corn tortillas are becoming U.S. They're versatile, and you can work them into interesting recipes: Mexican "lasagna", tostadas, homemade chips (an easy-do and utterly delicious—snip tortillas in quarters and fry in hot oil). I use corn tortillas as an everyday sandwich wrapper around any kind of filling I please—ham (with mustard), salmon (with mayo and dill relish), and even hot dogs (with all the fixin's) at hot dog roasts—toasting them over the fire is simple and authentic. You *must* heat them before using, and for that reason they don't travel well in lunches. My favorite in-house method is to toast them in a dry skillet until beginning to crisp and brown. You can pop them in a toaster, or steam a multiple amount in a foil packet in the oven.

Not all corn tortillas are created equal. The softer and flakier, the better. I really like Mission brand. If preservatives are a concern, beware: some corn tortillas contain paragraphs of them. Read labels to find a brand that suits your needs—and don't confuse corn tortillas with flour tortillas, which are definitely not gluten-free.

Couscous   (KOOS-koos): Coarsely ground durum wheat; not gluten-free.

Cream: The top layer of unhomogenized milk, rich in milkfat. There's no substitute for real cream in choice recipes, as dairy-sensitive find to their woe. I'm still on the search for a natural non-dairy "whipped cream" to top desserts that beg to be topped. Commercial non-dairy whipped topping is an option—if you can deal with the sugar plus the phonics-defying ingredients. Here's a sweet note: heavy cream can *sometimes* be tolerated because of the high fat ratio to milk (milk contains the lactose). Occasionally I convince myself I'm one of these few until, after too many surreptitious dips, I'm proven wrong.

I often use SOY SUPREME, a soy-based "sour cream" in recipes that need a little fluffy richness. It works well in baked goods and gelatins, though I've never used it solo as a topper. I'm just testing Silk brand soy creamer for coffee—and it may have potential as a cream stand-in, though I haven't flown high enough to whip it yet. If it would whip high and fluffy, my troubles in the cream department would vanish.

Dates: see DRIED FRUIT

Demerara Sugar (dehm-ah-REHR-ah): see SWEETENERS

Dextrin: A food additive made from either wheat or corn; it may or may not be gluten-free.

Dried Fruit: In this book, raisins, dates, apricots and figs. Dried fruits retain most vitamins, minerals and enzymes of fresh, but more concentrated. Dried fruits add moistness and flavor to gluten-free, low-sugar recipes. Use unsulfured dried fruits when possible. Sulfur helps fruits keep their color, and by comparison, unsulfured fruits can look unappealing. But taste them! Out of curiosity, I bought a ring of unsulfured, unsugared dried pineapple at a health food store. It was a knobby, unbecoming little thing, but I took a bite and the bright, untampered flavor surprised me. Now I want to buy dried pineapples every time I go back.

Raisins are high in potassium and make good lunch box "candy" as is, or tossed into trail mixes. *Dates*, rich with caramel overtones, I find hard to believe are fruit and not candy. They do tasty things to cakes and cookies. They're high in folic acid, potassium and fiber. Dates come pitted, either whole or in pieces. Use whole dates in cooking, and cut them if needed; date pieces are usually dusted with something (and that something is not always gluten-free). *Dried apricots* are king's fruits. Not as sweet, they're comfortable eating out of hand, and are high in vitamin A. Unsulfured apricots are especially tasty in baked goods. *Figs*, my favorites, are lightly sweet, full-flavored, and extremely high in calcium. Mission or Turkey figs are best in baked goods, Calimyrna (large, tan-skinned, soft-textured) are too good to tamper with. When snacking out of the bag, I wonder how a fresh fig tastes, and if it could get any better than this.

Dry Milk: Dehydrated, powdered milk is sometimes used in gluten-free breads to add sweetness, moisture, and protein—a good thing if you're not dairy-sensitive, a bad thing if you are. I find dry milk harder to tolerate than fresh milk—maybe because it's often used in condensed amounts.

Egg: Nutritious, protein-rich, and alas! one of the most common food allergens. Those of us who can't eat eggs miss more than just our breakfasts. Eggs have adeptly worked their way into almost every baked good you can name, and for good reason. They leaven and bind, lighten and add richness; all of which gluten-free baking would welcome with open arms. Eliminating eggs can be as difficult as eliminating gluten itself, and I grasp for clues like a detective.

I haven't found a one major substitute for eggs. Instead, I've collected an armory of small substitutes, ways to tweak and pull and cheat recipes without them knowing it. It helps to start with an understanding of how eggs work, then search for a stand-in to do the same job. Egg contains a high percentage of water, at least three different proteins, a spectrum of vitamins and minerals, and effective emulsifiers, including lecithin.

My simplest, most-used trick is to substitute a few tablespoons of water (and maybe a bit more leavening) for each egg. This works quite well in most cakes and cookies. If a recipe needs serious moisture (cakes, cornbread, quick breads), use a few tablespoons pureed fruit or vegetable per egg. Where more binding is needed, ground flaxseed can substitute, about 2 teaspoons per egg (mix with a few tablespoons water, or simply add the flax to dry ingredients, and the water to wet) (see FLAXSEED). Or use liquid soy lecithin (see LECITHIN), long known as a binder in whole-grain breads. It works beautifully for gluten-free breads, too, and makes a happy substitute for egg yolks in vanilla pudding, which vanilla pudding can't do without. You can buy a commercial egg substitute, but I haven't been able to fit it in my life.

Extracts: It was once thought alcohol-based extracts (i.e. vanilla, almond, maple) contain gluten because they have a grain alcohol base. It is now believed distilling destroys gluten; extracts containing grain alcohol are now considered gluten-free.

Farina: A hot cereal usually made from wheat; not gluten-free (see HOT CEREALS for gluten-free hot cereal suggestions).

Fats and Oils: Indispensable building blocks in baking and cooking, and essential to the human diet. Fats and oils run the gamut. There are so many kinds to bake and cook and fry and dress a salad with, and so much literature that says, "This oil is good for you!" or "This oil is bad!" that I feel unqualified to go in-depth on this subject.

Let me share what I know: there are three basic fats for cooking—unsaturated (both monounsaturated and polyunsaturated—liquid oils very important in your diet); saturated (solid oils essential in smaller amounts, but still essential); and transfats (anything hydrogenated, which humans can happily live without all the days of their lives).

It's not hard to cobble together a diet for self and family which contains oils in reasonably proper ratio. Use a lot of unsaturated fats, both poly- and mono-, a little saturated (about 1:4 with unsaturated), and avoid transfats (anything that says "hydrogenated"—think margarine and vegetable shortening).

How do you use them, and where? Learn to know your oils. Always use unsaturated oils, preferably those rich in good omegas for unbaked or uncooked applications. Unsaturated oils are olive, soy, corn, peanut, sunflower, safflower, grapeseed, canola and flax. Extra virgin olive is especially nice in salad dressing, and grapeseed oil in Vegenaise is wonderful (see VEGENAISE). Some of these oils have a very low smoke point, and heating them destroys good omegas, plus causes them to oxidize—and the body can't handle oxidized fats. The most versatile all-purpose unsaturated oil is light olive. It has a neutral flavor, which merges well into sweets or savories, and is fine for moderate-heat frying. It's my favorite oil; we buy it in gallons and use it in almost everything.

Since you need a little saturated fat, maximize on its better points and use it where it counts. Saturated fats are (from highest saturation on down): coconut oil, palm kernel oil, cocoa butter, butter, with lard somewhere among them. Saturated fat rarely goes rancid, and is heat-stable. So use it in high-heat applications (think coconut oil in oil-popped popcorn), or when flavor can't be sacrificed (think butter in butter cookies). If you can't do butter (my sincere sympathies!) see BUTTER to read about EarthBalance and other butter options.

Fava Bean Flour: see BEAN FLOURS

Figs: see DRIED FRUIT

Flaxseed: Small, flat seeds of the flax plant; the highest known source of omega-3 fatty acids. Flax is also high in linoleic acid (an immune booster) and lignan (a hormone balancer). In the allergy-free cooking world, flax does something valuable; *ground flaxseed*, in contact with a liquid, becomes mucilaginous, resembling egg white. This makes flax a natural binder, and I like to use it in recipes where I *really* want binding power. When I started using it in yeast breads, I immediately noticed a fluffier texture and extra lift which xanthan gum couldn't do alone (see EGG for more information about using flax as an egg substitute). Some people sprinkle ground flaxseed over breakfast cereal, both for the high omega-3s and the pleasantly nutty flavor. Don't use it raw excessively; raw flaxseed contains prussic acid. *Flaxseed oil* does not contain prussic acid, and unheated, contains omega-3s in abundance. It's a heavy oil; use sparingly. Substitute 10% flaxseed oil for the total oil in homemade salad dressing for a painless way to add omegas to your family's diet.

Fructose   (FRUHK-tohs, FROOK-tohs): see SWEETENERS

Garbanzo Beans   (gar-BAHN-zoh): see DRIED BEANS

Garbanzo Bean Flour (gar-BAHN-zoh): see BEAN FLOURS

Garlic: Onion's strong-minded cousin; known for thousands of years as the mightiest health weapon in the cook's hands. Garlic is one of my pet ingredients; raw, it gives zing; cooked, it subsides into sweet fullness, transforming plain fare into satisfying dishes. I keep fresh garlic at hand as I cook. You can, of course, buy garlic dried, chopped, powdered, slivered; but I beg you to become acquainted with the real garlic—inexpensive little packages of goodness. Not everyone shares my infatuation with garlic. For their sakes I learn to deal out garlic with a restrained hand. I haven't yet served anyone the classic chicken with forty cloves of garlic, or an Italian recipe I found the other day for pasta tossed with one-fourth cup of garlic, sautéed to a nutty brown. I'd like to taste that pasta—though I might have to go into exile afterward. If you're a garlic user, consider buying a garlic press. Even unpeeled cloves press easily through a higher-quality press (like Zyliss).

Gelatin: A thickening popular in desserts and salads; available unflavored, or flavored and sweetened. I've learned the ease of gelatin salads made with unflavored gelatin. It fits any flavor or sweetener of the moment. Remember this ratio: 1 package (or 1 scant tablespoon) unflavored gelatin for every 2 cups liquid. From your total liquid, use a small amount (cool) to soak the gelatin 5 minutes. Bring remaining liquid to a boil, pour over soaked gelatin and stir until dissolved. Taste, and add sweetener or lemon juice. Chill until set. There you have it! Mix and match as you please, dress it up or keep it simple. One more thing to remember: never use fresh or frozen pineapple, papaya, kiwi, figs, gingerroot or guava—the enzymes in these fruits will keep your gelatin from jelling.

Graham Flour: A type of whole wheat flour, not gluten-free.

Guar Gum: A gum made from a legume; sometimes used in place of xanthan gum (see XANTHAN GUM)

Honey: see SWEETENERS

Hot Cereal: The steaming bowls of cooked grain that appear on the table when temperatures drop; often oatmeal, steel cut oats, farina, or other gluten grain. If you've grown up on a bowl of oatmeal every morning, then a GF breakfast can seem a dreary thing. On a quest to bring back those tummy-warming breakfasts, I've looked for gluten-free hot cereals—and found some seriously good ones. One of the best is Bob's Red Mill Mighty Tasty Hot Cereal, a blend of gluten-free grains. Another is brown rice farina, a creamy farina made of nothing but brown rice. Right now I'm into rice bran—a few tablespoons in any hot cereal gives a smooth, rib-sticking consistency.

Jaggery   (JAG-uh-ree): see SWEETENERS

Kamut   (kah-MOOT): An early form of wheat; contains gluten.

Kasha   (KAH-shee): roasted buckwheat groats; gluten-free. In Europe, other grains can be called kasha which may not be gluten-free.

Lactose   (LAK-tohs): The sugar found in milk. Many people can't digest milk because their bodies don't make *lactase*, the enzyme which breaks down lactose. Celiac disease often is coupled with lactose intolerance. Researchers think *villi* in the colon manufacture lactase; when the villi are gone (which happens in celiac disease), lactose intolerance may result. Lactose intolerance can sometimes correct itself once you're on a celiac diet and the villi rebuild. Some dairy products are higher in lactose than others, with whey being the highest, hard cheeses and clarified butter the lowest. You can buy "lactose-free" milk (milk treated with lactase), which some dairy-sensitive people can tolerate.

Lecithin   (LEHS-uh-thihn): A fat in egg yolks and legumes; available as a soy-derived liquid for baking. It's a binder and emulsifier, and gives a lot to gluten-free breads, and (surprisingly) egg-free vanilla pudding. As an emulsifier, I suspect lecithin could play a leading role in homemade eggless mayonnaise, though I haven't as yet discovered how. I just spotted something containing "sunflower lecithin". If sunflower lecithin would replace soy lecithin on the market, soy allergy sufferers would rejoice.

Lemon, Lemon Juice, Lemon Zest: see CITRUS

Lime, Lime Juice, Lime Zest: see CITRUS

Margarine: see FATS AND OILS

Malt, Malt Flavoring, Malt Syrup, Malt Extract: All are made from barley, and contain gluten. (See also VINEGAR on *malt vinegar.*)

Maltodextrin: A food additive made from corn, potato, or rice in the U.S. If wheat is used in an imported product, it should be clearly labeled in the ingredients.

Maple Syrup: see SWEETENERS

Masa Harina (MAH-sah ah-REE-nah): Flour from dried *masa* (corn soaked in lime water, then ground); gluten-free. Masa is used to make tortillas and more authentic tortilla chips. Masa harina is more refined than other cornmeal; the lime soak removes the germ and hull of the corn. There's nothing quite like the real tortilla chips it makes, though! You know tortilla chips start with masa if the ingredients include "...and a trace of lime".

Mayonnaise: The creamy emulsion of egg and oil Americans like so well on their sandwiches. I missed mayonnaise after eggs were outlawed. Growing up in the Midwest, we ate potato salads rich with it, lettuce salad blanketed by it, and many, many dried beef sandwiches spread with it. The first years without egg, I tried to fill the empty mayonnaise spot with relishes, mustard, and butter. Then came Vegenaise. Vegenaise is an egg-free mayonnaise made with heart-healthy oils that tastes (can it possibly be?) better than the real thing. It fits seamlessly into every crack and crevice that mayonnaise used to go. The only distressing thing about Vegenaise is keeping the rest of the family out of it! Find Vegenaise in the refrigerator section of most health food stores, made from your choice of canola, olive or grapeseed oil.

Millet Flour: Flour ground from the grain millet; gluten-free. Because (oddly) I'm allergic to millet, I haven't experimented much with it, though others report its delicate, sweet flavor. Millet is a good-for-you grain, almost as high in nutrition as the nourishing non-grains, amaranth and quinoa. Whole millet can be cooked as a hot cereal.

Molasses: see SWEETENERS

Monosodium Glutamate, MSG: Derived from glutamic acid; a flavor enhancer often used in Oriental cooking. Many people react to MSG; because, though MSG is a natural element, it may be produced chemically in recent years. Some think synthetic MSG is responsible for allergy-like symptoms. And MSG can hide—often under the label "natural flavoring". Be wary of spice mixes, especially chili powder (see CHILI POWDER).

Nuts: High in protein, calcium, folic acid and monounsaturated fat, nuts are literally nutrition in nutshells. Unfortunately, many people are allergic to nuts (especially peanuts), but for those okay with them, nuts are a boon in gluten-free baking. They add richness and texture, boost the food value, and merge well into both salties and sweets. *Walnuts*, the most popular baking nut, are among the least expensive. They're especially nice, in excess, in dark chocolate brownies. *Pecans* toast beautifully in streusels, and complement anything apple-y, pumpkin-y or caramel-y. *Almonds* win honors for being the fittest in the nut world. They're rich in vitamin E and phytonutrients. Whole almonds are wonderful for out of hand eating, and I buy sliced almonds for my favorite Almond-Apricot Cookies (almonds are too hard to slice or sliver by hand). *Peanuts*, really legumes, are most popular in peanut butter. To avoid hydrogenated oils (see FATS AND OILS), try natural peanut butter. *Brazil nuts*, seeds from giant trees in the Amazon, are extremely high in selenium, an antioxidant. You can buy them unshelled, but arm yourself with a hammer. While most nuts complement chocolate, *hazelnuts* are the truest of chocolate's friends. Whole hazelnuts in dark chocolate is pure delight. *Macadamias*, smooth and rich, are the highest in fat of all the nuts. I once tasted whole honey-glazed macadamias, and may I not forget the taste of buttery nut against sweet, salty glaze. Macadamias complement white chocolate.

Nuts are high in monounsaturated fats, and they become rancid quickly, especially chopped, ground or sliced (whole nuts will keep a little longer, and unshelled twice as long). Buy them at a store with a rapid turnover, and keep them in the freezer.

Oats, Oat Flour, Oatmeal: Once considered taboo, oats now have a wider acceptance in the gluten-free world. Even after research, I can't tell you if oats are really gluten-free. One book says they are, another says they contain tiny amounts of gluten. Some blame this on cross-contamination (apparently oats are often processed with wheat). Packages of "gluten-free oatmeal" now grace health food stores with confidence. So far, I'm scared to experiment—I used to think oats made me sick. If oats are truly gluten-free, they would widen horizons considerably, because oats are versatile, full of soluble fiber, and high in iron, potassium, and B-vitamins. I think I'll wait and watch for more research, and when I'm positive, I'll welcome oats back with open arms.

Olive Oil: see FATS AND OILS

Onion: The pungent bulb of the lily family that has become the most popular flavor ingredient in savory dishes. Onions are rich in folate and vitamin C, and one green onion contains four times your daily quota of vitamin K. My mom grows rows and rows of onions—green onions, sweet onions, and pungent yellow and red keeping onions to last the winter. We eat an unbelievable amount of sweet onions on sandwiches (who doesn't like a big juicy ring on a burger!) and in salads (they're indispensable in Cauliflower-Lettuce salad). In cooking, where sweet onions can become insipid, yellow onions shine. It's amazing how something as tear-jerking pungent as a stout cooking onion can become sweet with a little heat. A life-lesson there, maybe.

Palm Sugar: see SWEETENERS

Pasta: Usually made from durum wheat; not gluten-free. Pasta has become such a part of American cuisine that even those without Italian ancestry miss pasta after a celiac diagnosis. We miss macaroni and cheese, spaghetti and meatballs, pasta salad. But pasta is back—check the gluten-free section of bigger groceries. The two popular kinds are corn and rice; I prefer brown rice, which cooks up tender and tasty. I read about pasta made from Jerusalem artichokes. I'd like to try it. Most gluten-free pasta is fragile cooked; stir with a light hand.

Piloncillo, Panela, Panocha: see SWEETENERS

Potato Starch, Potato Flour: Two distinctly different products; the first is made from uncooked potatoes, the second from cooked; both are gluten-free. I haven't used much potato flour, but potato starch is an important ingredient in gluten-free breads. Use it interchangeably with tapioca starch, cornstarch or arrowroot starch to lighten baked goods, though it gives a moister consistency. Combined with rice flour, it gives chocolate cake a delicate and moist crumb.

Quinoa   (KEEN-whah): A nutritious grain-like seed native to the Andes; gluten-free. I know little about quinoa except the quinoa flakes a friend gave me to try. (It made tasty and filling granola, which I'd happily eat every morning, but going out to buy more flakes, the price stopped me short—and gave me a sweet lesson on friends and generosity.) Reading about quinoa makes me want to know it better. I find quinoa is rich in an incredible array of nutrients: iron, phosphorus, B-vitamins, and vitamin E. It's said to have an amino acid profile similar to milk (with even more calcium), and is 16% protein, higher than any other grain (now I know why that granola was so satisfying). Don't grind your own unless it is washed of the bitter saponin which coats the kernels. Quinoa flour is available in health food stores.

Rapadura: see SWEETENERS

Rice: Starchy, mild, and digestible, rice is the celiac's friend. We eat it cooked in place of noodles in spaghetti, ground into flour in muffins, and drink rice milk on puffed rice. For most celiacs, rice becomes the grain on center stage, therefore we should insist on the healthiest and best.

Rice doesn't have to be monotonous, no matter how many times a day we eat it. With thousands of varieties grown every year in Asia and beyond, rice carries a lot of personality—and more is available in specialty food stores all the time.

Rice is categorized by the length of grain: *long-grain* cooks up dry, light, and fluffy, *short-grain* moist and sticky, *medium-grain* between the two. Each kind is suitable for certain recipes. Basmati rice is an aged aromatic rice with a very long grain. It lengthens even further as it cooks, and the light "strands" work well in stir-fries and substitutes for spaghetti (serve it fluffed, piping hot, with spaghetti sauce on the side). Jasmine rice is an aromatic rice with a nut-like flavor and shorter grain, and it cooks up soft and clingy— perfect in chicken and rice.

Brown rice, unmilled and unpolished, is high in an absorbable B-vitamin (in which celiacs are often deficient). It also contains rice bran, a soluble fiber, lysine, and calcium, iron and protein. Unpolished rice comes in most shades of brown under the sun—from almost black Chinese rice, to rusty Himalayan, to buff Wehani. I like to mix colors for rice casseroles or Cornbread-Wild Rice Stuffing. I find the texture of brown rice is best baked; the chewy bran has more time and moisture to cook to a smooth texture.

White rice, milled and polished, is lower in nutrients, and higher on the glycemic index, but contains a more absorbable protein. A little in a balanced diet is not a bad thing. It cooks much faster than brown rice, and I keep it in the cupboard for emergencies.

Wild rice, not a true rice, is nutty and satisfying. It's expensive; try mixing the beautiful black grains with other brown or red rices. They cook in about the same amount of time.

Though different rices absorb more or less amounts of water, a good rule of thumb for boiling or baking rice is to use 2 cups of liquid per 1 cup of rice. Salt varies; I like up to 1 teaspoon per cup of rice. My sister adds a splash of olive oil.

Rye: Rye, rye flour and all rye products contain gluten.

Semolina (seh-muh-LEE-nuh): A type of durum wheat; not gluten-free.

Sorghum Molasses (SOR-guhm): see SWEETENERS

Sorghum Flour (SOR-guhm): A staple grain in the Far East for thousands of years. Sorghum is finally emerging in America, mostly because of celiacs like us. Sorghum flour is gluten-free, and nutritious. It has a mild, lightly sweet flavor that pairs well with bean flours. I use it in yeasted breads.

Sour Supreme: A sour cream substitute made from soy. It merges into most recipes where sour cream should go. It is slightly less acidic. In dips and dressings, try perking it with vinegar or lemon juice. You can buy Sour Supreme at major grocery stores.

Soy, Soy Flour, Soy Milk: Soybeans are in almost everything, in many forms—as those allergic to soy discover when reading labels. To those not allergic, there's still cause for concern: most soy in America is genetically modified. (Recent studies suggest GMO grains may cause inflamed intestinal tracts, diarrhea, malabsorption—from which most celiacs are trying to recover!) For this reason, buy organic soy whenever possible. I find soy flour, soy nuts, and soy nut butter hard to digest. There are several other soy products I've come to know, however—soy yogurt, soy cheese, Sour Supreme, a very nice sour cream substitute, and Better Than Cream Cheese. See SOUR SUPREME; CHEESE.

Soy Sauce: A sauce made of fermented soybeans and often wheat or barley; often not gluten-free. Check labels carefully, front and back.

Spelt: A cousin to wheat; not gluten-free.

Sweeteners: A hodgepodge of sugars and sugary-tasting powders and syrups, varying in nutrition, taste, and source, united in one thing: they taste sweet. Most sugar comes from sugarcane, in every gradation from "raw" to highly refined, but they don't stop there. We can sweeten our cakes with cacti from Mexico, palms from India, or shrub leaves from Paraguay.

Sweetness is the first taste we crave and the last we lose—and is often contained in "comfort food". Thus the sweet tooth, I find, is a personal thing. Among hypoglycemics and diabetics, what one can happily live with, another can't. Because of this, where a recipe doesn't rely heavily on a sweetener for consistency, this cookbook will ask for "sweetener of choice". Where the sweetener matters, I specify.

Sugarcane, king of sweeteners, goes through an intricate process before it becomes the snowy refined sugar Americans love. Along the way, many other forms of sugar are born. *Jaggery* from India and *panela, piloncillo, panocha* and *rapadura* from Mexico and South America are the "rawest" of sugars, and are simply cane juice boiled until sugared. They contain much of the nutrients of cane; their flavor is earthy and molasses-ey; and they are about eighty-two percent sucrose. They usually come in hard, dense cones—you have to grate or melt them before using. Find them in the ethnic section of larger groceries. *Raw sugar, evaporated cane juice*, and *turbinado* are more refined. They are crystallized sugar minus the last refinings, and retain some of the molasses. Bake with them interchangeably with white sugar, though they will give a recipe a fuller flavor that I prefer. *Demerara* and *muscovado* are considered raw brown sugars, where molasses is retained, and the sugar dehydrated. Demerara has a faint caramel flavor, and muscovado hints of butterscotch (try it on hot cereal). *Brown sugar* is often refined sugar with molasses added. *White sugar* is sugarcane refined until there's virtually nothing left but sucrose. I avoid white sugar in my recipes for several reasons. One, white sugar contributes no nutrients (and nutritious food is so important in the celiac diet!), and two, I find the walloping dose of sucrose hard to handle.

Sugarcane also gives us liquid sweeteners. *Molasses* is the by-product spun off as sugar is refined; it comes in about three gradations of sweetness— light, robust and blackstrap. Many manufacturers add sulfur to extract the molasses. If you are allergic to sulfur, look for unsulfured molasses at bulk or health food stores. It's tastier anyway. I love earthy, acidic molasses teamed with cornbread. Blackstrap is not a common baking molasses, but it is high in iron, potassium and calcium. Some people take it by the tablespoon as a nutritional supplement—nicer tasting than most medicine!

This Northerner has never tasted *cane syrup*, pressed cane juice boiled until syrupy. Deep Southerners, I have read, produce it locally—and I dream of sampling it over warm biscuits. *Golden syrup*, a clear, brown syrup made of raw sugar, is much like our dark corn syrup. It's a British thing—and hard to find in America (versus imitations, made with corn syrup and molasses). I wonder why? It sounds delectable.

Now on to non-sugarcane sugars. I'll go from approximately highest to lowest on the glycemic index. *Honey* takes the honors of being the sweetest of the liquid sweeteners. My brother kept bees for a few years, and the whole monarchy of queens, workers, scouts and drones is fascinating.

The product of their hard work is sweet, concentrated nectar, with baking and eating characteristics all its own. It stars in yeast breads, homemade graham crackers, and hot cereal. I find it too sweet to eat solo, but, tamed into unctuous honey-butter, it's a natural on pancakes. Honey works well as a substitute for some liquid sweeteners, but can't be substituted for sugar in recipes without tweaking flour/liquid proportions. It tends to brown quickly and leave a bitter aftertaste in overbaked baked goods. *Maple syrup* is Waffle King and sweetens pumpkin pie (and anything warmly spiced) with talent. To substitute for sugar, you must adjust the recipe to accommodate the extra moisture. Don't confuse real maple syrup with *pancake syrup*, a fake substitute. *Palm sugar* is something I've never tried, but I read about it with interest. It's made from the sap of date or coconut palms much like maple sugar. It's said to have the color of jaggery (see preceding page), but with a buttery flavor. *Sorghum molasses* is made by evaporating the juice pressed from the stalks of the sorghum plant. It is thinner and slightly more acidic than sugarcane molasses. *Corn syrup* is a highly refined syrup overused as a cheap sweetener in processed foods. Because it's shiny and restricts crystallization, I do like it in specific candy recipes. *Brown rice syrup*, about three-quarters as sweet as sugar, is expensive, but has a light, neutral flavor. It's used a lot in dairy-free ice creams. Read the label; I once thought some rice syrups contain gluten (though I can't imagine why). *Xylitol* has unique traits other sugars don't share. It's antibacterial, so it's good for your teeth and it fights candida. Pure, crystalline xylitol is expensive, though you can sometimes find it cheaper in bulk. Substitute it 1:1 for sugar. Unbaked applications, like drinks, over cereal, in puddings, work very well. It doesn't perform like other sugars in the oven. And since it's antibacterial, don't use it in yeast breads, or you may have unleavened loaves! Xylitol is very processed; however, it has a low glycemic index; something to consider if you're diabetic or hypoglycemic. *Fructose* also has a low glycemic index, though it tastes sweeter than sugar (use about ⅔ cup as substitute per cup of sugar). It's my sister's chief sweetener, and her hypoglycemic husband tolerates it well. Like xylitol, fructose is fine unbaked and uncooked, but takes an experienced hand when baking. My sister has an arsenal of tricks in her cupboard, hard-won by years of experience, and she turns out very nice cakes and desserts, though she's never tamed it enough for cookies. Here are a few of her tricks: in creaming, fructose works best with partially melted versus softened butter. It also can't be used for egg-based cakes (i.e. angel food, sponge, chiffon) or with baking powder (Denise substitutes ½ teaspoon cream of tartar and ½ teaspoon baking soda per teaspoon of baking powder when using fructose). *Agave nectar* is a syrup evaporated from the sap of the agave plant (also called *century plant*), a succulent from Mexico. You can buy both light and amber in most supermarkets. Agave has the lowest glycemic index of the liquid sweeteners. It's my all-time favorite pancake topper; try warm pancakes dripping with the thick, vanilla-y syrup. Agave nectar also blends beautifully into beverages, and makes wonderful homemade root beer. Don't use agave in savories where its dessert-y overtones would be unwelcome. It won't give the caramelization we expect from sugars in cookies or candies, but it might work well in cakes. *Stevia*, the "un-sugar" of sugars, is an herb harvested from a shrub, and since it only *tastes* sweet, it has no calories, and doesn't affect the blood sugar in any way. And it is *really* sweet; use only ¼ to ½ teaspoon to replace one cup of sugar. Since stevia doesn't act like sugar, it's difficult to bake with. I like it best for beverages; a tiny pinch sweetens a cup of tea to perfection. Too much, and the sweetness will turn bitter. It's good in cold drinks, too; you'll notice in Old-Fashioned Lemonade I use it to supplement the main sweetener. Reading recipes, I noticed another baker's trick: use about ¼ teaspoon of stevia in baked goods, and cut your sugar by half. I intend to try this idea.

Tapioca, Minute Tapioca, Tapioca Starch: All made from the starch of the tuber of the cassava plant. *Tapioca starch* works well when extra lightness is needed in cake and cookie recipes (along with a base flour, such as brown rice flour). *Pearl tapioca* and *minute tapioca* broaden allergy-free desserts considerably. Tapioca is easy to digest, and thickens both fruit- and milk-based desserts nicely. Tapioca gets stringy if you stir it too much while cooking; cook at a low simmer and don't stir until dessert has cooled twenty minutes.

Teff: A tiny grain native to Africa, mild, nutritious, and gluten-free. I haven't experimented with teff, but my friend from Ethiopia tells about the fascinating way the natives eat it; ground, fermented overnight in a thin batter, then fried like crepes. Over this *injera* go savories, often stews and soups, seasoned with a fiery spice above the heat level of most Americans. Recently I laid up a supply of ground teff; Lord willing, *injera* is one of the next things coming up.

Triticale (triht-ih-KAY-lee): A grain that's a cross between wheat and rye; not gluten-free.

Turbinado Sugar (tur-bih-NAH-doh): see SWEETENERS

Vanilla Extract: see EXTRACTS

Vegetable Shortening: see FATS AND OILS

Vegenaise: see MAYONNAISE to read about this delicious egg-free mayonnaise substitute

Vinegar: The cruet of puckery liquid indispensable in the kitchen for thousands of years. Vinegar can be fermented from a wide range of saps, juices, and syrups. *Apple cider vinegar* is a hardworking vinegar with a pleasant fruity tang. I use it for pickles, salad dressings, and anything sweet and sour. *White distilled vinegar* is made from grain; because it's distilled, and distilling is thought to destroy gluten, it's considered gluten-free. White vinegar has a harsh, one-dimensional flavor; it makes a clear pickling syrup. *Balsamic vinegar*, made of sweet white grapes and aged in wooden kegs, is my personal favorite. It's sweet, musky and rich. A little goes a long way—it's best in conservative amounts as a seasoning. Strangely, I like it in barbecue sauce. Steer clear of *malt vinegar*, popular in Britain. It's made with barley, and is not distilled. It contains gluten.

Wild Rice: see RICE

Wheat: The wonderful, high-gluten grain that has nourished millions for centuries; the bane of every celiac's life. Serious celiacs must avoid all wheat and wheat-derived products in any amount, form, or guise.

Wheat Starch: What's left of ground wheat after the gluten has been washed out. Wheat starch is considered safe for celiac diets in some European countries. Tests have shown, however, that the residual gluten in the starch is far too high for safety. Wheat starch is not considered gluten-free in America.

Xanthan Gum   (ZAN-thuhn): A product made from fermented corn sugar, xanthan gum is an essential in my kitchen. Mixed with liquid, it forms an elastic texture which mimics gluten. But not all xanthan gum brands are the same. For several horrifying months last summer, while I was retesting, my baked goods were disastrous. I asked advice from everyone I dared—including my brother. "An ingredient must have changed," he said with soothing rationality. Ah ha! I'd used new xanthan gum, purchased from a once-trusted source. My heart in my throat, I ran off and bought a bag of Bob's Red Mill brand, flew home, and mixed up a cake. It baked soft and pillowy, like all good little cakes. I now recommend Bob's Red Mill brand (and *only* Bob's Red Mill) to celiac friends.

Xylitol   (ZI-lih-tol): see SWEETENERS

Yeast: Living, single-cell organisms that bakers have used to leaven bread for thousands of years. Unlike brewer's yeast, baker's yeast is gluten-free. You can buy several types of yeast, primarily regular or quick-acting dry yeast. I think the slower rise of regular dry yeast versus quick-acting gives bread a better flavor. Some bakers find quick-acting a real time-saver though, as it rises in about half the time.

Yogurt: Milk cultured with beneficial bacteria into tangy, spoonable goodness. Since the bacteria breaks down lactose, many lactose-intolerant are fine with yogurt. If you're among those fortunate, you not only retain a good breakfast, but yogurt can add a lot to gluten-free baking. Since I can't eat dairy yogurt, I haven't developed recipes with it. Substitute it for buttermilk or sour cream in your favorite recipes, like scones, muffins, or biscuits. For the unfortunates, try soy yogurt—O'Soy and Silk brands are the best.

Index

{ notes }

_____

_____

_____

_____

_____

_____

_____

_____

_____

_____

_____

_____

_____

_____

_____

_____

_____

_____

_____

_____

_____

_____

_____

_____

{ notes }

{ notes }

{ notes }

{ notes }